UNDERSTANDING SHINRAN

NANZAN STUDIES IN ASIAN RELIGIONS
Paul L. Swanson, General Editor

1   Jan NATTIER, *Once Upon a Future Time:*
    Studies in a Buddhist Prophecy of Decline, 1991.

2   David REID, *New Wine:*
    The Cultural Shaping of Japanese Christianity, 1991.

3   Minor and Ann ROGERS, *Rennyo:*
    The Second Founder of Shin Buddhism, 1991.

4   Herbert GUENTHER, *Ecstatic Spontaneity:*
    Saraha's Three Cycles of Dohā, 1993.

5   Mark R. MULLINS, SHIMAZONO Susumu, and Paul L.
    SWANSON, eds., *Religion and Society in Modern Japan:*
    Selected Readings, 1993.

Understanding Shinran

A Dialogical Approach

Hee-Sung KEEL

ASIAN HUMANITIES PRESS

Fremont, California

ASIAN HUMANITIES PRESS

Asian Humanities Press offers to the specialist and the general reader alike the best in new translations of major works and significant original contributions to our understanding of Asian religions, cultures, and thought.

Printed in the United States of America

Library of Congress Cataloging-in-Publication Data

Keel, Hee-Sung
    Understanding Shinran : a dialogical approach / Hee-Sung Keel.
      p.   cm. — (Nanzan Studies in Asian Religions ; 6)
    Includes bibliographical references and index.
    ISBN 0-89581-937-6 (cloth : alk. paper)
    1. Shinran, 1173–1263.   I. Title. II. Series.
BQ8749.S557K44 1995   95–13351
294.3'926—dc20   CIP

CONTENTS

FOREWORD

Jan Van Bragt

SHINRAN (1173–1262), THE SUBJECT OF THIS BOOK, is one of the most eminent figures on the Japanese religious scene, and his teaching unquestionably constitutes one of the pinnacles of Pure Land thought.

The Pure Land tradition is a form of religious doctrine and praxis that developed within Buddhism. It has its roots in India, primarily in the "Pure Land sūtras" and in some early commentaries; in China, it developed doctrinally in the treatises of the "patriarchs" T'an-luan (Jpn. Donran), Tao-ch'o (Dōshaku), Shan-tao (Zendō), and others, and spread throughout nearly all of Buddhism; finally, in Japan, with the teaching of Hōnen and Shinran, it took the form of a separate school and exclusive path.

Of the major traditions of Buddhism, Pure Land is probably the least known outside of Japan, especially in the West, where Buddhist scholars tend not to take it seriously. It is thus not superfluous to say a word in defense of the study of this form of religiosity. I shall argue that its study is of great importance for the study of Buddhism as a living historical reality and that it has a special importance for Christian theology.

How can one truly study Buddhism in its historical reality? Most scholarly introductions to Buddhism are like histories of the development of a religious philosophy, but living Buddhism is clearly more than a philosophy. It is a bountiful religion lived and treasured by ordinary people with their existential needs and their aspirations for the good and the beautiful. My thesis here is that a study of Pure Land Buddhism is one of the better means to discover the nonphilosophical *life* of Buddhism. The Pure Land tradition takes some religious impulses at work below the philosophical surface of all living Mahāyāna Buddhism to their extreme form, and thereby highlights them. It is impossible to describe this type of grassroots Buddhist life in a single sentence, but one could say that it is marked by a general focus on the person(s) of the Buddha rather than on the Buddhist Law or Dharma (one could speak here of a "buddhayāna" versus a "dharmayāna"), and by an existential need for "graspable" religious forms.

In any case, the following traits of this living Buddhism, which are clearly relevant to Pure Land Buddhism, can be mentioned: reliance on the Buddha, as expressed in the universally used liturgical formula of "The Three Treasures"; the practice of recitation of Buddha names, attested to in the earliest sources; the figure of the bodhisattva whose heroic vow to save all sentient beings inversely implies that people expect salvation from him; the great role of stupa worship and Buddha imagery; and, finally, the aspirations of the laity in a monk-dominated religion.

As to the importance of the study of Pure Land Buddhism for Christian theology, I tend to see the picture as follows. Among the various Christian encounters with other religions, that with Judaism may be of the greatest help in clarifying our Christian roots, and that with Islam may be of the greatest importance sociologically speaking, but the "confrontation" with Buddhism may hold out the greatest challenge and promise for the further development of Christian theology. Since space does not permit me to elaborate on this, I must immediately focus on the possible contributions of Pure Land doctrine to Christian theology.

The chapters of this book will make clear to the reader at least the following two points. First, many of the central religious themes and doctrinal problems in Pure Land Buddhism are very similar to those in Christianity. Second, Pure Land doctrine developed in a dialectical, and possibly problematic, relationship with the dominant Mahāyāna logic of *śūnyatā* (emptiness). Since one of the strongest challenges to Christian theology is precisely this doctrine of emptiness and formlessness, it follows that Pure Land doctrine might be enormously useful for Christian theology in that it has already theologically elaborated the religious themes it shares with Christianity in the framework of that Mahāyāna basic view.

The publication of *Understanding Shinran* is therefore a welcome event, since it adds substantially to the very short list of works introducing the Pure Land School to the world at large. Here, however, a few caveats are in order.

First, Hee-Sung Keel does not intend to describe the entire Pure Land movement, but directly only a cross-section of it, namely the Shinran event. It is, however, a cross-section taken from a very important moment in the development of the movement. This is the moment in which Pure Land Buddhism, after a long history of hidden and symbiotic existence, declared its independence and became, at least in Japan, a sociologically distinct form of Buddhism with its own organizations and rituals, its own "path," and, ideally, its own "theology."

Second, the aim of the author was not to write a general introduction to Shinran, but rather, as the title of the book indicates, to understand Shinran from a Christian standpoint and engage in dialogue with him. As a matter of fact, the book does not try to answer all the questions an outsider might have when reading Shinran's text, but instead focuses on the major gaps that appear to separate Shinran's thought from that of a Christian. That I nevertheless deem this book well suited to introduce this important religious movement to the "post-Christian" West is the result of a kind of hermeneutic paradox.

Should an introduction to a religion be written by a "neutral" academic observer or by an insider? Leaving aside the neutral observer—who may be a nonexistent entity or an "extensionless concept" anyway—let us concentrate on the insider. Theoretically, of course, the case for the insider seems stronger, since it is he who has the most intimate knowledge of the message to be conveyed. Experience does not bear this out, however, since the more important factor in the equation is generally the audience to whom the message must be conveyed. The introduction of thought is a work of mediation or bridge-building between a text and an audience to whom the text is "alien." The introduction must therefore take into account the frame of mind, the presuppositions, and the questions of the reader. It is, in other words, a work of "translation," and it is generally admitted, I believe, that translation is best done by a native speaker of the language into which the work in question is translated. And indeed, it is my belief that the few existing Western-language introductions to Shinran's thought, written by Pure Land insiders, preoccupied as they are with the concerns of the in-group, fail to really enlighten the Western reader.

In any event, from the viewpoint of the author's real aim, *Understanding Shinran* is a truly "strong" book, an "engaged and sustained hermeneutical effort at understanding," that never loses itself in irrelevant details. It probes deeply into the main points that appear to separate Shinran's thinking from Christian thinking, and honestly challenges the respective doctrines when the light emanating from the other seems to warrant it. In his effort to understand Shinran's doctrine of Other Power, Keel uses to the full his intimate knowledge of the Christian problematics of grace (as seen from a Protestant viewpoint). He also brings into play the Christian eschatological dialectic of the "already" and the "not yet," in order to come to a balanced understanding of Shinran's delicate position on the relationship between the present moment of faith and the future enlightenment through birth into the Pure Land. It is important to remark, however, that these Christian doctrines are not adduced for the sake of direct comparison nor as yardsticks with which to pass judgment on Shinran's doctrines, but are used strictly as tools for understanding.

Still, deep probing of a doctrinal system from the outside inevitably leads to the questioning of traditional tenets and presuppositions. At that point one enters the second—the most delicate and painful, but also the most beneficial—stage of the dialogue. Indeed, interreligious dialogue is hardly worth the effort if it does not involve mutual questioning and transformation—if it does not hold up to both partners a mirror wherein they can come to a truer self-knowledge. In this respect, the author is nothing if not bold. His own deeply held convictions lead him to apply some quite critical norms to the Pure Land texts and, even more so, to certain present-day trends and tenets among Shinshū theorists.

One of the book's strengths is its almost exclusive reliance on the Pure Land scriptures (which include Shinran's writings), with only an occasional hint from later interpretations. Thereby Keel not only gains the benefit of drinking from the very source but he is also not bound by historical constructs of Pure Land theorists and thus enjoys a freedom such as few Pure Land scholars could hope to enjoy. The "norms" that he applies are rooted, no doubt, in his own Christian faith. They are not argued for, however, in the light of that faith, but are presented instead as more general standards based on the science of religion. Among them, the two that play the most prominent role are: 1) the need for religion not to lose its transcendent, world-denying, character, and 2) the imperative for religion to have some intrinsic link to ethics, both individual and social.

I look forward to the reactions of Shinshū scholars to the author's provocative questioning of certain present-day Shinshū "theological" tenets. But will these scholars take up the challenge and accept the invitation to the "dialogical dance?" I sincerely hope so, for the sake of the dialogue, but past experience makes me a bit skeptical. At any rate, an almost necessary precondition would be the translation of Keel's book into Japanese. Any volunteers?

➢   ➢   ➢

Right at the beginning of his first chapter, Keel asks a basic question:

> Is this message of Hōnen [and Shinran]...still to be considered Buddhism? Is Buddhism still possible without the practice of morality (*śila*), mental concentration (*samādhi*), and wisdom-insight (*prajñā*)...?

Keel does not present a direct theoretical answer to this question, although he clearly treats the Pure Land School as in fact a form of Buddhism. At the beginning of his fifth chapter, he clearly expresses the basic differences between Pure Land Buddhism and other forms of Mahāyāna: its belief that enlightenment can be obtained, not in this life but only in the beyond of the Pure Land, and not by one's own efforts but only by Other Power; and its having an origin as a religion in a story rather than in a universal truth. He does not consider these differences to be sufficient reason to disqualify the Pure Land School from being Buddhism, but he insists that the Pure Land religiosity does not fit within the traditional Mahāyāna worldview, and that Shinshū scholars who consistently try to interpret it in terms of the wisdom of *śūnyatā* "dissolve the very paradoxicality of Shinran's salvation by faith." To this I want to say a wholehearted "Amen!" The remaining question might be whether the logic of emptiness captures the whole reality and dynamism of Mahāyāna Buddhism. The very existence of Pure Land Buddhism might be the clearest indication that it does not really do so.

We have Keel's book to thank for illustrating this aspect of Mahāyāna Buddhism, and for advancing the dialogue between Christianity and Buddhism one step further.

Introduction

THERE IS SOME IRONY in the fact that I, a Korean academic of Buddhism with a Christian background, should write a book on a major figure in Japanese Buddhism. For I had to struggle, intellectually as well as emotionally, with two kinds of tension arising from two seeming incongruities: the tension between "Korean" and "Japanese," and between "Christian" and "Buddhist." The awareness of this odd combination has constantly been with me as I worked on this subject. Let me elaborate a bit on these two tensions that nevertheless had a positive effect by sharpening my sense of *Problematik* in interpreting Shinran's thought.

First we have the rather unusual phenomenon of a Korean academic writing a book in English on Japanese Buddhism. It is widely recognized that there is a pressing need in Buddhist studies in the West for more English materials on Korean Buddhism. Why, then, should a Korean academic bother to add another volume in English to the already long list of books and articles on Japanese Buddhism, while it is still very difficult to come by a single decent volume on Korean Buddhism in general? For a Korean academic, this question cannot be answered simply by appealing to personal academic interest. A more convincing reason has to be found when one devotes all the time and effort necessary to produce a monograph on a Buddhist thinker of Shinran's magnitude.

It is no secret that Koreans are generally ill-disposed toward anything Japanese. The Korean academic world is on the whole no exception. The apparent neglect of Japanese studies among Korean scholars, especially in the areas of history, culture, and religion, is attributable in no small measure to this deep-rooted ill-feeling toward Japan as a nation, if not toward Japanese people themselves as individuals. While Korean scholars may be aware of the unique history and the rich cultural tradition of Japan, they still feel reluctant to study that history and tradition, let alone admire them. Although there is a growing awareness among the younger generation of Korean intellectuals that it is essential for Koreans to know their "close" neighbor more accurately, if only in order to "put" Japan "in its place," Japanese studies still remain a "forbidden" area among Korean scholars in general. All this may sound silly to a Western academician, but

1

the reality must be faced: a dark shadow always falls upon the minds of Korean academicians and intellectuals, including myself, when they seriously engage themselves in Japanese studies.

When it comes to Buddhist studies, Korean Buddhists are justifiably proud of their Buddhist heritage. They take a particular pride in pointing out that Japanese Buddhism was heavily indebted to Korean monks and artisans during its formative period. Korean scholars may have a high regard for current Japanese Buddhist scholarship, but this high regard does not extend to the faith and practices of Japanese Buddhism. Korean Buddhists tend to regard Japanese Buddhism as corrupt, in that the tradition of monastic celibacy has virtually disappeared. Korean Buddhists are also painfully aware that Japanese Buddhists "corrupted" the Korean sangha during the period of colonial occupation by introducing the practice of "monks taking wives" (*taech'ŏsŭng* 带妻僧), which led eventually to the division of the Korean sangha into celibate monks and married "monks." Korean Buddhists also look upon at least some forms of Japanese Buddhism—such as the Pure Land faith and the "worship" of the *Lotus Sūtra* in the Nichiren line of Buddhism—as highly eccentric and unorthodox, widely deviating from the orthodox Mahāyāna tradition. Even worse, many Koreans feel uneasy about the "infiltration" into their country of what they consider the jingoistic line of Japanese Buddhism, in particular the Sōka Gakkai. In short, Korean Buddhists do not have a favorable view of Japanese Buddhism and find no compelling reason to study it, let along learn from it. It is no wonder then that, as far as I am aware, there has not been a single book, in Korean or in English, produced by a Korean scholar on Japanese Buddhism.

The fact that I may be the first Korean to be writing a monograph on Japanese Buddhism is not unrelated to the fact that I am personally not a Buddhist, but "merely" a student of Buddhism and the history of religions in general. Nay, it is more than that. I am also a Christian with training in theology—a rare combination in Korean Protestantism! This, however, may explain to a great extent how I could be an exception to the general trend in Korean Buddhism mentioned above, and more particularly why I became interested in Shinran.

Here I must say something about the second undercurrent of tension flowing beneath my work, namely that between "Christian" and "Buddhist." This tension basically stems from the fact that my work here is more than an academic study of Shinran carried out from a "neutral" standpoint; it is rather the product of a strenuous hermeneutical effort to bridge the gap between two traditions that seem so close to each other and yet are so different. For me, the "tension" between Buddhism and Christianity is not simply the result of the obvious doctrinal conflict between the two religious traditions. To be a Christian inevitably forces an Asian who is aware of the great native spiritual tradition to make a spiritual *Auseinandersetzung*, a decision of choice one way or another. The question of truth inevitably comes up—all the more so when one has to deal with a figure like Shinran, whose message not merely comes so close to the Christian gospel but also carries a tremendous existential appeal.

Cultural relativism is ultimately not acceptable for me personally, as well as for many others. But I do not yet know how to resolve the tension and settle the problem of truth claims. Nevertheless, I am sure of one thing: the first step, and the best way, to deal with it is still a dialogue, "an engaged and sustained hermeneutical effort to understand a faith that is not my own." Despite John Cobb's call to go "beyond dialogue," I have therefore entitled my work "Understanding Shinran: A Dialogical Approach." The readiness to be "transformed" only comes when one has seen at least some *truth* in another faith through a serious effort to understand it, i.e., through a dialogue. In my case this dialogue was with Shinran's texts, along with other interpreters of his thought.

A genuine understanding in human affairs always occurs through a dialogue, and no genuine dialogue is possible without a position and commitment of one's own. To understand another faith, therefore, does not simply mean to "bracket" one's own faith (as phenomenologists would suggest), let alone give it up. Human understanding does not occur in a mental vacuum but in the "mingling of horizons" (*Horizonts-verschmelzung*), as Gadamer points out. Thus, in my dialogue with Shinran I have tried not to lose a healthy tension between my obligation to listen to the voices of others and my obligation to listen to my own voice; between a faithfulness to the "other" and a fidelity to myself.

But let there be no misunderstanding here. I do not intend my work to be an outright theological discussion of Shinran's thought. The dialogue I carry on with Shinran here is more implicit than explicit; it is not at the forefront or on the surface but behind and beneath the complicated intellectual work that is required for anyone who wants to understand Shinran accurately. In other words, the present work is intended to contribute not merely to the Buddhist-Christian dialogue but also to Shinran

3

studies, as well as to Buddhist studies in general.

How the two kinds of tension that I have explained above are related to each other to form a single force energizing my work can probably be seen by the following account of what concretely motivated my study of Shinran and what kind of issues I wanted to deal with in my work. What drew me at first to Buddhism was its clear world-transcending ("other-worldly" or "world-denying") character, its clean and thorough denial of the worldly values we ordinarily pursue, and its tremendous sense of freedom. One may criticize Buddhism for escapism from the world and society, but one cannot fail to be impressed by its heroic effort to attain complete freedom from this transitory world that is so full of conflict and suffering. As I came to study Mahāyāna Buddhist philosophy and Zen, however, I became convinced that Mahāyāna Buddhism contains within itself the danger of losing the transcendent perspective characteristic of Theravāda Buddhism, and hence of losing its tension with the world. The Mahāyāna doctrine of the identity of *saṃsāra* and *nirvāṇa*, its logic of *soku* 即 (identity), and the Zen affirmation of things as they are in their suchness (*tathatā*), I realized, can easily be turned into an uncritical acceptance of the world, its order, and its values. To be sure, the Mahāyāna affirmation of the world is not a simple direct affirmation unmediated by the logic of negation. The world of Emptiness (*śūnyatā*) is a world where all things are negated and not a single thing is allowed to stand on its own. But Emptiness is at the same time the world of fullness where all things are accepted as they are in all their particularity and diversity. It was especially the Chinese Hua-yen 華嚴 (Jpn. Kegon) philosophy and the Ch'an (Zen) traditions that, under the strong influence of native Taoist and Confucian philosophies, pushed this logic of affirmation to its extreme in reaction against the Indian mentality and worldview. The Zen affirmation of the world is totalistic, not selective or discriminate, just as its negation of the world is totalistic. Thus, when Zen affirms good and evil in its spirit of transcending dualism of any sort, it faces the danger of indiscriminately embracing both good and evil, just as beautiful and ugly things are reflected as they are in a clean mirror or a jewel, a favorite simile in Zen for the pure mind.

With this understanding of Mahāyāna and Zen—with which some may disagree—I turned my attention to other forms of Buddhism, especially the Pure Land faith as it is interpreted by Shinran. I recall vividly how much I was impressed by Shinran's thought when I had my first contact with it through Stanley Weinstein's course on the history of Buddhism at Yale, which I took as a divinity student more than twenty years ago. Going way beyond my previous conception of Buddhism, here was a thinker who immediately captured my heart with what appeared to be a Buddhist version of the doctrine of *sola fides* and *sola gratia* in which I was deeply immersed at the time. Although I could not pursue my interest in Shinran further at that time, Shinran remained in the back of my mind ever since.

My interest in Shinran was greatly enhanced when I came to know the works on Japanese thought by Ienaga Saburō, which came to my attention through Robert Bellah's article "Ienaga Saburo and the Search for Meaning in Modern Japan."[1] To read Ienaga's masterful presentation of the thought-world of the leaders of the so-called Kamakura New Buddhism (*Kamakura shin bukkyō* 鎌倉新仏教) in his *Chūsei bukkyō shisōshi kenkyū* (1955) was truly an eye-opening experience for me, and in my judgment it still has not been surpassed by any other treatment of the subject. I was particularly impressed by his interpretation that the truly innovative element in Shinran's Pure Land thought lies in his doctrine of *akunin shōki* 悪人正機, which teaches that the evil person is the true object (the "right spiritual capacity") for whom Amida's compassionate Vow is meant. Of no less interest to me was Ienaga's concern with the "logic of negation" (*hitei no ronri* 否定の論理) in Japanese thought in general,[2] the same concern as was expressed by Bellah's concept of the element of "transcendence" in Japanese thought. I came to be convinced through Ienaga's writings as well as through my own study of Shinran that if the element of transcendence or the logic of negation is to be found in Japanese thought, it is in Shinran that it is found in its purest form.

My sabbatical year in 1990 finally released me from a heavy burden of teaching that I had to carry for thirteen years without interruption. There was never a single doubt in my mind about what I would most like to do with my sabbatical. Thanks to a Japan Foundation Fellowship, my dream was realized, and I spent one full, happy year preoccupied with nothing but Shinran at the Nanzan Institute for Religion and Culture at Nanzan

---

[1] In Marius Jansen, ed., *Changing Japanese Attitudes toward Modernization* (Princeton: Princeton University Press, 1965).

[2] Ienaga Saburō, *Nihon shisōshi ni okeru hitei no ronri no hattatsu* (Tokyo: Kōbunkan, 1940).

University in Nagoya. During my research at Nanzan I had the fortune of discovering Ienaga's work on Tanabe Hajime, one of the key philosophical minds of modern Japan. Ienaga's book on Tanabe was as much a work on himself as on Tanabe, to whom he confesses to be deeply indebted. The same preoccupation with the logic of negation ran throughout this great work—the preoccupation with the clear-cut discontinuity between the relative and the absolute, immanence and transcendence, affirmation and negation, this world and the other world, and one's own power (*jiriki* 自力) and Other Power (*tariki* 他力). I quickly turned to Tanabe's *Philosophy as Metanoetics* (*Zangedō to shite no tetsugaku*) with a view to finding out what it was in Tanabe that inspired Ienaga so much, and in order to learn about Tanabe's interpretation of Shinran. What struck me most in Tanabe's interpretation of Shinran's thought was his emphasis upon the dialectic of the act (*gyō* 行) of repentance (*zange* 懺悔) on the one hand and faith and grace on the other. In emphasizing the need for the pure grace of Other Power to be mediated by the human act or practice of repentance, Tanabe touches upon a very important aspect in Shinran's thought, regardless of the correctness of his interpretation of Shinran. For Tanabe is concerned lest the failure to maintain a proper dialectical tension between the two should make Other Power a cheap grace lacking ethical seriousness.

To go back to the theme of negation and transcendence, the most crucial problem in interpreting Shinran's thought is, in my view, the question of how much it is to be interpreted in the light of traditional Mahāyāna ontology, and how much Shinran still retains the old Mahāyāna worldview of the continuity between the relative and the absolute, the impure land and the Pure Land, and *saṃsāra* and *nirvāṇa*. There appears to be a general tendency among modern interpreters of Shinran to emphasize the continuity between Shinran and traditional Mahāyāna philosophy. A good example of this can be found in Ueda Yoshifumi and Dennis Hirota's *Shinran*.[3] This study devotes a good portion of the book to a discussion of Mahāyāna ontology as essential for understanding Shinran. But is this really necessary? To the extent that this question is answered in the affirmative, it appears to me that the unique value of Shinran's thought is reduced. There is also some tendency

---

[3] Yoshifumi Ueda and Dennis Hirota, *Shinran: An Introduction to His Thought* (Kyoto: Hongwanji International Center, 1989).

among contemporary interpreters of Shinran to read Zen ideas into his thought, especially with regard to his view of attaining salvation here and now in this world, as if faith was understood by Shinran to be the same as the Zen experience of *satori*. The trouble I have with this kind of interpretation lies not so much in its clear deviation from Shinshū orthodoxy, as in the implication it has in terms of weakening the logic of negation and the dialectical tension, ontological as well as ethical, that is clearly present in Shinran's conception of salvation to be obtained in this world. For Shinran, no matter what our faith may be, this world can never be turned into a paradise, nor can the problem of human sinfulness be completely solved as long as we remain in this world.

I have indicated some of the concerns that I have brought into my study of Shinran. Along with my dialogue with Shinran, therefore, there is in this book another dialogue going on with some of the modern Japanese thinkers and interpreters of Shinran. The absence of transcendence and negation in Japanese thought in general is not a mere religio-philosophical problem; it constitutes in my mind the core issue, one directly related to the tragic history of modern Japan that culminated in the nuclear holocaust of Hiroshima and Nagazaki. For me, Shinran represents the best of Japanese thought. The seriousness and honesty with which he wrestled with the problem of human existence, the clear-cut rejection of the predominant this-worldly orientation of traditional Buddhism and the Shinto religiosity, the radical break with Buddhism as the state ideology, the intense preoccupation with individual salvation, and the humble spirit of egalitarianism with which he led the community of faith he had established, are clearly some of the universalistic elements in Shinran's thought that are of permanent value for humanity as a whole.

Although confined to a small group of people, there is an in-depth Buddhist-Christian dialogue going on in Japan. If I may be allowed to make a remark from the perspective of an observer living across the sea, let me say that if there is anything that Christianity can contribute to Japanese thought, it is its prophetic tradition of transcendence and negation, which have strongly characterized its orientation toward humanity and the world. Without belittling the importance that Nishida Kitarō's and Nishitani Keiji's philosophy of religion has for the Buddhist-Christian dialogue in Japan, I feel it should be pointed out that their predominantly Zen and *śūnyatā* (Emptiness) orientation can easily lead to overlooking the "infinite qualitative difference" between the absolute and the relative, the transcendent and the immanent, the divine and the human. This orientation, epitomized in Nishida's concept of "self-identity in absolute contradiction" (*zettai mujunteki jiko dōitsu* 絶対矛盾的自己同一) or his concept of absolute nothingness (*zettaimu* 絶対無), may be unable to get away from what Bellah calls the "cosmological myth" or "cosmological continuum." If there is anything that Japanese thought should learn from the dialogue, it is from Shinran and the Christian worldview rather than from the Nishida and Nishitani line of thinking. Indeed, the traditional concept of divine transcendence in Christianity is becoming more and more untenable for modern man, and Christian theology is in the process of searching for more satisfactory ways to conceptualize transcendence. And yet it is here that the potential fruitfulness of Christian dialogue with Buddhism undoubtedly lies. It must be kept in mind, however, that the sense of the distance between God and humans, the sense of the "otherness" of Other Power (Shinran), cannot be relinquished except at great cost.

Takizawa Katsumi, a Barthian and Nishida disciple at the same time who did much to activate the Buddhist-Christian dialogue in Japan, seems to have been aware of this problem but was unable to face it squarely because of the pervasive influence of Nishida in his thought. The consequence is that he neglects the very crucial elements of transcendence and negation that are clearly there in Barth and Shinran, and one-sidedly emphasizes the world of absolute affirmation, the "Immanuel" (God with us), or what he calls the primary contact between God and man. It is true that in doing this Takizawa tries to safeguard the primacy of divine initiative and the purity of Other Power—their givenness and objectivity prior to human decision and response. Yet he fails to do justice to the dialectical tension between divine affirmation and grace on the one hand, and sin and divine judgment on the other, in Barth and Shinran. Grace, whether in Barth or Shinran, presupposes an infinite distance between the divine and the human that can never be overcome by our human effort. A crucial question raised with regard to Shinran in this respect is whether this sense of the infinite distance is and can be maintained consistently in his thought. This again raises the question of how far his doctrine of sin and grace is really compatible with traditional Mahāyāna ontology—which after all does not seem to allow that qualitative difference and distance between the absolute and the relative—and the question of the extent to which the former is still to be interpreted in the light of the latter in Shinran.

It is time now to introduce briefly the main contents of this book, which consists of five chapters. Chapter 1, "The Easy Path," discusses the social and religious background of the emergence of Hōnen's sole-practice (*senju* 専修) movement of nenbutsu in the late Heian era of Japan (794–1160), the movement without which the appearance of Shinran is unthinkable. Chapter 2, entitled "Shinran, the *Bonpu*," examines his life and career, but without going into the extremely complicated details of his life—something that would, in any case, be beyond my present capability. It focuses on Shinran's keen awareness of human sinfulness and the sense of despair that led him radically to reinterpret the Pure Land Buddhist tradition he had inherited, including that of Hōnen, his master. Chapter 3 is on "Faith." Here I examine sympathetically, and critically, this central concept in Shinran's thought and cautiously probe the possibility of interpreting it somewhat differently from the more usual orthodox Shinshū understanding.[4] Chapter 4, "The Life of Faith," deals with Shinran's view of the nature of salvation attainable in this present world, and its moral implication; here the problem of faith and moral responsibility in Shinran is closely examined. Lastly, Chapter 5, "Form and Formlessness," probes Shinran's view of the Pure Land and Amida Buddha. After all, it is the story of Amida as Bodhisattva Dharmākara (Hōzō) that forms the basis of Shinran' soteriology. What is the ontological basis of this story of "forms," and how does it fit with the traditional Mahāyāna ontology of "formlessness"? These important issues are examined in the final chapter, and some comparative observations are made from the Christian soteriological perspective.

---

[4] "Shinshū" (True Sect) is the name of the Pure Land Buddhist tradition that takes Shinran as its founder.

1

The Easy Path

IN THE PREFACE to his great translation of Hōnen's biography, Ryugaku Ishizuka states:

> Japanese Buddhism, though tracing its origin to the Buddhism of China and India, has always had characteristic features of its own. But until Hōnen appeared, the Buddhism of all the three countries was fundamentally one. All Buddhist propagandists, Indian, Chinese and Japanese alike, down to Hōnen's time, had chiefly stressed the duty of observing the Buddha's precepts and meditation upon the truth, in order to [gain] the attainment in the present life of the heights of Buddhahood. On the other hand, Jōdo Buddhism's outstanding message was that, as common mortals are entirely too weak both in intellect and will to apprehend and observe all the strict requirements of the Law, as ordinarily taught by all the Buddhist sects, they should abandon such attempts as fruitless, and put their whole dependence upon the mighty power of the Buddha Amida's Primal Vow, and call upon his sacred name in the simple faith, that by his grace alone can they be born into the Buddha's land, however unworthy they may be.[1]

Is this message of Hōnen 法然 (1133–1212) still to be considered Buddhism? Is Buddhism still possible without the practice of morality (*śīla*), mental concentration (*samādhi*), and wisdom-insight (*prajñā*), the Three Learnings that have constituted the foundation of the traditional Buddhist path ever since it was taught by Śākyamuni Buddha?

So radically did Hōnen's message depart from tradition that it is no wonder it drew severe criticism and protest from the champions of the traditional path. Jōkei 貞慶 (1155–1213), an illustrious monk of the Hossō 法相 school based in Kōfuku-ji in Nara and a contemporary of

---

[1] *Hōnen, the Buddhist Saint,* trans. by Harper H. Coates and Ryugaku Ishizuka (New York and London: Garland Publishing, Inc., 1981), I: xx (Translator's Preface). "Original Vow" in the translation has been changed to "Primal Vow," which we will use throughout this book.

Hōnen, deplores the movement launched by Hōnen as follows in a petition submitted to the emperor:

> The sole-practice followers say: "The games of *go* (*iki*) and parcheesi (*sugoroku*) do not violate the sole-practice; neither are the relations between women and priests (*nyobon*) nor the eating of meat hindrances to birth in the Pure Land. Practicing the discipline in this Latter World is as rare as having a tiger in the marketplace. And it is a fearful mistake. A person who has scruples about committing evil is one who does not place his reliance on the Buddha."
>
> Because this kind of rough talk (*sogon*) spreads throughout the land and captures people's thoughts, it becomes an enemy of the Dharma. It is essential that the teaching of birth in Paradise promote the practice of the discipline, the karmic cause for birth in the Pure Land. If you ask why this is so, I reply that, were there no regulations, then it would be impossible to maintain the Six Roots of Merit; and when one permits the doors of the senses [to remain open] at will, then the Three Poisons [illusion, envy, anger] easily arise. When one entangles oneself in the conditions for illusion, then the window for meditating on the Buddha (*nenbutsu*) is not serene; and when one muddies the heart with envy and anger, the waters of the Jeweled Lakes (*hōchi*) cannot be clear. Is not the experience of these good karmic states the Pure Land itself? Accordingly, we intently employ the practices of the discipline as the karmic cause for birth in the Pure Land.... The movement is popular in the capital and in nearby provinces; and it is said that as far [north] as Hokuriku and the various provinces along the Eastern Sea (Tōkai) and other circuits, monks and nuns of the sole-practice movement successfully propagate these notions. Except by Imperial Edict, how can they be restrained? The purpose of this request is entirely concerned with these matters!
>
> The Buddha's Law and the Imperial Law are as body and mind: each should see to the well-being of the other, and then the welfare of the state will be assured. In these times the Pure Land movement has begun to arise and the activities of the sole-practice to flourish. But can we also say that these are times when the imperial power has been restored? Moreover, the Three Learnings [morality, wisdom, meditation] are about to be abandoned and the Eight Sects are declining. Time and again how the government of society is in disarray![2]

[2] Robert E. Morrell, *Early Kamakura Buddhism: A Minority Report* (Berkeley, California: Asian Humanities Press, 1987), 86–87.

If we do not have here an entirely accurate representation of the "sole-practice" (*senju* 專修) movement of nenbutsu launched by Hōnen and his followers, we certainly can hear the voice of an eminent monk of high aristocratic background who, alarmed at the rapid spread of the nenbutsu movement, is urgently calling for the intervention of the state to protect the Dharma. For him, the Buddha's Law and the Imperial Law are inseparable, and it is this traditional alliance, the very foundation of the established order, which he sees threatened by the new popular movement.[3]

It is not that Jōkei denies the Pure Land faith itself. How could he, seeing that it was also based upon the scriptures preached by the Buddha, and that it already had a long tradition in the land? In fact, he even mentions the nenbutsu and the ideal way it should be practiced. Nenbutsu, for him, is none other than to meditate (*nen* 念) upon the Buddha (*butsu* 佛), its literal and original meaning, and this can only be done properly when based upon the strict observance of the moral precepts and mental purification.[4] But it was precisely this idea of nenbutsu as a form of meditation that was being rejected by Hōnen in favor of the vocal recitation of the name of Amida Buddha (*shōmyō* 稱名 *nenbutsu*). Not only were practices such as precepts, meditation, worship of Buddhas, and other good acts and meritorious deeds declared by Hōnen to be unnecessary, but even the nenbutsu practiced as a form of meditation with a view to visualize the Buddha and his Pure Land was repudiated as another "difficult path" for ordinary people to follow. It was this radical departure from the meditational practice of nenbutsu, already a long-established tradition within Heian Buddhism, that marked the culminating point of ever-increasing popularization of the Pure Land faith and practice and brought about a revolutionary change in Buddhism.[5] In the words of Hōnen,

[3] Concerning the socio-political implication of Hōnen's nenbutsu movement, see Tamura Enchō, "Senju nenbutsu no juyō to dan'atsu" *Nihon bukkyō shisōshi kenkyū: Jōdokyō hen* (Kyoto: Heiraku-ji Shoten, 1959), 58–92.

[4] Jōkei's understanding of Pure Land Buddhism and nenbutsu is expressed in the Kōfuku-ji Petition that he drafted; see particularly article six, "The Error of Ignorance Concerning the Pure Lands," and article seven, "The Error of Misunderstanding the Nenbutsu" in Morrell, *Early Kamakura Buddhism*, 80–85.

[5] Concerning the difference between Hōnen's nenbutsu and the traditional Tendai nenbutsu as represented by Genshin's *Ōjōyōshū*, see Inoue Mitsusada, "Fujiwara jidai no Jōdokyō no tokushitsu" *Shintei Nihon Jōdokyō seiritsushi no kenkyū* (Tokyo: Yamakawa Shuppansha, 1975), 112–21.

Let devotees of the present day give up their so-called meditations as if they were required by the Law. Even though a man would meditate upon the images of the Buddhas and Bodhisattvas in Paradise, the fact is he is incapable of picturing to himself the Buddhas as represented in the images made by such famous sculptors as Unkei and Kōkei. Even though he tries to meditate upon the things which beautify the Land of Bliss, he finds it hard even to picture to his mind the beauties of the flowers and fruit of the cherry, plum and peach of this world with which he is so familiar. So simply believe the words in Zendō's Commentary, which says, "That Buddha is now present in the Land of Bliss, having already attained enlightenment. All ye sentient beings ought to know that His great Primal Vow was not in vain, and that if you call upon His name you shall without fail be born into the Pure Land. Put your whole trust in that Primal Vow and call upon His name with all your heart. If you thus call, the three mental states will come of themselves."[6]

The idea of sole-practice (*senju*) originates from Shan-tao 善導 (Zendō, 613–681), the Chinese Pure Land master whom Hōnen deeply respected and faithfully followed and in whom the doctrinal development of the Chinese Pure Land thought reached a culminating point.[7] From a wide variety of Buddhist practices, Shan-tao chose five as the "right practices" (*shōgyō* 正行): recitation of the Pure Land sūtras, contemplation on Amida and the Pure Land, worshiping Amida, calling upon Amida's name, and praising Amida and offering to him. For Shan-tao, "right practices" meant the practices that are solely based upon the Pure Land sūtras and directed solely to Amida and his Pure Land. Hence, for him the right practices meant the sole-practice, whereas their opposite, the "sundry practices," were the above-mentioned five kinds of acts devoted to other Buddhas and objects of devotion. Shan-tao then went a step further when he singled out from the five right practices the calling upon the name of Amida Buddha as the "true act of settlement (of enlightenment in the

---

[6] Coates and Ishizuka, *Hōnen*, 398. The "three mental states" refer to sincere mind, deep mind, and the aspiration for enlightenment by directing merit, which are mentioned in the *Sūtra of Contemplation on the Buddha of Immeasurable Life (Kan muryōjubutsu kyō)* as the necessary state of mind for practicing nenbutsu.

[7] For Shan-tao's Pure Land thought, see Mochizuki Shinkō, *Chūgoku Jōdo kyōrishi* (Kyoto: Hōzōkan, 1942), 180–96; see also Shan-tao's passages on the sole-practice quoted in Hōnen's major work, *Senjaku hongan nenbutsu shū*, in Shinshū Shōgyō Zensho Hensansho, ed., *Shinshū shōgyō zensho* (Kyoto: Ōyagi Kōbundō, 1941; hereafter SSZ), I: 934–40.

Pure Land)" in distinction to the other four practices, which he called "auxiliary acts." Shan-tao, however, did not reject auxiliary acts, nor by sole-practice did he mean nenbutsu only.

It was Hōnen who drew a radical conclusion from Shan-tao's soteriology by eliminating all practices other than nenbutsu as unnecessary and made Shan-tao's sole-practice synonymous with the exclusive practice that rejects all practices other than nenbutsu. In the well-known passage in his *Senjaku hongan nenbutsu shū* (Passages on the nenbutsu selected in the Primal Vow; hereafter, *Senjaku shū*), an epoch-making document in the history of Japanese Buddhism, Hōnen states:

> If you desire to free yourself quickly from birth-and-death, of the two excellent teachings leave aside the Path of Sages and choosing, enter the Pure Land way.
>
> If you desire to enter the Pure Land way, of the two methods of practice, right and sundry, cast aside all sundry practices and choosing, take the right practice.
>
> If you desire to perform the right practice, of the two kinds of acts, true and auxiliary, further put aside the auxiliary and choosing, solely perform the act of true settlement. The act of true settlement is to say the Name of Buddha.[8]

As the above words indicate, the idea that one has to select (*senjaku* 選擇) one practice to the exclusion of others preoccupied Hōnen's mind in his quest for salvation. For him, nenbutsu was *the* practice because it was the act "selected in the Primal Vow" (*senjaku hongan* 選擇本願)—hence, the title of his work, "Passages on the Nenbutsu Selected in the Primal Vow."[9]

It was indeed this idea of selecting one practice as the only way of salvation and concentrating on it single-heartedly that characterized the entire new Buddhist movement that followed Hōnen, what the scholars

[8] Quoted in *The True Teaching, Practice and Realization of the Pure Land Way: A Translation of Shinran's Kyōgyōshinshō* (Kyoto: Hongwanji International Center, 1983; Shin Buddhism Translation Series), I: 136; *Senjaku shū, SSZ*, I: 62.

[9] This is the way the title of Hōnen's work is translated in the above translation of Shinran's *Kyōgyōshinshō*. Literally, "selected" modifies the "Primal Vow" rather than the "Nenbutsu," and thus "The Passages on the Nenbutsu of the Primal Vow Selected [by Amida]" would be the more accurate literal translation of the title. In terms of the meaning intended by Hōnen, however, it is after all the nenbutsu that is selected in the Primal Vow (selected) by Amida.

have called the Kamakura New Buddhism (*Kamakura shin bukkyō* 鎌倉 新佛教) as against the traditional eight sects.[10] Representing the *Zeitgeist* of the time when the Heian regime was crumbling and the feudal order of the Kamakura era (1185–1333) was emerging, Hōnen heralded the radically new approach to the problem of human salvation, the "easy" and popular way that, however, demanded a total devotion. He was followed by others like Shinran, one of his dedicated followers who further radicalized his Pure Land message; Nichiren, who preached chanting the name of the *Lotus Sūtra* (*daimoku* 題目) instead of the name of Amida Buddha as the only way of salvation; and Dōgen, who insisted upon mere sitting in meditation (*shikan taza* 只管打坐) as the only path to attaining Buddhahood. The age in which these figures appeared and delivered their messages of salvation was profoundly different from the height of the Heian period when the Buddhist sangha, supported by the state and the nobles, offered an eclectic and comprehensive system of practices designed to harmonize various doctrines and appeal to people of diverse backgrounds and capacities. Schools and denominations were there before the rise of the new Buddhist movements, but they were neither sectarian nor exclusivistic in their methods of practice leading to liberation from birth-and-death. Different voices were heard on salvation, but they were neither so urgent nor so straightforward as the messages of salvation delivered by the leaders of the new Buddhist movements. Clearly, times had changed, and it is to the social condition of the late Heian period to which we must turn our attention if we are to have an adequate understanding of the rise and spread of these sectarian movements that eventually came to dominate Japanese Buddhism.

The twelfth century was a period when fundamental change of profound consequence was taking place in Japanese society.[11] The cen-

---

[10] The idea of "selecting" (*senjaku*) as the chief motif of the Kamakura New Buddhism is pointed out in Chiba Jōryū, Kitanishi Hiromu, and Takagi Yutaka, *Bukkyōshi gaisetsu: Nihon hen* (Kyoto: Heirakuji Shoten, 1969), 94–95. The best introduction to the fundamental spirit and nature of the Kamakura New Buddhism is still, in my mind, Ienaga Saburō's *Chūsei bukkyō shisōshi kenkyū* (Kyoto: Hōzōkan, 1955; revised and enlarged edition), 1–109. My discussion of Kamakura Buddhism is heavily indebted to it. See also Stanley Weinstein, "The Concept of Reformation in Japanese Buddhism," *Studies in Japanese Culture*, ed. by Saburo Ōta (Tokyo: Japan Pen Club, 1973), II: 75–86.

[11] The following discussion of the social change in twelfth-century Japan is primarily based upon George Sansom, *A History of Japan to 1334* (Stanford: Stanford University Press, 1958).

tralized imperial system, based upon the Chinese model and the legal bureaucratic system devised after the Taika reform in the seventh century, had nearly collapsed and Japan was entering into a medieval feudal order led by powerful local military leaders and landowners. According to the social order envisioned, and to a certain degree implemented, by the Taika reformers and the imperial loyalists, all the land and people belonged to the imperial house as its public domain. But the privatization of some land and the people attached to it had already begun in the Nara period. The so-called manors (*shōen* 莊園) of the powerful noble families in the court and the capital and the influential monasteries and shrines began to eclipse the economic basis of the imperial system. George Sansom describes the rise and development of the manor as follows:

> Thus the manor was strictly speaking an illegal growth, but it developed upon such a scale and served the interest of so many powerful persons that the state was bound to recognize it, the more so since almost all the nobles and officials in the capital and all the great monasteries and shrines lived upon income received from manorial rights. It was for this reason that the illegal and the legal systems grew up side by side without any great conflict.[12]

The economic erosion of the imperial system by the manors reached its peak during the tenth and eleventh centuries, when the powerful Fujiwara families wielded an almost absolute power. Along with the development of the manors, the privileged lands that were exempt from taxation and administrative control by the local government, there also was growth in the power of the local landlords and magnates, who had either their own lands or acted as the administrators on behalf of absentee landlords in the capital. In order to protect and extend their large estates, the landlords had to retain military power and often resorted to naked physical power; this led to the rise of the professional warrior class. The decline of the central imperial authority, economic and military as well as administrative, reached its lowest point in the latter half of the twelfth century, when the real power of the whole country belonged to the two most powerful military families, the Taira and the Minamoto. The rivalry and conflict between these two great warrior families accounted for much of the social confusion of twelfth-century Japan.

[12] Sansom, *History of Japan*, 356.

The established Buddhist orders, whose power and prosperity had been thoroughly enmeshed with the secular socio-political system since Nara, contributed in no small measure to the bleak social atmosphere of the late Heian era. The disorderly conduct of the monk-soldiers, especially those of the Tendai headquarters at Enryaku-ji, the rivalry between powerful Tendai monasteries such as Enryaku-ji and Onjō-ji as well as between Enryaku-ji and Kōfuku-ji of Nara (which was being patronized by the Fujiwara family), added to the general social confusion of the time. Tōdai-ji and Kōfuku-ji, the symbols of old Nara Buddhism, were ravaged by Taira troops in revenge for the monasteries' support of the Mochihito revolt (1180). Upon hearing this news, the Regent Kujō Kanezane wrote as follows in his diary, the *Gyokuyō* 玉葉:

> Although this may indeed be attributed to the fate of the times, my sorrow at the time [when I heard the news] was deeper than when you would have lost your parents. I was born accidentally in this time, and have met these circumstances. This is in accordance with my past karma; would I therefore have anything to depend on in my next life? If the world becomes settled, I would be able to fulfill my long-cherished aspiration to retire quickly to mountains and woods. The old aspiration to have the right mind at the moment of death is the most essential thing in my life.[13]

As if to match this social turmoil, nature also wrought tremendous havoc in twelfth-century Heian Japan. George Sansom describes the grim social condition in the following way:

> Though the misfortunes of the late Heian period are of earlier origin than the rise of the Taira clan, the last years of their power saw an awful accumulation of disasters. Whatever its cause, the failure of the regime was plainly attested by the frequency of robbery, arson, and murder in the very heart of the imperial city, offences which the armed forces of the Taira were unable to suppress. The government did resort to drastic measures, arresting and punishing criminals with ferocity; but the results were not good. The condition of the city was lamentable. It has been described in a celebrated work called *Hōjō-ki*, which is the notebook of a not very unworldly recluse living in a small hut in one of its suburbs. His name was Kamo Chōmei. His work contains, as well as an obviously first-hand description of Fukuwara, a striking account of material conditions in the capital in the years from 1177 to 1182. It is a dreadful tale of

---

[13] Quoted in Akamatsu Toshihide, *Shinran* (Tokyo: Yoshikawa Kōbunkan, 1961), 24.

storms, earthquakes, conflagrations, plagues, starvation, and cold, when infants could be seen clinging to the breasts of their dead mothers and shivering men stole images of the Buddha for firewood and corpses remained unburied. In the city proper, excluding the suburbs, over forty-two thousand corpses lying in the street were counted in two months. It was a world of pollution, and famine struck not only the capital city, but also all the surrounding provinces and the western seats of Taira power.[14]

In view of this disastrous situation in late Heian society, it was only natural that the idea of the age of the Last Dharma (*mappō* 末法) appealed with great force to thoughtful Buddhists of the time.

The idea of the progressive decline of the Buddhist dharma, although of Indian origin, was systematically formulated in China, especially after the severe persecution of Buddhism in the sixth century. According to this formulation, the Buddhist dharma is to undergo three stages of progressive decline. There were several divergent theories on the three stages. One of them, the most popular during the late Heian period, held that after the *parinirvāṇa* of the Śākyamuni Buddha the period of the Right Dharma (*shōbō* 正法) continued for one thousand years, during which both the teaching and the practice existed and people attained enlightenment through them. It was then followed by the period of Semblance Dharma (*zōhō* 像法), which lasted another thousand years during which there were the teaching and practice but no enlightenment. Finally, the period of Last Dharma (*mappō* 末法) set in to last for ten thousand years, during which there would remain only teaching but no practice or enlightenment.[15] According to this theory, the *mappō* period would begin in Japan in the latter half of the eleventh century—according to the traditional Chinese dating of the Buddha's *parinirvāṇa* (941 BC)—when Heian society already showed serious signs of disintegration.

Although the idea of *mappō* had been known in Japan long before the late Heian period, now for the first time it became "real" and found

---

[14] Sansom, *History of Japan*, 286. Fukuwara, in present-day Hyōgo Prefecture, is the location to which the capital was temporarily moved in 1180.

[15] For a brief discussion of the various theories of the three periods, see Inoue, *Jōdokyō seiritsushi*, 108–12; Tamura, "Mappō shisō no keisei," *Nihon bukkyō shisōshi kenkyū*, 277–308. Weinstein's article, "The Concept of Reformation in Japanese Buddhism," discusses the significance of the *mappō* idea for the leaders of the Kamakura New Buddhist movements, 79–80. On the idea of the decline of Buddhism, see Jan Nattier's recent comprehensive study, *Once Upon a Future Time: Studies in a Buddhist Prophecy of Decline* (Berkeley, California: Asian Humanities Press), 1991.

19

wide acceptance among people from all walks of life. Sufferings were visible everywhere and the impermanence of life was not a mere doctrinal teaching. As Tamura Enchō puts it:

> Although the concept of *mappō* in Japan was taken as announcing the common fate of the nobility in the process of downfall, rather than being a problem concerning the easiness and difficulty of practice and the possibility of attaining Buddhahood, the conflicts and confusions caused by the Taira and the Minamoto, along with the natural disasters that accompanied them, finally made even the lower classes of common people experience vividly the advent of *mappō*.[16]

Buddhism started out as a religious movement addressing the problem of suffering and impermanence of life; it began as a religion promising liberation from these fundamental problems of human life. Yet it was precisely this fundamental mission of Buddhism that the established Buddhism of late Heian society proved unable to fulfill. Reasons for this failure were many. First of all, there was the obvious fact that the Buddhist sangha was extremely corrupt and at least partly responsible for the social turmoil of the day. The established Buddhism was also part and parcel of the crumbling old order, sinking with it and desperately trying to hold on to the secular privileges it had been used to.

It is one of the greatest ironies of history that Buddhism, a religion that began with such a clear rejection of worldly values and order, was universally turned into a religion of the society and the state, a social and cultural religion that guarantees worldly security and happiness. This universal metamorphosis of Buddhism, however, was perhaps nowhere more thoroughly established than in the late Heian Buddhism. As a religion completely submerged in the earthly spirit of Shinto and even institutionally amalgamated with it, as a religion that lost the transcendent orientation toward the world and was satisfied with praying and performing magical rituals for the welfare of the nobility in this world as well as in the next life, it was far from being in a position to satisfy the souls crying out for liberation from the very conditions of human existence. Its message of this-worldly promises did not interest those seeking salvation from the world; its message of Buddha-nature inherent in every human being did not convince those who had a deep awareness of the massive presence of

[16] *Hōnen* (Tokyo: Yoshikawa Kōbunkan, 1959), 63–64.

evil and sinfulness in themselves as well as in their society; its promise of realizing Buddhahood in this very body (*sokushin jōbutsu* 即身成佛) and its vision of the world consisting of dharmas mutually interpenetrating and harmonizing were no longer persuasive to those who were possessed by the idea of the *mappō* and witnessing the complete disintegration of their society.

Clearly, the last days of the Heian era called for a religious message that promised supramundane salvation and not worldly security; a religion of individuals, not a religion of the state and family; a religion that looks at humanity and the world without the old religious perspectives and squarely faces the stark realities of life. The traditional answers appeared not merely unconvincing but also unworkable in the age of *mappō*. The yearning for salvation was more urgent than ever, but the old messages were unacceptable.

How then to get out of this dilemma? How to take the reality of *mappō* seriously and yet find liberation still possible? This was the central issue that agonized the many religious souls of the late Heian period. The answer lay in finding an "easy path" of salvation that could work for everybody, high and low, men and women, monks and lay, good and evil alike. And it was Hōnen who ushered in this new approach by boldly formulating an "easy path" and setting the tone for all the new forms of Buddhism that were to follow him.

Basing his judgment upon Tao-ch'o's (562–645) *Passages on the Land of Happiness*, Hōnen declared at the outset of his *Senjaku shū*:

> The present time is the age of the Last Dharma, the evil age of five defilements. The Pure Land Path is the only road through which we can enter [into enlightenment].[17]

The traditional Path of Sages (*shōdōmon* 聖荀門) can no longer work. There are two reasons for this: "We are too far removed from the great sage (Śākyamuni Buddha), and the truth is profound but our understanding feeble."[18] Here we find Hōnen's deep awareness of the time (*ji* 時) and the capacity (*ki* 機) of people to practice the path of enlighten-

---

[17] *SSZ*, I: 929. "The five defilements" (*gojoku* 五濁) refer to the five marks of degeneracy that accompany the Last Dharma-age: the impurities of the age (kalpa), impurity in view, impurity of blind passion, degeneration of sentient beings' mind and body, and the shortening of their span of life (Nakamura Hajime, *Bukkyōgo daijiten*, 1981, p. 369).

[18] *SSZ*, I: 929.

ment, an awareness that underlay his message of the sole-practice of nen-butsu. We have to pay careful attention to our own capacity and the time we are situated in, lest our whole effort come to nothing: "The practice of the Buddhist path requires that we truly weigh ourselves well and discern the time."[19]

This was not a mere general statement but one based upon his own existential awareness. Hōnen weighed his own capacity in the following way:

> Having a deep desire to obtain salvation, and with faith in the teachings of the various Scriptures, I practice many forms of self-discipline. There are indeed many doctrines in Buddhism, but they may all be summed up in the three learnings, namely the precepts, meditation and knowledge, as practised by the adherents of the Lesser and Greater Vehicles, and the exoteric and esoteric sects. But the fact is that I do not keep even one of the precepts, nor do I attain to any one of the many forms of meditation. A certain priest has said that without the observance of the *śīla* (precepts), there is no such thing as the realization of *samādhi*. Moreover the heart of the ordinary unenlightened man, because of his surroundings, is always liable to change, just like monkeys jumping from one branch to another. It is indeed in a state of confusion, easily moved and with difficulty controlled. In what way does right and indefectible knowledge arise? Without the sword of indefectible knowledge, how can one get free from the chains of evil passion, whence comes evil conduct? And unless one gets free from evil conduct and evil passions, how shall he obtain deliverance from the bondage of birth and death? Alas! What shall I do? What shall I do? The likes of us are incompetent to practice the three disciplines of the precepts, meditation and knowledge.

It was in the midst of this deep frustration and despair, combined with an intense longing for salvation, that Hōnen came to find the light in the message of the nenbutsu taught by Shan-tao. Hōnen continues his story:

> And so I inquired of a great many learned men and priests whether there is any other way of salvation than these three disciplines, that is better suited to our poor abilities, but I found none who could either teach me the way or even suggest it to me. At last I went into the Library at Kurodani on Mount Hiei, where all the Scriptures were, all by myself, and with a heavy heart, read them all through. While doing so, I hit

---

[19] Quoted in Tamura, *Hōnen*, 64.

upon a passage in Zendō's *Commentary on the Meditation* [*Contemplation*] *Sūtra*, which runs as follows:—"Whether walking or standing, sitting or lying, only repeat the name of Amida with all your heart. Never cease the practice of it even for a moment. This is the very work which unfailingly issues in salvation, for it is in accordance with the Primal Vow of that Buddha." On reading this I was impressed with the fact that even ignorant people like myself, by reverent meditation upon this passage, and an entire dependence upon the truth in it, never forgetting the repetition of Amida's sacred name, may lay the foundation for that good karma, which will with absolute certainty eventuate in birth into the blissful land. And not only was I led to believe in this teaching bequeathed by Zendō, but also earnestly to follow the great Vow of Amida. And especially was that passage deeply inwrought into my very soul which says, "For it is in accordance with the Primal Vow of that Buddha."[20]

The light of salvation that shone upon Hōnen here was not so much the practice of nenbutsu as such—which was a known practice at the time—as the Primal Vow of Amida who, out of his deep compassion for the sentient beings unable to follow the Path of Sages, laid the foundation for an "easy" way of salvation. The nenbutsu became the sole-practice for Hōnen because he suddenly realized that "it is in accordance with the Primal Vow of that Buddha." It was this discovery of the power of the Primal Vow that led Hōnen to the exclusive practice of nenbutsu as the sole-practice sufficient for salvation.[21]

Unlike other Pure Land thinkers before him, as we have mentioned, Hōnen did not understand the nenbutsu as a form of meditation, which would have made it another "difficult" practice. Ishizuka has aptly written,

---

[20] Coates and Ishizuka, *Hōnen*, 185–87.

[21] The vow that Hōnen is referring to is the eighteenth Vow, the most important among the forty-eight Vows, uttered and fulfilled by Bodhisattva Dharmākara (Hōzō). The story of this bodhisattva, which constitutes the basis of the Pure Land faith and practice, is given in the *Larger Sūtra of Immeasurable Light* (*Daimuryōju kyō*). Since the knowledge of this story is presupposed in our treatment of Hōnen's and Shinran's thought, readers who are not familiar with it are referred to chapter 5 of this book, where a summary of it is given. At any rate, in the eighteenth Vow Dharmākara presents a minimum practice of nenbutsu done in sincere faith as the condition for birth in the Pure Land. Since all of his Vows, the story goes, came to be fulfilled as the karmic reward of his long and arduous bodhisattva practice, it is believed that, therefore, those who practice nenbutsu will without fail attain birth in the Pure Land.

Meditation was the predominant feature of all nenbutsu practice before Hōnen. Genshin taught that in the act of invocation of the sacred name a mental picture should be formed of the compassionate Buddha, while Kakuban kept in mind the significance of the virtues inherent in the invocation, which, to him, was much the same as the *Dhāraṇī* or mystic incantation of the Shingon. With Yokwan that alone was an efficacious invocation of the Buddha which was invariably preceded by mental concentration, and, without this, a million repetitions would be useless. Thus all the types of nenbutsu before Hōnen were so dependent upon this subjective element of meditation, that if a devotee should be mentally too dull to apprehend all the implications of his act of invocation or fail at any point in his meditation, the efficacy of his nenbutsu was all but entirely negatived.[22]

According to Hōnen, nenbutsu as the easy path reflects Amida Buddha's universal compassion to save all sentient beings regardless of their conditions, spiritual, social, or material. Asking why Amida particularly chose in his Vow the nenbutsu, rather than other practices, as the practice necessary for our birth in the Pure Land, Hōnen says that, although it belongs to the ultimate mystery of the Buddha's mind, he chose nenbutsu because it can be easily practiced anywhere and at any time, and by all classes of people, even the poorest.[23] It is also "the most excellent way, because Amida's name represents all the virtues inhering in him, or, in other words, stands for his very personality, and so when one calls his name he reveals himself just as anyone responds when his name is called."[24]

In a letter of Hōnen we find his glowing faith in Amida's compassionate will, manifested in his Vow for universal salvation:

When we consider the capacity of the sentient beings living in the age of Last Dharma for the birth in the land of utter bliss, we should not doubt our birth because of the paucity of our practice; a single or ten invocations are enough for it. We should not doubt because we are sinners; it is

---

[22] Coates and Ishizuka, *Hōnen*, 42 (Historical Introduction). *Nembutsu* in the translation has been changed to "nenbutsu," which we will use throughout this book. Genshin (942–1017), Kakuban (1095–1143), and Yokwan (Yōkan; 1054–1132) are all important monks who had been involved in some form of Pure Land practice prior to Hōnen, but they did not champion the sole-practice of nenbutsu as Hōnen did.

[23] *Senjaku shū, SSZ,* I: 943–45.

[24] Coates and Ishizuka, *Hōnen*, 45 (Historical Introduction).

said that Amida does not dislike the person who has deep roots of sin. Nor should we doubt because the times have waned; even the sentient beings living after the dharma has completely disappeared can still attain birth, how much more would those living in the present age [of Last Dharma]? We should not doubt because we are evil; [even Zendō] confessed himself to be an ordinary being laden with blind passions. Although there are numerous Pure Lands throughout the ten directions, we aspire for the Western Paradise because even the sentient beings who have committed ten evils and five grave offenses can be born there. Among all the Buddhas we take refuge in Amida because he comes in person to welcome us when we utter his name three to five times. Among all the practices, we have recourse to nenbutsu because it is Amida's Primal Vow. Now, when we ride on the Primal Vow of Amida and aspire for the birth, it being Amida's Vow, there is no reason that it cannot be attained. In order to ride on the Primal Vow, all you need is simply to have a deep faith. To be born in the body of a human being, which is hard to be born in; to meet with the Primal Vow, which is hard to meet with; to awaken the aspiration for enlightenment, which is hard to awaken; to leave the village of transmigration, which is hard to leave; to attain birth in the Pure Land, which is hard to be born into, is the joy of joys. Although we believe that even those who have committed ten evils and five grave offenses can be born in the Pure Land, we should be careful not to commit even a trifle sin. Even a sinful person can be born, how much more would a good person? Believing that even the practice of a single or ten invocations is not without benefit, we should call upon the Buddha ceaselessly. One can attain birth even with a single invocation, how much more would one who makes many invocations?[25]

The easy practice made possible by Amida's Vow requires an act of faith: "In order to ride on the Primal Vow, all you need is simply to have a deep faith." Here we see another spiritual characteristic of the new popular Buddhist movements that began with Hōnen, namely the emphasis on faith. The easy practice, however easy it may be, still requires the faith to accept it; if nothing else, the faith to accept the unbelievably easy path and to practice it single-heartedly.

An important consequence of this emphasis in the new Buddhist movements on the easy path and faith was that the traditional division within Buddhism between monks (*shukke* 出家) and laity (*zaike* 在家) was turned into a distinction between believers and non-believers. Now the

---

[25] Quoted in Tamura, *Hōnen*, 49–50; *Saihō shinan shō*, SSZ, IV: 220–21.

identity of the lay Buddhists became much sharper and stronger and that of the religious less pronounced than in the traditional Buddhism. If faith and the easy practice are the only conditions for our salvation, it is only natural that the religious authority of the monks becomes relativized. What matters now is whether or not you have faith, not the ability to follow the arduous path to enlightenment preached in traditional Buddhism. Hōnen himself is said to have led a pious religious life, one in which he adhered to the precepts required of the monk who has renounced the secular life. But it was only a matter of time before others would come along who would draw a bold logical conclusion from the new religiosity initiated by Hōnen.

The sense of crisis brought to the traditional Buddhist teaching by the widespread belief in the idea of the *mappō*, the emphasis on easy practice and faith, the exclusive loyalty to a single path of salvation, and the emergence of lay Buddhists with a clear sense of religious identity, were phenomena unheard of in the long history of monastically oriented Buddhism, not merely in Japan but indeed the world over. These trends gave rise to an entirely new form of Buddhist community, essentially resembling the early Christian church, which was radically different from the traditional sangha. It was a community of believers with an egalitarian spirit, a community with a strong sense of belonging on the basis of an individual decision of faith. It consisted of believers who responded to the message of liberation from the world and considered themselves as being "in the world" but not "of the world," and of a new type of religious leaders who considered themselves "neither monk nor lay"—as Shinran, a dedicated follower of Hōnen, was later to describe himself.

An organization of voluntary choice, this new form of religious community reflected the rise of social consciousness in the commoners of the late Heian society.[26] The religious message was no longer confined to the élite few but addressed to everybody without distinction of religious standing, social status, sex, age, education, and knowledge, or even of moral merit and demerit. Often put into the popular *kana* script, easy to read and understand, the message of the "easy path" called forth a response of faith from people no longer satisfied with the subservient role they had to play within the structure of traditional Buddhism. In many

---

[26] See Tamura Enchō, "Senju nenbutsu no juyō katei," *Nihon bukkyō shisōshi kenkyū,* especially 42–57.

respects, indeed, these new movements in Buddhism resembled the Reformation in the West.

Let us now turn to the main concern of our study, Shinran, often called "the Luther of Japan," a figure whose appearance is unthinkable without Hōnen but who eventually came to eclipse his master, not only in the revolutionary message he delivered but also in his fame and the influence he exerted upon later generations.

2

Shinran, the *Bonpu*

SHINRAN 親鸞 (1173–1262) HAS BEEN HONORED by his followers as a saint (*shōnin* 聖人), but he would be the first person to disclaim the title if he were to hear it today. It is one of the great ironies of history that a person who had lived his entire life in constant awareness of his own ineradicable sinfulness came to be revered as a saint. The irony does not stop there. The one who did not want to be regarded as a teacher—the true teachers being Śākyamuni Buddha and the other Pure Land masters before him—or a leader, and the one who never even dreamed of being the founder of an independent sect, came to be honored as the founder of the largest Buddhist sect in Japan today. Yet a saint Shinran was, albeit in a very different way from the traditional Buddhist way of sainthood that was attained through a strenuous pursuit of spiritual perfection. Shinran, in contrast, became a saint by thoroughly giving up the effort to become a saint. His was a paradoxical way of sainthood.

Religion, whatever its transcendent origin may be, begins, as far as the human side is concerned, with an awareness of the problems intrinsic to human life: human finitude and frailty, the impermanence and transience of worldly things, sin and evil, inevitable sufferings, and the unexpected tragic events that shake up the "secure" order of life. Religion thus promises another world that is absolutely free from these problems, a transcendent order of being, epistemological or ontological, that is beyond the turmoils of this world. All religious traditions work with these two aspects of "reality" and with the inevitable tension felt between them. When a religious system becomes established and its doctrines generally accepted in a given society, however, it tends to settle comfortably within that society, have its view of reality skewed by that society, and thus lose sight of the problems that gave rise to it in the first place. It becomes so successful in persuading, or very often "forcing," people to believe in the ideal world it preaches, that it becomes oblivious to the harsh realities of life and out of touch with reality. It becomes intoxicated by its ideal vision of the world and mechanically repeats its message, while the social situation has changed radically and the new problems call for new answers.

This, probably, is one of the reasons that secular thinkers have criticized religion for covering up the reality of the world and seeking escape from it by making false promises of an unknown and unverifiable world somewhere beyond or behind (or hidden). And this, probably, was what led the young Barth to issue the following harsh warning on religion:

> Religion, so far from being the place where the healthy harmony of human life is lauded, is instead the place where it appears diseased, discordant, and disrupted. Religion is not the sure ground upon which human culture safely rests; it is the place where civilization and its partner, barbarism, are rendered fundamentally questionable.... Religion must beware lest it tone down in any degree the unconverted man's judgment. Conflict and distress, sin and death, the devil and hell, make up the reality of religion. So far from releasing men from guilt and destiny, it brings men under their sway. Religion possesses no solution of the problems of life; rather it makes of the problem a wholly insoluble enigma. Religion neither discovers the problem nor solves it: what it does is to disclose the truth that it cannot be solved. Religion is neither a thing to be enjoyed nor a thing to be celebrated; it must be borne as a yoke which cannot be removed. Religion is not a thing to be desired or extolled: it is a misfortune which takes total hold upon some men, and is by them passed on to others...[1]

The charge that religion is guilty of dishonesty for not facing up to the realities of life and the world may without much dispute be applied to the established Buddhism of the late Heian society, for it did not pay serious attention to the agonies of *mappō*, the age of the Last Dharma. The same cannot be said for Shinran's religious message, however. For it was above all his naked exposure, unmitigated by the traditional Buddhist answers, to the harsh realities of life, especially to the massive presence of evil in man, that led him to search for a new path of human salvation. What strikes us particularly in Shinran's life and work is the fact that, rather than the general rhetoric of the traditional laments regarding human misery caused by ignorance, greed, and anger, we are able to hear in him the highly personal voice of a man agonizing over his own plight.

[1] Karl Barth, *The Epistle to the Romans*, trans. by Edwyn C. Hoskyns (London: Oxford University Press, 1933), 258.

The entire works of Shinran, including his most systematic work, the *Kyōgyōshinshō* 教行信證,[2] ring with the voice of a man in deep existential anguish over his own state of "sinking in an immense ocean of desires and attachments."[3] And it is this voice of an "unsaved soul," Shinran, the *bonpu* 凡夫 (ordinary person) laden with "deep and heavy karmic evil and raging blind passions,"[4] more than any of his religious messages, that still speaks forcefully to the hearts of modern men and women. Perhaps we may be allowed to say that the existential seriousness and honesty with which he grappled with the problem of his own sinful nature is as meaningful as the answer he eventually came up with. In fact, as we shall see later, the awareness of the problem and the answer itself are inseparable parts of the same reality for Shinran. The answer at which he arrived was opened up to him because he refused to be satisfied in a facile manner with the traditional answers, including those of the Pure Land masters before him, and pushed the problem to its utmost limit, where he had to give up the effort to solve it, and where this giving up turned out to be the only genuine answer to the problem.

Shinran's message of the grace of Amida is unthinkable without his relentless struggle with the presence of inexhaustible sin and evil in himself. One who does not know "the reality of religion" under the "law" does not truly know what grace is. What Barth says about St. Paul's agony under the law may equally be said without any hesitation about Shinran's experience:

> Apprehension of the meaning of religion depends upon the clarity with which the dominion of sin over the men of this world is disclosed to our view. When we recognize the peculiar sinfulness of the religious man and see sin *abounding* in him, we are able to understand the meaning of *grace more exceedingly abounding*, and the necessity that the divine mercy should act in spite of sins.[5]

---

[2] The original title of the work is *Ken jōdo shinjitsu kyōgyōshō monrui* 顯浄土眞実教行證文類 [Passages revealing the true teaching, practice, and realization of the Pure Land]. But it is commonly referred to as the *Kyōgyōshinshō* [Teaching, practice, faith, realization], and we will also use this common title. More will be said about this work later.

[3.] Shinran's own description of himself in *The True Teaching, Practice and Realization of the Pure Land Way* (Kyoto: Hongwanji International Center, 1985; Shin Buddhism Translation Series), II: 279; *Kyōgyōshinshō, SSZ*, II: 80. Hereafter, this translation will be referred to as *True Teaching*.

[4] *Tannishō, SSZ*, II: 773.

[5] Barth, *The Epistle to the Romans,* 257.

It is impossible to think of Shinran without Hōnen, whose dedicated and loyal disciple he remained to the last minute of his life. But it was Shinran who drew the ultimate conclusion from the message of his master and pushed it to the extremity of paradoxicality, giving it the boldest formulation. And it was above all Shinran's profound awareness of the human predicament that added a new depth and intensity to Hōnen's message of nenbutsu. As Ienaga Saburō notes, whatever the points of doctrinal difference between Hōnen and Shinran may be, the fundamental religious difference between them is to be found in Shinran's thought that an evil person possesses the true capacity to receive Amida's salvific work (*akunin shōkisetsu* 悪人正機説, or *akunin shōinsetsu* 悪人正因説).[6] The *Tannishō* reports the following famous words of Shinran:

> Even a good person can attain birth in the Pure Land, so it goes without saying that an evil person will.
>
> Though such is the truth, people commonly say, "Even an evil person attains birth, so naturally a good person will." This statement may seem well-founded at first, but it runs counter to the meaning of the Other Power established through the Primal Vow. For a person who relies on the good that he does through his self-power fails to entrust himself wholeheartedly to Other Power and therefore is not in accord with Amida's Primal Vow. But when he abandons his attachment to self-power and entrusts himself totally to Other Power, he will realize birth in the Pure Land.
>
> It is impossible for us, filled as we are with blind passions, to free ourselves from birth-and-death through any practice whatever. Sorrowing at this, Amida made the Vow, the essential intent of which is the attainment of Buddhahood by the person who is evil. Hence the evil person who entrusts himself to Other Power is precisely the one who possesses the true cause for birth.
>
> Accordingly he said, "Even the virtuous man is born in the Pure Land, so without question is the man who is evil."[7]

---

[6] Ienaga Saburō, *Chūsei bukkyō*, 4–5. There are scholars who do not attribute this particular idea to Shinran himself but to Hōnen or his other disciples (or even to Shinran's followers) and do not find much difference in this respect between Hōnen and Shinran; see Tamura's discussion of this matter in his "Akunin shōkisetsu no seiritsu," *Nihon bukkyō shisōshi kenkyū*, 93–123. Ienaga also discusses this problem and defends his view, 8–14.

[7] *Tannishō: A Primer*, trans. by Dennis Hirota (Kyoto: Ryukoku University Translation

It is perhaps no exaggeration to say that in this paradox of evil lies the crux of the entire teaching of Shinran. And behind this, needless to say, lay his profound awareness of the thorough depravity and sinfulness of human beings—not the least, of his own being.

SHINRAN GOES TO HŌNEN

The year 1201 was the crucial turning point in Shinran's life. It was in that year that he, after twenty years of life as a Tendai monk on Mt Hiei, the headquarters of the Tendai Order, decided to leave it and go to Hōnen. The significance of this action, and the fact that it was a radical change in his life, is tersely expressed by Shinran at the end of his *Kyōgyōshinshō*:

> I, Gutoku Shinran, disciple of Śākyamuni, discarded sundry practices and took refuge in the Primal Vow in 1201.[8]

It was in this year, therefore, that Shinran abandoned the traditional path of self-power and took refuge in the Other Power, the compassionate Vow of Amida that saves sinful beings just as they are.

We do not know exactly what led him to make this radical decision, but one thing seems clear: the traditional path of Buddhist practice that he followed on Mt Hiei did not work for him and he had to search for an alternative way of salvation. To be more exact, Shinran found himself to be utterly incapable of following the traditional "difficult path" because he found his passion-ridden nature hard to overcome. That he was in a very desperate situation is well attested to by the following words about his relationship to Hōnen:

> I have no idea whether the nenbutsu is truly the seed for my being born in the Pure Land or whether it is the karmic act for which I must fall into hell. Should I have been deceived by Hōnen Shōnin and, saying the Name, plunge utterly into hell, even then I would have no regrets. The person who could have attained Buddhahood by endeavoring in other practices might regret that he had been deceived if he said the nenbutsu and so fell into hell. But I am one for whom any practice is difficult to

---

Center, 1982), 23–24. Unless otherwise indicated, the *Tannishō* quoted hereafter refers to this text and translation.

[8] *True Teaching*, IV: 614; *SSZ*, II: 202.

accomplish, so hell is to be my home whatever I do.[9]

Shinran's wife, Eshinni, describes his attitude in one of her letters:

> People would say all types of things about where the master [Hōnen] might go. They would even say that he was headed for an evil rebirth (*akudō* 悪道). Whenever people spoke such things, [Shinran] would reply, "I am one who believes that I would even go [with him], since from realm to realm and from rebirth to rebirth I am lost already.[10]

Shinran's going to Hōnen was therefore a sort of "gamble," because he was not yet convinced that it was the right choice. But he had to gamble because he had no other choice; incapable of any practice, he felt that he was "lost" and that hell was his "destiny" anyhow. The full implication of his decision and the new faith he found evolved only gradually over the long span of his life. But the one thing that was clear to him was that he had to give up his moral fight with himself and find a new way of liberation that was not contingent upon this endless and hopeless fight. Shinran found this new path in Hōnen's message of the sole-practice of nenbutsu, which was rapidly gaining popularity in the capital.

What kind of religious life did Shinran have and what kind of practices did he follow on Mt Hiei? Amidst the general obscurity surrounding the twenty years of Shinran's career as a Tendai monk on Mt Hiei, one thing is now recognized as certain, thanks to the letter of Eshinni—that he was a *dōsō* 堂僧 on the mountain. On the basis of current scholarship, Alfred Bloom says the following about *dōsō* and its significance for Shinran:

> The *Dōsō* were priests of fairly low status in the organization of Mt Hiei and probably served either in the Jōgyōzammaidō or the Hokkedō. Though they have been confused with the *Dōshū*, another type of servant priest, it now appears that they were especially concerned with the ceremonies of the Continuous Nenbutsu performed in the Jōgyōzammaidō. As such they were particularly important because of their intimate connection to the development of Pure Land doctrine and practice. Ryōnin, the founder of the Yūzunenbutsu teaching in 1103, is an outstanding example of *Dōsō*.[11]

---

[9] *Tannishō*, 23.

[10] Quoted in James C. Dobbins, *Jōdo Shinshū: Shin Buddhism in Medieval Japan* (Bloomington and Indianapolis: Indiana University Press, 1989), 25.

[11] Alfred Bloom, "The Life of Shinran Shōnin: The Journey to Self-Acceptance,"

The "Continuous Nenbutsu" (or Uninterrupted Nenbutsu, *fudan nenbutsu* 不断念佛) practiced in the Jōgyōzanmaidō was a variation of the *jōgyōzanmai* 常行三昧 or the Samādhi of Constant Walking, which was brought to Mt Hiei by Ennin when he returned from T'ang China in 847. The Samādhi of Constant Walking, one of the four *samādhi*s practiced in the Tendai system of meditation established by Chih-i, is based upon the *Hanjuzanmai kyō* (*Pratyutpannasamādhi-sūtra*), which teaches constant circumambulation of the Buddha's statue for ninety days, accompanied by the uninterrupted uttering of Amida Buddha's name with a view to seeing the appearance of Buddhas before one's eyes. The Continuous Nenbutsu also consisted in the constant recitation of the name of Amida Buddha, but it differed from the Samādhi of Constantly Walking in the length of the practice. That is, it was usually practiced from three to seven days instead of the original ninety days.[12] It was by no means an easy practice, and Shinran must have led a life of strenuous discipline in order to practice this hard path. Bloom continues:

> The knowledge that Shinran was a *Dōsō* and intimately involved in Pure Land thought already during his stay on Mt Hiei provides a context for understanding the religious anxiety and dissatisfaction which he experienced. As a *Dōsō*, he was exposed to Pure Land concepts concerning the evil character of the age and human existence. He was probably confronted frequently with the transiency of life, because the Continuous Nenbutsu services were sponsored by individuals mainly to acquire merit which could be transferred to a relative to ensure his good destiny. In this way Pure Land teachings penetrated Shinran's mind and contributed to the deepening of his religious sensitivity.[13]

This should not be taken, however, as a suggestion that the Continuous Nenbutsu was the only major activity occupying Shinran's religious life on Mt Hiei. In view of the extensive knowledge of Buddhist scriptures that Shinran demonstrates in his writings, there can be little doubt that he applied himself very hard to scriptural studies, especially those in the Tendai and Pure Land tradition as transmitted on Mt Hiei.[14]

Numen, 15 (1968): 6. See also Akamatsu, *Shinran*, 31–33.

[12] Akamatsu, *Shinran*, 33–34.

[13] Bloom, "The Life of Shinran," 6.

[14] Concerning the influence of Tendai tradition on Shinran while he was on Mt Hiei, see Matsuno Junkō, *Shinran—Sono kōdō to shisō* (Tokyo: Hyōronsha, 1971), 51–66.

It is also highly likely that Shinran engaged in various other forms of Buddhist practices and meditations to which he could have been exposed during his twenty years of life in this eclectic center of Buddhism. But none proved successful for him, as he confessed: "I am one for whom any practice is difficult to accomplish." We may be able to find in the following words of the *Kyōgyōshinshō* an echo of his own experience:

> But it is hard for the foolish and ignorant, who are ever sinking in birth-and-death, to perform acts with the mind of meditative practices, for this is to cease thinking and to concentrate the mind. It is also hard to perform acts with the mind of non-meditative practices, for this is to discard evil and practice good. Thus, since it is hard even to visualize forms and fix the mind on them, [Shan-tao] states:
>
> > One may dedicate a lifetime of a thousand years, but still the dharma-eye will not be opened.
>
> How much harder indeed is it to realize formlessness and cessation of thought. Therefore he states:
>
> > The Tathāgata already knows that foolish beings of the latter age possessed of karmic evil and defilements are incapable of visualizing forms and fixing the mind on them. How much harder is it to seek realization without visualizing forms; it is like a person lacking transcendent powers building a house in the air.[15]

Tradition has it that Shinran visited various shrines on Mt Hiei in order to seek an escape from his spiritual impasse. One such visit turned out to have a decisive impact on his life. According to Eshinni's letter, Shinran once left the mountain and went to the Hexagonal Hall (Rokkakudō) in Kyoto—which enshrined the bodhisattva Kannon and which was allegedly founded by Shōtoku Taishi—to spend a hundred days in vigil there, to pray concerning his afterlife. On the dawn of the ninety-fifth day, he received a vision in which Shōtoku Taishi appeared to him with a message. Deeply moved by this, Shinran left the hall early in the morning and went to Hōnen "in order to meet the Venerable one who can be of help for his afterlife."[16]

If this can be any clue as to what kind of religious concern preoccupied Shinran on Mt Hiei, we can conclude he was above all anxious about his future destiny, an anxiety that was intimately connected with his deep

---

[15] *True Teaching*, IV: 501–02.

[16] Quoted in Akamatsu, *Shinran*, 43–44.

consciousness of sin. As Tamura Enchō points out, it was not so much the sense of the transitoriness of worldly things as the sense of karmic sinfulness and the resulting concern for afterlife that led Shinran (and Hōnen as well) to aspire after birth in the Pure Land.[17] The sense of the impermanence of the world, which was not unusual even among the nobility of the late Heian, could be easily accommodated within the traditional piety of the day, but the sense of one's own ineradicable sinfulness was something that called for an entirely new solution—one that can only come from *outside* oneself, i.e., from Other Power (*tariki* 他力), the Transcendent.

Shinran's visit to the Hexagonal Hall practically signified his break with the Buddhism of Mt Hiei. Perhaps it was not merely his own predicament but also the general decay he found in the religious atmosphere of the Tendai Order on the mountain that led Shinran to leave. The influx of unqualified monks into this center of the socioreligious establishment, the violent behavior of the monks as they applied pressure and voiced threats to the government in order to secure material benefits, the constant conflict between the student monks (*gakushō* 学生) and the priests (*dōshū* 堂衆), and the routine performance of rituals dedicated to gain worldly benefits—all these must have deeply disturbed a sensitive religious mind seeking a fundamental solution to a pressing problem: liberation from the world of birth-and-death.

Why, then, did Shinran go to Hōnen in particular? What was the connection between the message he received from Shōtoku Taishi and his decision to go to Hōnen? What was the content of the message? According to the letter of Eshinni cited above, it had been enclosed on a separate sheet of paper in the same letter, addressed to her daughter Kakushinni. Unfortunately, this sheet is not extant today.[18] Various theories have been proposed regarding the matter, but Akamatsu's view seems most persuasive.[19] According to him, Shinran received the following verse from Shōtoku Taishi, who was considered a manifestation of the bodhisattva Kannon:

> When the devotee finds himself bound by his past karma to come in contact with the female sex, I will incarnate myself as a most beautiful

[17] Tamura Enchō, *Nihon bukkyō shisōshi kenkyū*, 10–14.

[18] Akamatsu, *Shinran*, 46–47.

[19] See his discussion of this extremely complicated matter in *Shinran*, 46–65.

36

woman and become his object of love; and throughout his life I will be his helpmeet for the sake of embellishing this world, and on his death I will become his guide to the Land of Bliss.[20]

Then the *Shinran denne* [The illustrated biography of Shinran], upon which the story of this dream is based, continues:

"This," continued the Bodhisattva, "is my vow. Thou, Zenshin, shalt announce the signification of this my vow to the world and make all sentient beings know of it." At this time, Zenshin still in a state of trance looked eastward facing directly the Rokkakudō, and descried a range of high mountains, on the highest peak of which was found congregating an immense number of people. He addressed them as commanded by the Bodhisattva, and when he imagined that he had come to the end of his address, he awaked from the dream.[21]

Although this verse cannot directly explain why Shinran particularly chose to go to Hōnen—except for the allusion to the birth in Pure Land—it is significant at least in two respects. First, it throws light upon the kind of problem that was vexing the young monk Shinran at the age of twenty-nine. Secondly, it gives us an explanation for Shinran's marriage later on. The vow of celibacy that he took as a monk, irresistible sexual desire, and the resulting concern for his future destiny, are all indirectly revealed in the dream.

Most likely it was in order to solve this problem once and for all that Shinran surrendered himself to Hōnen's teaching. Even though Hōnen himself is said to have led a celibate life with strict adherence to the pre-

[20] Gesshō Sasaki and Daisetz T. Suzuki, trans., *The Life of Shinran Shōnin (Godenshō)*, in *Collected Writings on Shin Buddhism* by Daisetz Teitarō Suzuki, The Eastern Buddhist Society, ed. (Kyoto: Shinshū Ōtaniha, 1973), 170; *Honganji Shōnin Shinran denne*, SSZ, III: 640.

[21] Suzuki, *The Life of Shinran Shōnin*, 170; *SSZ*, III: 640. There are several editions of this *Shinran denne* (with different titles) or the *Godenshō* [Biography], which is the earliest Shinran biography; the one quoted here is that preserved in the Nishi Honganji Temple. There is an important difference between them concerning the year when this dream is supposed to have taken place; see Akamatsu's discussion in *Shinran*, 46–65; see also Matsuno Junkō, *Shinran—Sono kōdō to shisō*, 67–90. Matsuno agrees with Akamatsu in viewing the problem of sexual desire as the chief factor in Shinran's conversion to Hōnen's message, but he does not endorse the view that this particular dream provided the direct occasion for the conversion. This story of the dream in *Shinran denne* is based upon *Shinran muki* 親鸞夢記 [Record of Shinran's dream], of which there also are several versions, thus complicating matters further. See the above references in Akamatsu and Matsuno; see also Dobbins, *Jōdo Shinshū*, 23–24, for a brief discussion of this problem.

cepts, there was definitely a revolutionary spirit in his message of nenbutsu, which liberated people once and for all from the heavy burden of the monastic precepts. Note the following admonition of Hōnen, for instance:

> When you live the present life, spend your life reciting nenbutsu; if anything impedes your nenbutsu, throw it away, whatever it may be. If you cannot say nenbutsu as a wandering monk (*hijiri* 聖), say it taking a wife; if you cannot do it with a wife, do it as a wandering monk.[22]

For Hōnen, attaining birth in the Pure Land through nenbutsu was the sole purpose of life on earth; it was the *summum bonum* that all human beings have to pursue with their utmost power at any cost and compared with which all other matters become secondary. Hōnen's biography records the following dialogue:

> "If we only put our trust in Amida's Primal Vow, there is no doubt whatever about our future destiny, but what are we to do with the present world?" "Well, the thing to do is to make the nenbutsu practice the chief thing in life, and to lay aside everything that you think may interfere with it. If you cannot stay in one spot and do it, then do it when you are walking. If you cannot do it as a priest, then do it as a layman. If you cannot do it alone, then do it in company with others. If you cannot do it and at the same time provide yourself with food and clothing, then accept the help of others and go on doing it. Or if you cannot get others to help you, then look after yourself but keep on doing it. Your wife and children and domestics are for this very purpose, of helping you to practice it, and if they prove an obstacle, you ought not to have any.... How tenderly should we care for our bodies, and how earnestly should we practice the nenbutsu, when we know that our destiny is birth in the Pure Land...."[23]

Another dialogue is also very significant:

> "Is there any difference in the *Ōjō* [Birth in the Pure Land] rank of those who keep the precepts and repeat the nenbutsu but a few times, and those who break them but say the nenbutsu very often?" Hōnen replying pointed to the mats on which they were sitting, and said, "It is because the mats exist that we can say of them that they are either worn out or not. If there were no mats how could they be worn out or otherwise? In like manner in these wicked days we may say that the precepts [them-

---

[22] Quoted in Akamatsu, *Shinran*, 66; *Wago tōroku*, *SSZ*, IV: 683.

[23] Coates and Ishizuka, *Hōnen*, II: 737.

selves] are neither kept nor broken, for the monks themselves are such in name only, as Dengyō Daishi very clearly states in his *Mappō Tōmyōki* (Record of the light in the Latter Days of the Law). So there is nothing to be gained by discussing the question of the breaking or the keeping of the precepts. It is for just such common mortals as this, that the Primal Vow itself was made in the first place, and so we cannot be too eager and diligent in our calling upon the sacred name."[24]

In short, according to Hōnen, the issues of whether or not to keep the precepts, whether or not to marry, are no longer primary in the world of Amida's Primal Vow. Salvation does not depend on them but on the whole-hearted practice of nenbutsu. Would this not be the kind of message that would liberate Shinran from the lonely struggle he was waging with himself on Mt Hiei?

Hōnen was already sixty-nine years old when Shinran took refuge in him, and twenty-six years had passed since he launched the movement of the sole-practice of nenbutsu (1175). Hōnen's masterpiece, the *Senjaku shū*, had already been completed, and the movement he had launched was rapidly spreading in the capital. It is highly likely that Shinran had already been aware of this movement and its message even before he joined it, but the actual decision to join it only came after the aforementioned religious experience at the Hexagonal Hall. It is said that Shinran visited Hōnen's residence in Yoshimizu for one hundred days without missing a single day to learn the new path to salvation,[25] and he was given a new Buddhist name, Shakkū 綽空, by Hōnen. The culmination of Shinran's contact with Hōnen, which was to last for six years until 1207, the year of their exile, came when Hōnen granted him permission in 1205 to make a copy of the *Senjaku shū*, which was being circulated rather secretly among a select group of disciples. Shinran recalls this event at the end of his *Kyōgyōshinshō*:

> I, Gutoku Shinran, disciple of Śākyamuni, discarded sundry practices and took refuge in the Primal Vow in 1201. In 1205 Master Genkū [Hōnen], out of his benevolence, granted me permission to copy his *Passages on the Nenbutsu Selected in the Primal Vow*. In the same year, on the fourteenth day of the fourth month, the master inscribed [the copy] in his own hand with an inside title, "Passages on the Nenbutsu Selected

---

24 Coates and Ishizuka, 736–37 (translation slightly adjusted).

25 Akamatsu, *Shinran*, 43.

in the Primal Vow," with the words, "Namu-amida-butsu: as the act that leads to birth in the Pure Land, the nenbutsu is taken to be fundamental," and with [the name he had bestowed on me,] "Shakkū, disciple of Śākyamuni." That day, my request to borrow his portrait was granted, and I made a copy. During that same year, on the twenty-ninth day of the seventh intercalary month, the master inscribed my copy of the portrait with "Namu-amida-butsu" and with a passage expressing the true teaching:

> If, when I attain Buddhahood, the sentient beings of the ten quarters say my Name as few as ten times and yet are not born, may I not attain supreme enlightenment. The Buddha has now actually attained Buddhahood. Know that the momentous Primal Vow is not in vain, and that when sentient beings say the Name, they unfailingly attain birth.

Further, since my name "Shakkū" had been changed in accord with a revelation in a dream, on the same day he wrote the characters of my new name [Zenshin 善信] in his own hand. At that time, the master was seventy-three years of age.... Thus, suppressing tears of both sorrow and joy, I record the circumstances that have resulted [in my compilation of this book].[26]

It was probably in this same year of 1205 that Shinran received from Hōnen the permission to marry and was granted the name Zenshin, which was the name revealed to him in that dream in the Hexagonal Hall.[27] Even in 1204, when Shinran signed the *Shichikajō kishōmon* 七箇条起請文 [Seven-article pledge] drafted by Hōnen in order to curb the loose conduct of some of his disciples and avoid conflict with the established Buddhist order, Shinran attached the word "monk" (*sō* 僧) to his old name Shakkū.

In 1207, however, we find Shinran describing himself as "neither a monk nor a layman" (*sōni arazu zokuni arazu* 非僧非俗) and adopting the pejorative epithet *toku* 禿 (stubble-haired) for himself. This was when his new life with Hōnen came to an abrupt end as a result of the persecution of the nenbutsu movement. Shinran recalls this tragic event with indignation at the end of his *Kyōgyōshinshō*:

---

[26] *True Teaching*, IV: 614–16; *SSZ*, II: 202–203.

[27] Akamatsu, *Shinran*, 71–74. It is not known with certainty whom Shinran married at this time, but Akamatsu is inclined to think that Shinran married only once, and that thus it was Eshinni, the author of the famous letters; see 74–78.

The emperor and his ministers, acting against the dharma and violating human rectitude, became enraged and embittered. As a result, Master Genkū—the eminent founder who had enabled the true essence of the Pure Land way to spread vigorously [in Japan]—and a number of his followers, without receiving any deliberation of their [alleged] crimes, were summarily sentenced to death or were dispossessed of their monkhood, given [secular] names, and consigned to distant banishment. I was among the latter. Hence, I am now neither a monk nor one in worldly life. For this reason, I have taken the term Toku ["stubble-haired"] as my name. Master Genkū and his disciples, being banished to the provinces in different directions, passed a period of five years [in exile].[28]

Even when one considers that imperial authority was not, in the late years of Shinran's life when the above statement was written, what it used to be, it was not a small act of courage on the part of Shinran to indict the emperor and his ministers of "acting against the dharma and violating human rectitude." If Shinran was still carrying a smoldering grudge in his late years over the unjust persecution he and his master had suffered from the authorities decades ago, how much more anger and frustration would the young Shinran have felt at the time of his actual exile? At any rate, here we see Shinran saying that he was deprived of monkhood and consequently became "neither a monk nor a layman." Does this suggest then that Shinran had not yet been married before the exile and that he adopted that designation for himself unwillingly?

The word *toku*, it has been pointed out, was used during Shinran's times to refer to those monks who were living a life of moral laxity unbefitting persons who had renounced secular life, monks who had "broken the precepts without any sense of remorse" (*hakai muzan* 破戒無慚).[29] Shinran added another word *gu* 愚 ("foolish") to it and made *gutoku* ("foolish and stubble-haired") his surname. In contrast to those to whom this ignominious designation was attached by other people, Shinran did not hesitate to use it of himself—not gladly, presumably, but with conviction and courage. Unlike others, Shinran broke the precepts literally "without any sense of remorse." In other words, he was a "criminal of conscience" who had broken without religious compunction the precept of celibacy. It is even possible that his openly married life, based

[28] *True Teaching*, IV: 613–14; *SSZ*, II: 201–202.

[29] Miyazaki Enjun, "Shinran Shōninden sobyō," in *Shinran no kenkyū. Miyazaki Enjun chosakushū*, I (Kyoto: Shimonkaku Shuppan, 1986), 23; Dobbins, *Jōdo Shinshū*, 26–27.

upon a new type of religious conviction, was one of the reasons the authorities picked him out among the numerous disciples of Hōnen to be punished.[30] For him, being married and leading a religious life as a "monk" were not incompatible at all. For he believed that in the Last Dharma-age there is in the first place no precept to be broken, and no monk except in name only. Quoting the *Mappō tōmyōki*, Shinran boldly says:

> Next, after the end of the semblance dharma-age, there are no precepts whatsoever. Recognizing the momentum of the times, the Buddha praises those who are monks in name only, declaring them to be the field of merits for the world, in order to save the people of the last dharma-age.[31]

Numerous monks, indeed, broke the precept of celibacy and led an illicit married life. As the *Shaseki shū* 沙石集 says, "One has rarely heard in past years of a religious man (*shōnin*) during this last age (*matsudai* 末代) who has not taken a wife."[32] Akamatsu points out that around the time of Shinran's birth one who hid his marriage was considered a venerable one (*shōnin*), but that during the time of Shinran's later years not only were there few *shōnin* who did not marry, there also were few who bothered to hide it.[33] Shinran did not hide it either. Illicit as Shinran's marriage was, it was nevertheless based upon a clear religious conviction, acquired through Hōnen's teaching, that, with precept or without, married or not, the sole purpose of life is to attain salvation through nenbutsu. The traditional path of "self-power" had already been given up and was no longer meaningful for Shinran. Calling himself "neither a monk nor a layman" and "foolish stubble-haired" was therefore an act of defiance or protest against the traditional Buddhist community—as well as against the authorities—who were, in his mind, holding on to the no longer workable Path of Sages, turning people into hypocrites. It signaled at the same time the emergence of a new type of religious identity that cut across the traditional bifurcation of the Buddhist community into the monks (*shukke*) and the laity (*zaike*).

---

[30] Akamatsu, *Shinran*, 115–16.

[31] *True Teaching*, IV: 551; *SSZ*, II: 173.

[32] Quoted in Dobbins, 26. The *Shasekishū* [Collection of sand and pebbles) is a collection of Buddhist stories composed around Shinran's time. See Morrell's translation, *Sand and Pebbles* (1985).

[33] Akamatsu, *Shinran*, 62–63.

Because of the persecution, the *Tannishō* records, "Hōnen Shōnin and seven disciples were banished, and four executed. The Shōnin was exiled to Hata in Tosa Province [the present-day Kōchi Prefecture on Shikoku] under the criminal's name of Fujii Motohiko, male, aged seventy-six [or seventy-five?]. Shinran was exiled to Echigo Province [present-day Niigata Prefecture] under the criminal's name Fujii Yoshizane, aged thirty-five."[34] Why was Shinran, of all the many disciples of Hōnen, particularly included among the seven exiled? We have already mentioned his married life as a possible reason for this. Beside this, however, there must have been something in his thought, too, that distinguished him from other disciples of Hōnen.

It is well known that among Hōnen's disciples opinions were divided among those who believed the practice of nenbutsu itself was more important (*kigyōha* 起行派), and those who held that faith, i.e., the mental attitude with which one should say the nenbutsu was more important (*anjinha* 安心派).[35] Concerning this problem of the relative priority of practice and faith, Dobbins points out the following significant fact:

> Of the many interpretations of the nenbutsu in circulation, those emphasizing practice or the effort of the believer were closer to the position of the traditional schools of Buddhism and were therefore more likely to be tolerated. Those which rejected practice and highlighted faith were frequently blamed for social unrest and hence became perennial targets of suppression. Among the eight nenbutsu priests sentenced to exile in 1207 [seven, if we exclude Hōnen], Kōsai, Shōkū, Gyōkū, and Shinran are known to have stressed faith in their teachings.[36]

In other words, Shinran may have become a special target because his teaching was considered to be more radical than others, in that it regarded the traditional Buddhist practices, including the observance of the precepts, as irrelevant for salvation, which is attainable only by the power of Amida's Vow to save sentient beings laden with blind passions. And Shinran showed his belief in action by taking a wife.

[34] *The Tanni Shō: Notes Lamenting Differences* (Kyoto: Ryukoku University Translation Center; Ryukoku Translation Series II, 1962), 84.

[35] Mochizuki Shinkō, *Ryakujutsu Jōdo kyōrishi* (Tokyo: Nihon Tosho Center, 1977 [reprint]), 251–55.

[36] Dobbins, *Jōdo Shinshū*, 19 (brackets mine).

THE AWARENESS OF KARMIC EVIL

We have seen that it was above all Shinran's deep awareness of evil in himself that led him to break with the Buddhism of Mt Hiei and join Hōnen's nenbutsu group. Since this is such an important element in understanding Shinran's life and thought in general, we should devote more space here to his understanding of himself as a *bonpu* and his view of humanity.

Shinran's deep awareness of the thorough depravity of his own being seems to have persisted throughout his entire life, hence not merely before he found the light of salvation in Hōnen's teaching but even after his discovery of Amida's world of grace. The *Tannishō* records the following significant dialogue between Shinran and his disciple:

> I asked the Master, "Although utterance of the Name emerges from within me, I scarcely experience such joy that I leap and dance, and I have no aspiration to go to the Pure Land quickly. Why is this?"
>
> He replied, "I, Shinran, have also had this question, and the same thought occurs to you, Yuien-bō!
>
> "When I reflect deeply on my failure to rejoice that my birth in the Pure Land is settled—something for which a person should dance with joy in the air and on the earth—I realize all the more clearly, through this very absence of joy, that my birth is indeed settled. What suppresses the heart that ought to take joy and prevents me from rejoicing is the activity of my blind passions. But the Buddha, knowing this beforehand, said that he would save 'the foolish being full of blind passions'; such, then, is the compassionate Vow of Other Power. Realizing that it is precisely for the sake of such people as myself, I feel it all the more trustworthy."[37]

Here we see Shinran turning the very sign of his sinfulness, "the absence of joy" (which does not disappear even after his encounter with Other Power), into an even greater reason to believe in the compassionate Vow of Amida.

Many important details about Shinran's life still remain in obscurity and are the subject of scholarly speculation,[38] but one thing seems cer-

---

[37] *Tannishō*, 27 (translation slightly amended; see p. 71 of the same translation).

[38] Some important items still unclear are: Shinran's mother; the motives behind his entering the priesthood; his religious life on Mt Hiei and the specific reason for leaving it and joining Hōnen's nenbutsu movement; how many times he married and when; the rea-

tain: that Shinran lived his entire life in constant awareness of his own sinfulness, so hard to uproot, and its converse, an infinite gratitude to Amida Buddha who had already achieved his salvation through the compassionate Primal Vow. The *Tannishō* records:

> Shinran would often say,

> When I consider deeply the Vow of Amida, which arose from five kalpas of profound thought, I realize that it was entirely for the sake of myself alone! Then how I am filled with gratitude for the Primal Vow, in which Amida settled on saving me, though I am burdened thus greatly with karma.[39]

Shinran's awareness of evil in himself seems to have grown sharper with his discovery of the world of Amida's compassionate Vow. His own depravity came into greater relief when it was put alongside Amida's mind:

> I know nothing of what is good or evil. For if I could know thoroughly, as is known in the mind of Amida, that an act was good, then I would know the meaning of "good." If I could know thoroughly, as Amida knows, that an act was evil, then I would know "evil." But for a foolish being full of blind passions, in this fleeting world—this burning house— all matters without exception are lies and gibberish, totally without truth and sincerity. The nenbutsu alone is true and real.[40]

When one is so evil that one does not truly know what evil is, all the distinction of good and evil on the level of common sense is blasted as "lies and gibberish." This was, paradoxically, what Shinran came to realize through his encounter with Amida's grace. His awareness of sin and evil, rather than disappearing or diminishing, gained depth and clarity, causing Shinran to cling all the more to the source of salvation coming from other than himself.

---

son he went to the Kantō area after his release from exile instead of returning to Kyoto; his activities in the Kantō area; and the reason he left the Kantō area in his later years. The present chapter is not intended to be a biographical study of Shinran in a strict sense but only sketches what I consider to be important aspects of his life, with a special focus on his awareness of evil as the leitmotif of his life and thought.

[39] *Tannishō*, 43.

[40] *Tannishō*, 44.

This sense of inexhaustible evil remained with Shinran to the last minute of his life and made him humble and "poor in spirit," always looking up to Other Power, where alone he found the light. Nowhere else, perhaps, is this sense of ineradicable sinfulness more forcefully expressed by Shinran than in his *Gutoku hitan jukkai* 愚禿悲歎述懷 [Lamentation and confession of Gutoku Shinran], which was composed when he was eighty-six years old:

Although I have taken refuge in the true teaching of the Pure Land,
The mind of truth hardly exists in me;
Moreover, I am so falsehearted and untrue
That there cannot be any mind of purity.

Each of us shows an outward appearance
Of being wise, good, and diligent,
Possessing so much greed, anger, and wrong views,
We are filled with all kinds of deceit.

My evilness is truly difficult to renounce;
The mind is like a serpent or scorpion.
Even doing virtuous deeds is tainted with poison,
And so is called false practice.

How shameless and unrepentant a person am I
And without a heart of truth and sincerity;
But because the Name is transferred by Amida,
Its virtue pervades the ten directions.[41]

The fact that Shinran lived his life always deeply aware of his own sinfulness is best witnessed by the epithet he adopted for himself when he was exiled to Echigo: "Gutoku." By thus calling himself "foolish and stubble-haired," he indicated his view of himself as an ordinary man (*bonpu*) and his status as "neither a monk nor a layman," his own description of himself after the exile.[42] Shinran continued to use this epithet for the rest of his life, not in order to demonstrate his humility but as a sign that he had given up the attempt to be more than "a foolish being full of blind passions" (*bonnō gusoku bonpu* 煩悩具足凡夫) and a sign of his calm

---

[41] *Shōzōmatsu Wasan: Shinran's Hymns on the Last Age* (Kyoto: Ryukoku University Translation Center, 1980; Ryukoku Translation Series VII), 94–97 (translation altered); *SSZ*, II: 527. The concept of the Name "transferred" by Amida will be discussed below in Chapter Three.

[42] *True Teaching*, IV: 613–14; *SSZ*, II: 201–202.

acceptance of himself as such an ordinary being in the light of the grace he had found in Amida's "Vow Ocean."

We should not misunderstand Shinran's awareness of evil in himself as something merely based upon his moral self-reflection. Sin and evil, for Shinran, was of karmic origin and determination. They had the nature of a deep-rooted karmic hindrance that had been accumulated in him throughout innumerable past lives in the world of birth-and-death. Thus Shinran seems to have been possessed of a deterministic sense of human sinfulness:

> Good thoughts arise in us through the beckoning of past good, and we come to think and do evil through the working of karmic evil. The late master [Shinran] said, "Know that every evil act done—even so slight as a particle caught on a strand of rabbit's fur or sheep's wool—has its cause in past karma."[43]

Although these words are quoted in the *Tannishō* in order to show that any moral merit or demerit we may have is completely of no account for our salvation (which is only possible through Amida's compassionate Vow), it is a good indication of Shinran's sense of the karmic determination of our moral acts. The implication is that there are really no good acts that we can claim as *our* acts. Whether good or evil, all of our acts, being under karmic influence beyond our control, merely demonstrate our moral helplessness and our ultimate sinfulness, which can only be overcome through Amida's salvific work of grace—something that is beyond the law of cause and effect, or that is under an entirely different kind of karmic law, the karmic law of Other Power. For Shinran, therefore, good and evil are fundamentally of a religious dimension beyond moral judgment:

> Shinran characterizes evil as "karmic" (in such terms as *akugō* and *zaigō*, literally "evil karma")…. For Shinran, all our acts, whether good or evil by moral or ethical standards, are evil in a religious sense, being defiled by ignorance and passions. Moreover, this evil is karmic, meaning that it stretches back infinitely into the past. Since the beginningless past, all our acts have worked only to bind us to samsaric life. Because of aeons of repetition and habit, we harbor unknowable evil in the depths of our existence. Hence, to become aware of the roots of our existence is to know the basic nature of the self as pervaded by passions and ignorant

---

[43] *Tannishō*, 33.

clinging. This attachment traps us completely, and we cannot let go.[44]

Thus, from the perspective of karmic human nature, our ordinary moral distinctions lose their meaning. To be sure, Shinran uses the terms "good" and "evil" in an ordinary relative sense as well. But, from the absolute point of view that he came to attain through his discovery of the world of Amida's true goodness, all our human moral distinctions crumble; we are all sinners, laden with deep-rooted karmic evils. Hence, our actions, good or evil, cannot escape their karmic nature, which only causes us to sink deeper into the sea of suffering. It was this deep karmic sense of evil that made Shinran confess that he was incapable of any practice whatever. No matter what practice he tried, even the "easy practice" of nenbutsu, Shinran felt that he could not escape from what he was, "a foolish being full of blind passions." This was the source of his sense of despair. Shinran says:

> In all small and foolish beings, at all times, thoughts of greed and desire incessantly defile any goodness of heart; thoughts of anger and hatred constantly consume the Dharma-treasure. Even if one urgently acts and urgently practices as though sweeping fire from one's head, all these acts must be called "poisoned and sundry good" and "false and deceitful practice." They cannot be called "true and real action." To seek to be born in the land of immeasurable light through such false and poisoned good is completely wrong.[45]

Inseparably related to this deterministic sense of the karmic force of evil in Shinran was his keen awareness of the spiritual crisis of his time, which he understood as the period of *mappō*, the age of Last Dharma. The awareness of the time (*ji* 時) and the awareness of human capacity (*ki* 機) reinforced each other in Shinran; they went hand in hand, not merely as a general theory of *mappō* but also as his personal experience. How seriously Shinran took the idea of *mappō* is well shown by the Japanese hymns he composed on the three ages of dharma, the *Shōzōmatsu wasan*. They are introduced with the following lamentation:

> For sentient beings of the Last Dharma-age with the five defilements practice and enlightenment are now beyond reach; and the teachings of Śākyamuni that had remained have all passed into the Dragon Palace.[46]

[44] Ueda and Hirota, *Shinran*, 156–57.

[45] *True Teaching*, II: 234; *SSZ*, II: 62.

[46] *SSZ*, II: 516.

It is not only that people are unable to cultivate and achieve enlightenment, they even have no desire to achieve Buddhahood, no desire to save others. They have no faith to accept the true teaching of the Path of Pure Land, but, full of doubt, slander and persecute it. Devoid of the true and real mind (*shinjitsushin* 眞実心), they have no desire to be born in the Pure Land and have no joy when they hear the message. While professing to practice the Buddhist path, people "inwardly revere and practice other teachings"; they worship heavenly gods and earthly deities and are absorbed in divinations and sacrificial rituals. The titles "monk" and "dharma-master" are misused. These are some of the signs of the *mappō* that Shinran deplores in his hymns.

Shinran also devoted a considerable amount of space to the theme of the Last Dharma-age in the sixth chapter of his *Kyōgyōshinshō*. In a passage that is almost like the conclusion to the whole book, Shinran declares:

> Truly we know that the teachings of the Path of Sages were intended for the period when the Buddha was in the world and for the right dharma-age; they are altogether inappropriate for the times and beings of the semblance and last dharma-ages and the age when the dharma has become extinct. Already their time has passed; they are no longer in accord with beings.
>
> The true essence of the Pure Land way compassionately draws all of the innumerable evil, defiled beings to enlightenment without discrimination, whether they be of the period when the Buddha was in the world, of the right, semblance, or last dharma-age, or of the time when the dharma has become extinct.[47]

And in the postscript to the work, Shinran says:

> Reflecting within myself, I see that in the various teachings of the Path of Sages, practice and enlightenment died out long ago, and that the true essence of the Pure Land way is the path to realization now vital and flourishing.[48]

Thus, for Shinran, who was gripped by a sense of internal crisis (the inability to get rid of karmic evil and sinfulness) as well as of external crisis (the Last Dharma-age), the only way out was the Path of the Pure

[47] *True Teaching*, IV: 532; *SSZ*, II: 166.
[48] *True Teaching*, IV: 613; *SSZ*, II: 201.

Land. The teaching should be in agreement with the time and people's capacity, and therefore the Path of the Sages (*shōdōmon* 聖道門) is no longer practicable for people living in this age of *mappō*. One should carefully discern the time in which one lives and one's own spiritual capacity:

> Thus, the multitudes of this evil, defiled world, ignorant of the distinctive characteristics of the latter age, revile the behavior and attitude of monks and nuns, but all people of the present, whether monk or lay, must take measure of their own capabilities.[49]

Shinran sharply criticized the followers of the Path of Sages who, not realizing the time and the capacity, still held on to unworkable traditional notions and practices. Thus, in his preface to the chapter on faith in the *Kyōgyōshinshō*, he says:

> But the monks and laity of this latter age and the religious teachers of these times are floundering in concepts of "self-nature" and "mind-only," and they disparage the true realization of enlightenment in the Pure Land way. Or lost in the self-power attitude of meditative and non-meditative practices, they are ignorant of true faith, which is diamond-like.[50]

Although all these words of Shinran concerning evil in human beings primarily date from the period in his life when he was firmly settled in Pure Land faith, probably long after his encounter with Hōnen, they must have their origin in the spiritual predicament that he experienced through twenty years of life as a Tendai monk on Mt Hiei and that ultimately led him to depart from that life forever. And this sense of the unbridgeable gap between what he was and what he wanted to be, between his own state of being and Buddhahood, afterwards never left him—to form, as we shall see, a major ingredient of his thought.

SHINRAN IN EXILE

Whatever the specific charge under which Shinran was sentenced to exile, the four years in the Echigo region were another important turning point in his life. Away from the capital and his hometown, separated from his

---

[49] *True Teaching*, IV: 537; *SSZ*, II: 168.

[50] *True Teaching*, II: 201; *SSZ*, II: 47. "Faith" is the translation of *shinjin* 信心, which the translators of the Shin Buddhism Translation Series decided to leave untranslated; we will discuss this important matter in Chapter Three, on the concept of faith in Shinran. We will consistently replace *shinjin* with "faith" throughout this book.

revered teacher, and under the harsh living conditions of a strange place, Shinran now had to stand firmly on his own feet, not merely economically—no longer a monk but a responsible head of a household—but also in religious faith and thought. Yet, it was most likely through this experience of living among the uncultivated common people of the northern region that his thought world began to mature and assume a different tone from that of his master.

In the northern region of Hokuriku on the Japan Sea, Shinran was exposed to a new way of life that must have deepened his understanding of human existence. He witnessed the life of the common people who had to struggle for existence under adverse material circumstances, pursuing jobs such as hunting and fishing that automatically involved them in the sin of killing living beings; he met ignorant and uncultured people who could not even read a single character, not to mention the difficult Buddhist scriptures, poor people who could not afford to perform for themselves costly meritorious acts of donation to the sangha.

Although Shinran himself had already renounced the privileges and pretensions of a monk and considered himself no more than a common man in the spiritual sense, a *bonpu*, his actual contact with these "real" common people during his exile must have awakened in him a new awareness of the reality and problems of human existence, deepening his sense of identity with humble folk who, by their very lowliness and ignorance, were probably more open to the message of the Pure Land gospel than the learned and more sophiscated people in the capital. In his *Yuishinshō mon'i* (Notes on the "essentials of faith alone"), explanations of the Chinese passages quoted in the work of Seikaku 聖覚 (a disciple of Hōnen), Shinran says:

> "To abandon the mind of self-power" admonishes the various and diverse kinds of people—masters of Hīnayāna or Mahāyāna, ignorant beings, good or evil—to abandon the conviction that one is good, to cease relying on the self, to stop reflecting knowingly on one's evil heart, and further to abandon the judging of people as good and bad. When such shackled foolish beings—the lowly who are hunters and peddlers—thus wholly entrust themselves to the Name embodying great wisdom, the inconceivable Vow of the Buddha of unhindered light, then while burdened as they are with blind passion, they attain the supreme nirvāṇa. "Shackled" describes us, who are bound by all our various blind passion. Blind passion refers to pains which torment the body and afflictions

51

which distress the heart and mind. The hunter is he who slaughters the many kinds of living things; this is the huntsman. The peddler is he who buys and sells things; this is the trader. They are called "low." Such peddlers, hunters, and others are *none other than we, who are like stones and tiles and pebbles.*[51]

Worth noting here is the expression, "burdened as they are with blind passion, they attain the supreme *nirvāṇa*." For the only form of salvation meaningful to the "hunters and peddlers" who had no other choice of livelihood was the one that can be attained despite the passions and sins that they were bound to commit by their karmic destiny. And they are, says Shinran, "none other than we, who are like stones and tiles and pebbles." Shinran continues:

> When we entrust ourselves to the Tathāgata's Primal Vow, we, who are like bits of tile and pebbles, are turned into gold. Peddlers and hunters, who are like stones and tiles and pebbles, are grasped and never abandoned by the Tathāgata's light.[52]

Later on we will have a chance to examine the meaning of being "grasped and never abandoned by Tathāgata's light." It is a gift granted by Amida Buddha to the person who turns to him in faith for salvation. Although Shinran's Pure Land thought may not yet have been fully developed in the period of exile, it was through his experience of life among the poor and ignorant that he must have deeply realized who the people are who really need the compassion of Amida and to whom the message of his grace should be addressed. Finding among them an image of himself as a "foolish being full of blind passions," Shinran's heart must have reached out to them in sympathy.

Although his *Ichinen-tanen mon'i* (Notes on once-calling and many-calling), a sort of commentary on the work by Ryūkan 隆寛, another disciple of Hōnen, was composed very late in his life, Shinran explains why he put them on paper:

> That people of the countryside, who do not know the meanings of characters and who are painfully and hopelessly ignorant, may easily understand, I have repeatedly written the same things again and again. The

---

[51] *Notes on "Essentials of Faith Alone": A Translation of Shinran's Yuishinshō-mon'i* (Kyoto: Hongwanji International Center, 1979; Shin Buddhism Translation Series), 40 (italics mine); *SSZ*, II: 628–29. Hereafter, this translation will be referred to as *Faith Alone*.

[52] *Faith Alone*, 40–41; *SSZ*, II: 629.

educated reader will probably find this writing peculiar and may ridicule it. But paying no heed to such criticism, I write only that foolish people may easily grasp the essential meaning.[53]

For Shinran, it was precisely to these common people who had nothing to boast about—socially, morally, or religiously—and nothing to contribute to their afterlife that the unconditional boundless compassion of Amida's Other Power was extended, just as it was to his own being, deeply "sinking in an immense ocean of desires and attachments," that Amida's grace had reached out through his master Hōnen. Would it be wrong to find in the following passage, recorded in the *Tannishō*, a reflection of his life with the poor and ignorant in the Hokuriku region?

> "If it were only though observing precepts and upholding rules that one were able to entrust oneself to the Primal Vow, how could we [ever] become free of birth-and-death?" [Shinran said]. Even such wretched beings [as we], upon encountering the Primal Vow, in reality come to "presume" upon it. But even so, evil acts not possessed [karmically] in one's existence can hardly be committed. Further, "Those who make their way in this world drawing nets in the seas and rivers and angling, and companions who carry on their lives hunting beasts in the moors and mountains and taking fowl, and people who pass [their lives] conducting trade or cultivating paddies and fields, are all the same" [Shinran said].[54]

The inevitability of an "immoral life" of breaking the precepts, the karmic determination of evil acts, utter renunciation of all human efforts to contribute to one's salvation, and the purely gratuitous character of the salvation made possible by Amida's Vow Power, which requires us to meet no condition other than the simple act of entrusting ourselves—all these elements Shinran may already have learned under Hōnen; but they were deepened and crystallized into clearer consciousness in him through the praxis of the Pure Land teaching he had received from his master among the poor and the ignorant. Seen in this way, Shinran's exile turned out to be a blessing in disguise. As Shinran himself is said to have confessed: "And again, if my Great Teacher, the Venerable Genkū, were not sent away into a remote province by the authorities, how should I ever

---

[53] *Notes on Once-calling and Many-calling: A Translation of Shinran's Ichinen-tanen mon'i* (Kyoto: Hongwanji International Center, 1980; Shin Buddhism Translation Series), 50; *SSZ*, II: 619–20. Hereafter, this translation will be referred to as *Once-calling*.

[54] *Tannishō*, 95–97.

live a life of banishment? And if I did not live a life of banishment, how could I hope to have the opportunity to convert the people living far away from the centre of culture? This too must be ascribed to the virtue of my Venerable Teacher."[55]

SHINRAN IN KANTŌ

Shinran's evangelizing activity in the Echigo region, however, must have been rather limited, seeing that he was a "criminal" sentenced to exile. He seems to have occupied himself more with study and reflection on the meaning of the Pure Land teaching he had received from Hōnen. In a list, dating from the early fourteenth century, of his direct disciples, only one person from Echigo is mentioned, and most of them come from the Kantō area.[56]

Shinran moved to the Kantō region with his family in 1214, about three years after the ban had been lifted. We do not know for certain why he chose to move to the Kantō region instead of returning to Kyoto. Perhaps the situation in Kyoto was perceived to be fraught with danger, the nenbutsu movement still being under prohibition there; perhaps he saw more opportunity, evangelically or economically, in the Kantō area, which was emerging as the new center of political power with Kamakura as the seat of the bakufu.[57] Or, perhaps, Shinran was simply unable for some reason to leave Echigo until 1214, and by this time Hōnen had already passed away (1212), so he found no reason to go back to Kyoto. At any rate, he seems to have been actively engaged in evangelizing work in the Kantō region and quite successful in gaining converts to the Pure Land faith.

The adherents of the new faith in the Kantō region met regularly in a place called a *dōjō* 道場, meaning a "place for [cultivating] enlightenment." Kakunyo, the third-generation patriarch of the Shinshū, says of it:

> Among all the disciples to whom Shinran personally imparted his teachings long ago, there were none who established temples. He suggested that they construct a *dōjō* simply by altering an ordinary dwelling place

---

[55] Suzuki, *The Life of Shinran Shōnin*, 171; *SSZ*, III: 641.

[56] Dobbins, *Jōdo Shinshū*, 27.

[57] See Matsuno's brief discussion of the various reasons proposed for Shinran's move to the Kantō: *Shinran*, 215–17.

slightly, perhaps by extending its roof.[58]

Dobbins describes the religious life centering around *dōjō* during and after Shinran's time:

> *Dōjō* of this type were not unique to the Shinshū, but were prevalent throughout the Pure Land movement. The local congregation affiliated with the *dōjō* became known as nenbutsu members (*nenbutsushu*) or as religious companions (*monto*). In the formative years of the Shinshū, nenbutsu members met once a month for worship services, usually on the twenty-fifth to commemorate the day Hōnen had died. After Shinran's death, most congregations changed to the twenty-eighth of each month, in memory of Shinran's death day. The centerpiece of worship in the Shinshū *dōjō* was usually a large inscription of Amida's name (*myōgō honzon*) hung over a simple altar. This kind of religious object was an innovation of Shinran's. Up to that time the center of Buddhist worship had been artistic images of the Buddha, usually carved or painted. Such icons were available primarily to the upper classes, who had the wealth to commission artists to execute religious works of art. Shinran's creation of the Amida inscription supplied the ordinary believer with a simple and accessible object of reverence for use in worship, thereby freeing religious objects from the artistic domain controlled by aristocratic society. The actual content of *dōjō* worship varied from place to place, but was dominated by nenbutsu chanting. In addition, simple sermons, the recitation of scriptures, and the singing of hymns such as Shinran's *wasan* also became common features.

Dobbins concludes:

> All these components—the *dōjō*, the religious inscription, and the elements of worship—provided lowborn believers with a ready outlet for their religious inclinations and with a degree of participation in religion denied them under Japan's traditional system of temples. This fuller religious life, centering around the *dōjō*, was the reason for its popularity among peasants, and was the key to Shinshū growth during the fourteenth and fifteenth centuries.[59]

In short, *dōjō* was not the traditional Buddhist monastery exclusively meant for the monks who had renounced the world. No such institution was now necessary for the new movement of faith, in which there was no

---

[58] Quoted in Dobbins, *Jōdo Shinshū*, 66.

[59] Dobbins, *Jōdo Shinshū*, 66.

distinction between monks and lay, men and women, high and low, young and old, and where the only requirement was sincere faith to give up one's self-power and rely on Amida's Other Power and say the nenbutsu in gratitude for the salvation made possible by Amida's Vow. *Dōjō* was in this sense a completely open place easily accessible to anybody regardless of religious, moral, social, or material conditions.

Thus a thoroughly egalitarian community of believers came into being, a community of humble hearts who confessed their sinfulness and took refuge in the compassionate Vow of Amida to save such helpless beings. To be sure, there were leaders of the *dōjō* who had more knowledge about this new faith than others had, and there were some among them who made false authoritarian claims for themselves or resorted to coercive measures to put the believers, the *monto*, under their control.[60] But they deviated from Shinran's teaching, and Shinran did not approve of their behavior. For Shinran, nobody can make a special claim before Amida Buddha. Equally sinful beings who are equally in need of Amida's mercy, the leaders of the *dōjō* are by no means people of higher religious standing than others. Shinran himself set the example for this new type of humble leadership:

> That there apparently are disputes over "my disciple," "somebody else's disciple" among companions in the singlehearted practice of the nenbutsu is a circumstance beyond comprehension. [I], Shinran, do not have even a single disciple. The reason [is]: if I brought a person to say the nenbutsu through my designs (*hakarai*), then he would probably be a disciple; [but] to call "my disciple" the person who says the nenbutsu through receiving the working of Amida is utterly preposterous.[61]

This is why Shinran called his "followers" "fellow companions" (*dōbō* 同朋) and "fellow practicers" (*dōgyō* 同行).[62] Behind this utter humbleness and spiritual egalitarianism was Shinran's thorough awareness that no one has anything to boast of before Amida's mercy, an awareness based upon his profound sense of human sinfulness and its converse, that is, Amida's

---

[60] Akamatsu, *Shinran*, 237–40, 307–16.

[61] *Tannishō*, 67.

[62] This is often pointed out by scholars, and I follow it here; but a careful examination of the actual usage of these terms by Shinran seems to indicate that Shinran used them only when he was referring to the relationship between his disciples rather than to his own relationship with them; see the *Mattōshō*, SSZ, II: 688, 692, and the *Tannishō*, SSZ, II: 790.

grace as the sole ground for our salvation. Shinran, of course, learned this from his teacher Hōnen. No discipline of meditation, no observance of precepts, no accumulation of karmic merit through good acts, no learning and wisdom, no distinction in birth or social standing is worth anything before Amida's compassionate Vow. It was precisely for those who were unable to claim any of these merits for themselves that Amida uttered his Vow of compassion. All we need to do on our part, therefore, is to call upon his Name in sincere faith in accordance with what the Vow says. Shinran said:

> Know that the Primal Vow of Amida makes no distinction between people young and old, good and evil; only the entrusting of yourself to it is essential. For it was made to save the person in whom karmic evil is deep-rooted and whose blind passions abound.[63]

Or,

> In reflecting on the ocean of great faith, I realize that there is no discrimination between noble and humble or black-robed monks and white-clothed laity, no differentiation between man and woman, old and young. The amount of evil one has committed is not considered, the duration of any performance of religious practices is of no concern. It is a matter of neither practice nor good acts, neither sudden attainment nor gradual attainment, neither meditative practice nor non-meditative practice, neither right contemplation nor wrong contemplation, neither thought nor no-thought, neither daily life nor the moment of death, neither many-calling nor once-calling. It is simply faith that is inconceivable, inexplicable, and indescribable.[64]

All worldly values, moral merits, and even religious achievements are relativized and equalized before Amida's sheer goodness, which calls for nothing but our simple faith to respond to it. What is amazing, moreover, is that for Shinran even the faith of all people is essentially equal. The *Tannishō* reports the following significant dialogue between Shinran and fellow disciples of Hōnen:

> Shinran remarked, "My faith and the Master's are the same."
> Quite unexpectedly, Seikan-bō, Nenbutsu-bō, and others among his fellow practicers argued, "How can your faith equal the Master's?"

[63] *Tannishō*, 22.

[64] *True Teaching*, II: 249; *SSZ*, II: 68.

Shinran responded, "The Master possesses vast wisdom and learning, so I would be mistaken if I claimed to be the same in these respects, but in faith that is the attainment of birth, there is no difference whatever. The Master's faith and mine are one."

The others remained skeptical, however, sharply asking how that could be. So finally they all decided that the argument should be settled in front of Hōnen.

When they presented the matter, Hōnen said, "My faith has been imparted by Amida; so has Shinran's. Therefore they are one and the same. A person with a different faith will surely not be born in the Pure Land to which I will go."[65]

SHINRAN ON NENBUTSU

Shinran, no doubt, would have been glad to see his "disciples" make the same assertion about their faith and his own. It is not that the faith of all people are the same in strength or weakness but that it is essentially of one kind or quality, it being "imparted by Amida" and not the result of our own efforts. And it is this sameness of faith that formed the basis of the egalitarian community of believers formed around the *dōjō*.

The idea that faith is imparted to us by Amida is attributed to Hōnen in the above dialogue. It was Shinran, however, more than anyone else among the Pure Land thinkers, who emphasized the sheer gratuitous character of Amida's grace and our salvation. Deeply aware of the thorough depravity of human nature, Shinran, as we shall see, realized that there is absolutely nothing that we can genuinely contribute to our salvation, including even the act of nenbutsu and faith. For Shinran, therefore, the practice of nenbutsu and the mind of faith should by no means be considered as "our" act and "our" mind. If they are, they can never be the cause for our birth in the Pure Land despite the fact that they are stipulated in Amida's Vow as requisites for that birth. Even the act of nenbutsu and faith are not ours but given to us by Amida Buddha himself. In other words, they are not to be counted as the last claim we can make before Amida's grace, the last contribution we can make to our salvation. For this reason Shinran says:

[65] *Tannishō*, 42.

For the practicer who says it, the nenbutsu is not a practice, it is not a good deed. It is said not to be a practice because it is not performed out of one's own efforts and designs. It is not a good deed because it is not brought about through one's efforts and designs. Since it is totally Other Power and free of self-power, for the person who says it, the nenbutsu is "non-practice," it is "not-good."[66]

Here we have probably the core of Shinran's soteriological thought; namely, his emphasis on the pure Other Power that excludes any form or vestige of self-power, even in the act of nenbutsu. And it is this aspect of Shinran's thought that differentiates it from that of Hōnen, despite the fact that Shinran had no intention of departing from his master's teaching. Simply put, for Shinran nenbutsu is not another form of practice we can perform for our salvation, or another form of good act that we can contribute to our birth in the Pure Land, however "easy" it may be as a practice.

For Hōnen, nenbutsu was clearly a practice—one chosen by Amida out of his compassion for those who are incapable of any other practice, the "easy practice" that anybody can perform and thereby attain birth in the Pure Land. But there was simply no "easy" practice for Shinran, who had a more thoroughgoing pessimistic view of human nature than Hōnen. No matter what we do, in so far as it is *our* act, it is overlaid with selfish motivation and sinful desires. Nenbutsu is no exception in this respect. Therefore, it has to come from none other than Amida himself who instituted it in his Vow in the first place, if it is going to be an act that leads us unfailingly to the Pure Land. If it is our act, then it is subject to the fluctuation that inevitably characterizes all our acts, i.e., the differences found among us in the amount of effort we put in as well as in the psychological state in which we perform it, making our birth in the Pure Land uncertain and insecure as well. In short, for Shinran, Amida not only chose nenbutsu in his Vow; he also makes it possible for every believer to perform nenbutsu as a genuine, "true and real" act.

The idea that the act of nenbutsu itself is given to us by Amida is certainly not found—at least, not literally—in the eighteenth Vow that both Hōnen and Shinran regard as embodying the highest truth concerning the true intention of Amida's salvific will. The eighteenth Vow simply states that Amida will not attain Buddhahood should the sentient beings

---

[66] *Tannishō*, 26.

of the ten quarters, with sincere mind of faith, call upon his Name up to ten times yet fail to be born in his land. Nor is that idea found (at least not explicitly) in Hōnen. To be sure, Hōnen is said to have remarked, "In nenbutsu no reasoning is [true] reasoning." What he meant by this was that nenbutsu is to be practiced with a simple faith without thinking about or speculating on its reason or meaning (*gi* 義), because it was the practice selected by Amida's sheer wisdom and compassion, which no human reasoning can fathom.

Shinran also said the same thing: "In nenbutsu no reasoning is [true] reasoning, for it is indescribable, inexplicable, and inconceivable."[67] But Shinran takes "reasoning" (*gi*) here as meaning the "calculation" (*hakarai*) that we make with a view to obtaining salvation for ourselves. It means self-power for Shinran, nenbutsu being the Other Power. Hence, we see Shinran quoting Hōnen's words in the following way with his explanation:

> Since this is the Vow of Tathāgata, Hōnen said, "In Other Power, no reasoning is true reasoning." "Reasoning" [*gi*] is a term which connotes calculation [*hakarai*]. Since the calculation of the person seeking birth is self-power, it is called reasoning. Other Power is entrusting ourselves to the Primal Vow and our birth becoming firmly settled; hence it is altogether without reasoning.[68]

Thus, for Shinran, the nenbutsu is not to be practiced as an act of self-power, a subtle form of it, but purely as an act done by Other Power. To use the technical expression, Shinran says that it is "directed to us" (*ekō* 廻向) by Amida. This is why it is called by Shinran "Great Practice."[69] Therefore the entire focus in Shinran shifts from nenbutsu as a practice to faith in Other Power.

Needless to say, Hōnen did not regard nenbutsu as a self-power act either, but not because he saw it as an act directed to us by Amida, as Shinran did, but because he saw it as chosen by Amida as the easy practice for everybody. For Hōnen, nenbutsu is "not our self-power act" in the sense that its efficacy is grounded upon Amida's Primal Vow and its

---

[67] *Tannishō, SSZ*, II: 778.

[68] *Letters of Shinran: A Translation of Mattōshō* (Kyoto: Hongwanji International Center, 1978; Shin Buddhism Translation Series), 23 (translation altered); *SSZ*, II: 658–59.

[69] *Kyōgyōshinshō, SSZ*, II: 5.

fulfillment. Following Shan-tao, Hōnen says: "Whether walking or standing, sitting or lying, only repeat the name of Amida with all your heart. Never cease the practice of it even for a moment. This is the very work which unfailingly issues in salvation, *for it is in accordance with the Primal Vow of that Buddha.*"[70] Therefore, for Hōnen too, the Vow is ultimately more important than the nenbutsu, if we may put it this way. This is why Hōnen once said that there is no difference whatsoever between the nenbutsu recited in pure mind and the one done in deluded mind; the latter is not a bit inferior to the former. To a disciple of his who expressed doubt on this view, Hōnen said:

> This doubt arises because you still do not understand the Primal Vow. It is in order to save sentient beings of evil karma that Amida Buddha launched the ship of the universal Vow in the great ocean of birth-and-death. Whether it is a heavy stone or a light hemp, all get aboard the ship and reach the other shore. Likewise, the Primal Vow being excellent, there is no other thing for any sentient being than simply calling upon the Name.[71]

This clearly shows that Hōnen did not regard the efficacy of nenbutsu as depending upon the subjective condition of our mental state or act, because nenbutsu is ultimately grounded upon Amida's compassionate Vow. In this sense, Hōnen also held that nenbutsu should not be considered as our merit.

Yet this does not mean that he did not regard nenbutsu itself as our act, something we can perform. Hōnen did not go that far, and this is where Shinran further radicalized—or drew the final conclusion from, we might say—the Other Power-oriented soteriology of Hōnen.

Hōnen not only practiced nenbutsu diligently himself, he also strongly exhorted his followers to practice it as much as they could. The more we do it, the better, he taught, leading some people to think of it as a kind of meritorious act.[72] In this respect, it has to be pointed out that there was a certain ambivalence in Hōnen's attitude toward nenbutsu, and it was this ambivalence that gave rise to the disputes among his disciples concerning

---

[70] Coates and Ishizuka, *Hōnen*, I: 187 (italics mine).

[71] Quoted in Fugen Daien, *Shinshū gairon* (Kyoto: Hyakkaen, 1950), 160.

[72] See his words on nenbutsu cited in chapter one. Some of his typical teaching regarding the importance of continuous practice of nenbutsu is found in Coates and Ishizuka, *Hōnen*, I: 408; II: 441, 528.

the nature and method of nenbutsu practice, despite his warning that it has no reasoning as its reason. The dispute particularly focused on the issue of the so-called "once-calling" (*ichinen* 一念) and "many-calling" (*tanen* 多念). It is important to consider this debate briefly if we are to have an adequate understanding of why Shinran took the position he did with regard to nenbutsu.[73]

If the efficacy of the Name is grounded upon the Vow and the practice by which Amida (as Bodhisattva Dharmākara) fulfilled the Vow, and not upon the nenbutsu itself, nor upon it as our act, then why should one repeatedly say the nenbutsu? Is the continuous practice necessary at all, especially in view of the fact that the Vow says that ten utterances, or even one, is enough to ensure our birth in the Pure Land? Insisting upon the continuous practice of nenbutsu is tantamount to doubting the power of the Vow itself. Thus ran the argument of those who opposed "many-calling" and said that a single utterance of nenbutsu based upon faith is enough.

Those who favored the diligent practice of nenbutsu, on the other hand, based their argument on the Pure Land scriptures and writings, especially Shan-tao's, which emphasize the continuous practice of nenbutsu. For them, nenbutsu is still a form of practice, albeit an easy practice selected by Amida Buddha for us so that everybody can be saved. Although the ground of the efficacy of nenbutsu lies entirely in Amida's Vow and practice, saying the nenbutsu is nonetheless incumbent upon us, and the more we do it, the better. Neglecting even this easy practice results in Buddhism with no practice and leads to the danger of antinomianism, the temptation of the "licensed evil" (*zōaku muge* 造悪無礙) that presumes upon the power of the Vow and is not afraid to commit evil acts without regard for moral restraint. Moreover, the proponents of the "many-calling" believed that nenbutsu expiates our past evil karma. We should therefore continuously utter the nenbutsu in order to expiate whatever sins we may have committed up to the last moment of life and make sure that Amida appears with his holy host to welcome us at our deathbed. Since we do not know when we will meet our death, we should do our best to say the nenbutsu whenever we have the opportunity.

---

[73] *Once-calling*, 4–8 (Introduction) gives a good account of this debate; the following discussion of mine is indebted to it.

We have already mentioned that there is a certain ambivalence inherent in Hōnen's position on the matter. Hōnen said: "As to entrusting, you should believe that birth is settled with a single utterance; as to practice, you should continue throughout your life."[74] Although Hōnen meant by this that faith and practice should not hinder each other, it was precisely this discrepancy between faith (entrusting) and practice, that gave rise to the above disputes. One thing that is certain is that Hōnen was a diligent practicer of nenbutsu throughout his life and taught others to do so. One interpretation takes this as a possible concession to pressure from traditional Buddhism:

> Resolution of this controversy from Hōnen's position lay in maintaining the delicate balance between emphasis on continual recitation, which could easily lead to nenbutsu as an act of self-power, and emphasis on complete entrusting to Other Power, which, pursued doctrinally, seemed to deny any need for continued attention to the Name at all. But as a revolutionary thinker, Hōnen had to defend his new-found path against attack from older schools by reiterating that the nenbutsu was indeed a practice in the Buddhist tradition, although it originated from an entirely different source. By doing so, he exposed himself to the same criticism he had leveled against the traditional forms of practice—dependence on self-power.[75]

Be that as it may, for Shinran the whole debate of once-calling and many-calling is essentially based upon a misunderstanding of the nature of nenbutsu. For him, nenbutsu is never to be regarded as another way of piling up merit for oneself so that one can enter the Pure Land, an easy method to attain the difficult goal. There is no easy practice for Shinran, who found himself incapable of a single practice. It is for this reason that, as we have seen, he calls nenbutsu "non-practice" and "non-good." If it is going to be a practice that brings about our birth in the Pure Land, it has to be a Great Practice made possible only through Amida's directing (*ekō*) to us his own true and real act.

Traditionally, nenbutsu was considered an act by which we can easily accumulate merit and transfer (*ekō*) it toward our (and others') birth in the Pure Land. But Shinran changed this notion completely. *Ekō* is not

---

[74] Quoted in *Once-calling*, 6 (Introduction); see Coates and Ishizuka, 395, for the context in which Hōnen said this.

[75] *Once-calling*, 7–8 (Introduction).

our act but Amida's, for we really have nothing to "transfer." Thus he declares at the outset of his chapter on practice in the *Kyōgyōshinshō*:

> Reverently contemplating Amida's directing of virtue for our going forth to the Pure Land, I find that there is great practice, there is great faith.[76]

And this is why Shinran calls nenbutsu "not directing virtue (merit)":

> The nenbutsu is not a self-power practice performed by foolish beings or sages; it is therefore called the practice of "not-directing virtue [on the part of beings]."[77]

For Shinran, salvation, if it comes at all, comes only from Other Power. Practice, if it is really possible, should therefore come from Other Power, too. Ultimately, therefore, salvation as he understands it is not a matter of practice but of faith that renounces self-power and relies solely on Amida's Vow, which does everything for you—not merely selecting the nenbutsu as *the* practice but also enabling you to practice it as the Great Practice. Shinran says:

> This practice arises from the Vow of great compassion, which is known as "the Vow that all Buddhas extol the Name," "the Vow that all Buddhas say the Name," and "the Vow that all Buddhas praise the Name." It might also be called "the Vow of directing virtue for our going forth" and "the Vow in which the saying of the Name is selected."[78]

In short, Shinran sees nenbutsu, based upon the fulfillment of the above Vow, as ultimately the cosmic activity of the Buddhas that, through faith, becomes expressed as our practice. This is the nenbutsu as Great Practice.

We have dwelt upon Shinran's conception of nenbutsu at some length because it constitutes the core and the most innovative aspect of his Pure Land soteriology vis-a-vis the tradition he had inherited, including perhaps Hōnen's teaching. He did not arrive at this view immediately after his conversion to Hōnen's nenbutsu movement. It was the product of a long process of reflection on the meaning of the message he had received from Hōnen. Shinran himself describes in three steps the process through which he came to have this final paradoxical understanding of nenbutsu as "non-practice."

[76] *True Teaching*, I: 71; *SSZ*, II: 5.
[77] *True Teaching*, I: 136; *SSZ*, II: 33.
[78] *True Teaching*, I: 71; *SSZ*, II: 5.

Thus I, Gutoku Shinran, disciple of Śākyamuni, through reverently accepting the exposition of [Vasubandhu,] the author of the *Treatise*, and depending on the guidance of Master [Shan-tao], departed everlastingly from the temporary gate of the myriad practices and various good acts and left forever the birth attained beneath the twin śāla trees. Turning about, I entered the "true" gate of the root of good and the root of virtue, and wholeheartedly awakened the mind leading to the birth that is non-comprehensible.

Nevertheless, I have now decisively departed from the "true" gate of provisional means and, [my self-power] overturned, have entered the ocean of the selected Vow. Having swiftly become free of the mind leading to the birth that is non-comprehensible, I am assured of attaining the birth that is inconceivable. How truly profound in intent is the Vow that beings ultimately attain birth![79]

This is the famous passage in his *Kyōgyōshinshō* on the so-called "three Vows conversions" (or turning about; *sangan tennyū* 三願轉入). It is a carefully worded passage full of allusions, and the full understanding of it requires a knowledge of the total doctrinal system of Shinran's thought. Essentially, Shinran talks about how he went through three different approaches to the Pure Land truth as represented by the three Vows—the nineteenth, twentieth, and the eighteenth among the forty-eight uttered by Amida—according to his highly idiosyncratic interpretation.[80]

---

[79] *True Teaching*, IV: 531; *SSZ*, II: 166.

[80] These three vows, as found in the *Kyōgyōshinshō* translation (Shin Buddhism Translation Series), are as follows:

19: If, when I attain Buddhahood, the sentient beings of the ten quarters—awakening the mind of enlightenment and performing meritorious acts—should aspire with sincere mind and desire to be born in my land, and yet I should not appear before them at the moment of death, surrounded by a host of sages, may I not attain the supreme enlightenment (vol. IV, pp. 476–77).

20: If, when I attain Buddhahood, the sentient beings of the ten quarters, on hearing my Name, should place their thoughts on my land, cultivate the root of all virtues, and direct their merits with sincere mind, desiring to be born in my land, and yet not ultimately attain it, may I not attain the supreme enlightenment (vol. IV, p. 512).

18: If, when I attain Buddhahood, the sentient beings of the ten quarters, with sincere mind entrusting themselves, aspiring to be born in my land, and saying my Name perhaps even ten times, should not be born there, may I not attain the supreme enlightenment. Excluded are those who commit the five great offenses and those who slander the right dharma (vol. II, p. 205).

First, Shinran followed the temporary gate (*kemon* 假門) which seeks birth in the Pure Land by producing merit for it through the practice of "myriad practices and various good acts [meditative and nonmeditative]"; but this only leads to an imperfect expedient realm, not the true realm of the Pure Land as realized by the fulfillment of Amida's Vow. This path probably refers to what Shinran was practicing as a Tendai nenbutsu monk on Mt Hiei. Then Shinran had recourse to the true gate (*shinmon* 眞門), which relies on nenbutsu as "the root of good and the root of virtue," but this, too, leads to a provisional form of birth in the Pure Land because it also lacks faith in Other Power and regards nenbutsu as another form of meritorious act of self-power. This was probably how Shinran initially understood Hōnen's message of nenbutsu when he left the practice on Mt Hiei and went to Hōnen. But, partly through his own deep reflection on the meaning of Amida's Vow and nenbutsu, and partly through the influence of other disciples of Hōnen, especially those who favored "once-calling" and emphasized faith more than practice, Shinran completely discarded the conception of nenbutsu as another form of practice and entered into "the ocean of the selected Vow." Now it is not the nenbutsu as such that is crucial, but the power of the Vow as the expression of Amida's compassion, and hence our complete trust and faith in it.

The crucial mistake of the first two paths is that, while they claim to follow the Pure Land way, they in fact lack true faith in Other Power; thus the one tries to transfer his or her own meritorious deeds toward one's birth in the Pure Land, while the other tries to turn nenbutsu into another form of one's own merit and hence mix the pure Other Power with self-power. They spoil the pure grace of Other Power and transform it into "self-power within Other Power."[81] Shinran deplores this stubborn

---

According to Shinran's interpretation, the nineteenth Vow represents the gist of the *Smaller Sūtra of Immeasurable Life* (*Amida kyō*), the twentieth Vow represents the gist of the *Sūtra of Contemplation on the Buddha of Immeasurable Life* (*Kanmuryōju kyō*), and the eighteenth Vow represents the gist of the *Larger Sūtra of Immeasurable Life* (*Daimuryōju kyō*), which is the highest truth. These three texts constitute the basic threefold scriptures (*Jōdo sanbu kyō*) of the Pure Land tradition.

[81] *True Teaching*, II: 250; *SSZ*, II: 69. In other technical doctrinal terms, these two paths, respectively corresponding to the path of salvation taught in the nineteenth and the twentieth Vow, belong to the path of Crosswise Departing (*ōshutsu* 横出), in contrast to the path of Crosswise Transcendence (*ōchō* 横超) represented by the eighteenth Vow, which was the third and final position Shinran arrived at; see also *True Teaching*, II: 261–62; *SSZ*, II: 73. In his *Mattōshō*, Shinran defines "self-power within Other Power" as follows: "That there is self-power within Other Power means that there are people who seek to attain birth

wilfulness of self-power, which turns even the most gracious gift of Amida into a subtle form of one's own merit and thus makes us fail to benefit from genuine Other Power:

> Sages of the Mahāyāna and Hīnayāna and all good people make the auspicious Name of the Primal Vow their own root of good; hence, they cannot give rise to faith and do not apprehend the Buddha's wisdom. Because they cannot comprehend [the Buddha's intent in] establishing the cause [of birth], they do not enter the fulfilled land.[82]

It is hard to tell when Shinran arrived at his final position, which even lets go of nenbutsu as one's act and lets Amida's Vow be everything. The following story, however, is interesting and may throw some light upon the development of Shinran's puristic Other Power–oriented soteriology. On his way from Echigo to Kantō he is said to have made a resolve to recite "one thousand copies of the three Pure Land sūtras" in order to "benefit sentient beings." By the time he had done it for four or five days, however, it occurred to him that the best way to repay his debt to Amida Buddha was through teaching others to have faith like his own (*jishin kyōninshin* 自信教人信), so that they could also say nenbutsu and partake of the same joy and peace he was experiencing. Thus he stopped reciting the sūtras.[83]

This story is significant in many ways.[84] First of all, reciting the Pure Land scriptures is one of the five "right practices" (*shōgyō* 正行) recommended by Shan-tao, but rejected by Hōnen in favor of the sole-practice of nenbutsu. Even though it was meant to benefit other beings by generating merit for them, Shinran was still found practicing it. It may be considered a vestige of the old practice of "continuous nenbutsu" that he used to perform as a monk on Mt Hiei, and it shows that his break with the merit-oriented Pure Land practices was still not complete at this point

---

through sundry practices and disciplines and through meditative and non-meditative nenbutsu; such people are people of self-power within Other Power." *Letters of Shinran: A Translation of Mattōshō*, 53. Hereafter, this will be referred to as *Letters*.

[82] *True Teaching*, IV: 530; *SSZ*, II: 165–66. "Fulfilled land (*hōdo* 報土) refers to the true realm of the Pure Land as realized by the fulfillment of Amida's Vow. Attaining it is called "inconceivable birth," as contrasted with the other two provisional forms of birth, "the birth attained beneath the twin śāla trees," and "the non-comprehensible birth."

[83] Akamatsu, *Shinran*, 137–48.

[84] I follow Akamatsu's interpretation of this event.

in his life and that this experience itself may have marked a crucial turning point in his complete break with the merit-oriented practice of self-power. We may further interpret this experience of Shinran as something that made him completely renounce the idea of nenbutsu as a merit-producing practice as well and concentrate on faith as being the most essential. What people need, he concluded, is the same experience of faith and the joy it brings, not the merit that *they* can generate and that, however great it may be, can only tie them to this world of birth-and-death. We would not be far from the truth if we see Shinran here fighting off the temptation of self-power and this-worldly attachment at the same time.[85] Thus Shinran acquired through this experience a renewed commitment to the authentic mission he would have to carry out in the new region to which he was moving.

That Shinran definitely rejected the idea of merit-producing practice of nenbutsu for himself as well as for others is clearly indicated by the following words:

> I have never said the Name even once for the repose of my departed father and mother. For all living things have been my parents and brothers and sisters in the course of countless lives in many states of existence. Upon attaining Buddhahood in the next life, I must save every one of them.
>
> Were saying the Name indeed a good act in which a person strove through his own powers, then he might direct the merit thus gained toward saving his father and mother. But this is not the case. If, however, he simply abandons such self-power and quickly attains enlightenment in the Pure Land, he will be able to save all beings with transcendent powers and compassionate means, whatever karmic suffering they may be sinking into in the six realms and the four modes of birth, beginning with those with whom his life is deeply bound.[86]

For Shinran, it is presumptuous to think about the transference of merit because there is simply no merit we can produce in the first place, not even through nenbutsu. Thus if we are going to help others, we had bet-

---

[85] Kasahara Kazuo stresses the latter aspect only when he interprets this event as betraying the temptation for Shinran to compromise the pure other-worldly orientation of his message with the worldly concerns of the Kantō people as he would face them in the coming mission. See *Shinshū ni okeru itan no keifu* (Tokyo: Tōkyō Daigaku Shuppankai, 1962), 124–28.

[86] *Tannishō*, 25.

ter attain enlightenment first before we can perform altruistic activities. One's birth in the Pure Land, therefore, is the supreme value each individual can pursue here on earth.

The rejection of all forms of merit-oriented practices and devotion solely to Amida's Other Power led Shinran to renounce magical practices and beliefs, fortune-telling, and praying to various deities for the sake of securing worldly benefits. He clearly condemns those who practice such things as non-Buddhist:

> "Other teachings" applies to those who incline toward the Path of Sages or non-Buddhist ways, endeavor in other practices, think on other Buddhas, observe lucky days and auspicious occasions, and depend on fortune-telling and ritual purification. Such people belong to non-Buddhist ways; they rely wholly on self-power.[87]

Shinran deplores those who follow these non-Buddhist ways as a sign of *mappō*:

> Lamentable it is that people, whether of the Way or of the world,
> Choose auspicious times and lucky dates,
> Worship heavenly gods and earthly deities,
> And are absorbed in divinations and rituals.[88]

Or,

> Lamentable it is that these days
> All in Japan, whether of the Way or of the world,
> While performing the rites and rituals of Buddhism
> Worship the spirits and ghosts of heaven and earth.[89]

We would be inclined to think that Shinran's puristic approach to Buddhism, which rejects the mundane benefits of faith and solely emphasizes supramundane salvation, may have made his message less attractive to people in the Kantō region, where he seems to have carried out active evangelizing work. In fact, this was to remain one of the major problems facing the Shinshū community throughout its history. Yet it may have been precisely this puristic message of supramundane salvation available to all believers that appealed all the more strongly to the lay people who

[87] *Once-calling*, 43.

[88] *Shōzōmatsu Wasan*, 101; *SSZ*, II: 528.

[89] *Shōzōmatsu Wasan*, 104 (translation altered); *SSZ*, II: 528.

were being awakened to a deeper religious need, especially the Kantō merchant class that was enjoying greater socioeconomic power, just as happened in the days of the Śākyamuni Buddha.[90] As far as the prospect of future salvation was concerned, at any rate, there was complete equality among the believers, no matter what their social background was.

Moreover, the prohibition of non-Buddhist practices was not merely a negative teaching. Behind it was the positive conviction that there was no other being, Buddha or god, who excels Amida Buddha, and no other practice that surpassed nenbutsu, which embraces within it all the virtues that can come from other deities and Buddhas. Consider the following remark in the *Tannishō*:

> The person of the nenbutsu treads the great path free of all obstacles. For the gods of heaven and the deities of earth bow in homage to a practicer of faith, and those of the world of demons or of non-Buddhist ways never hinder him; moreover, the evil he does cannot bring forth its karmic results, nor can any good act equal in virtue his saying of the Name.[91]

Thus Shinran instilled in the hearts of the believers a strong sense of fearlessness and freedom from anxiety over any evil that might occur to them in this world as a result of capricious supernatural forces—a sense of ultimate confidence in life based upon faith in Other Power. For this reason, we may even be able to say that Shinran "desacralized" the world to a certain degree by purging it of the supernatural activities of unseen forces—at least, purging it as a psychological force in the lives of the believers.

We must note in this context that Shinran included in his teaching the so-called "ten benefits in the present life" that come from faith, among which are found "the benefit of being protected and sustained by unseen powers," "the benefit of our karmic evil being transformed into good," and "the benefit of being protected and cared for by all the Buddhas."[92] From this, it is clear that he did not deny the existence of

---

[90] See Akamatsu's discussion of this problem, *Shinran*, 173–84.

[91] *Tannishō*, 26; see also Akamatsu Toshihide and Kasahara Kazuo, eds., *Shinshūshi gaisetsu* (Kyoto: Heirakuji Shoten, 1963), 56–57.

[92] *True Teaching*, II: 257; *SSZ*, II: 72. Shinran also composed *Genze riyaku wasan* 現世利益和讃 (Hymns on the benefits in the present life), which includes more materialistic benefits such as ending misfortunes and lengthening life; see *Jōdo Wasan: The Hymns on the Pure Land* (Kyoto: Ryukoku University Translation Center, 1965; Ryukoku Translation Series IV), 130–44.

unseen forces and deities in the universe—in this sense, he was neither a monotheist nor a complete desacralizer—but he taught that they cannot obstruct the practicer of nenbutsu and that all the benefits they may bring are already included in the nenbutsu itself. Worshipping them is a sign of doubting and betraying Amida's all-sufficient Vow Power, and hence should be prohibited. At the same time, though, it is clear that Shinran could not ignore the this-worldly concerns of the believers completely; to a certain degree he had to accommodate them in his message.

At any rate, in view of the fact that Buddhism had been thoroughly amalgamated with this-worldly Shinto faith ever since its coming to Japan, the significance of Shinran's prohibition of such mixed faith and practices can hardly be exaggerated. We could even assert, perhaps, that for the first time in the history of Buddhism, an authentic message of supramundane liberation was addressed to the lay believer without a major compromise, although it was a message vastly different from that of Śākyamuni Buddha some 1700 years before.

Shinran's thought matured and took a definite shape during his stay in the Kantō area. This is demonstrated by his composition during this period of the *Kyōgyōshinshō*, his most important and systematic work. Although the exact time at which he composed the work is still subject to debate, one thing remains certain—that he composed an early draft of it at Inada (Hitachi Province) in 1224, when he was fifty-two, if not earlier. And it is very likely that "the ideas contained in [it] were very much a part of his message to Kantō believers."[93] Something of the spirit in which Shinran composed it is revealed in the following words of the preface:

> This, then, is the true teaching easy to practice for small, foolish beings; it is the straight way easy to traverse for the dull and ignorant. Among all the teachings the Great Sage preached in his lifetime, none surpasses this ocean of virtues. Let the one who seeks to abandon the defiled and aspire for the pure; who is confused in practice and vacillating in faith; whose mind is dark and whose understanding deficient; whose evils are heavy and whose karmic obstructions manifold—let this person embrace above all the Tathāgata's exhortations, take refuge without fail in the most excellent direct path, devote himself solely to this practice, and revere only this faith.[94]

[93] Dobbins, *Jōdo Shinshū*, 31; see also his discussion of the composition, structure, and main content of the *Kyōgyōshinshō*, 31–38.

[94] *True Teaching*, I: 58; SSZ, II: 1.

Then, in the postscript to the work, Shinran expresses his overflowing joy and gratitude:

> How joyous I am, my heart and mind being rooted in the Buddha-ground of the universal Vow, and my thoughts and feelings flowing within the dharma-ocean, which is beyond comprehension! I am deeply aware of the Tathāgata's immense compassion, and I sincerely revere the benevolent care behind the masters' teaching activity. My joy grows ever fuller, my gratitude and indebtedness ever more compelling. Therefore, I have selected [passages expressing] the core of the Pure Land way and gathered here its essentials. Mindful solely of the profundity of the Buddha's benevolence, I pay no heed to the derision of others. May those who see and hear this work be brought—either through the cause of reverently embracing the teaching or through the condition of [others'] doubt and slander of it—to manifest faith within the power of the Vow and reveal the incomparable fruit of enlightenment in the land of peace.[95]

Shinran continued to work on his text after its first draft had been made. It took basically the present form in 1247 at least, if not earlier, when he allowed a disciple of his to make a copy of it. He was then seventy-five years old, so it was well after he had left Kantō and returned to Kyoto. Despite the exuberant joy and gratitude in which he wrote his work, we cannot overlook the fact that it is permeated by a continuing sense of his own sinfulness and the despair arising from it. The following passage that occurs toward the end of his exposition of faith is typical:

> I know truly how grievous it is that I, Gutoku Shinran, am sinking in an immense ocean of desires and attachments and am lost in vast mountains of fame and advantage; so that I rejoice not at all at entering the stage of the truly settled and feel no happiness at coming nearer the realization of true enlightenment. How ugly it is! How wretched![96]

The sense of joy and the sense of despair were inseparable in Shinran. The more he became aware of the boundless grace of Amida, the more keenly he realized the unfathomable depth of his sinfulness; the more he despaired over the ineradicable presence of evil in his own being, the more he exulted over the infinite compassion of the Vow. He seems to have lived his entire life with these two opposite feelings closely interlocked, either experiencing them simultaneously or oscillating between

[95] *True Teaching*, IV: 616–17; *SSZ*, II: 203.
[96] *True Teaching*, II: 279; *SSZ*, II: 80.

the two. As we shall see later, for Shinran, salvation, as far as it is experienced here in this defiled world, comes only in the form of a paradoxical experience, joy in the midst of sorrow, hope in the midst of despair. This is what he meant when he said that the person of faith "realizes *nirvāṇa* without severing blind passions."

SHINRAN RETURNS TO KYOTO

Shinran returned to Kyoto around 1235, the year in which the Kamakura bakufu took severe actions against the nenbutsu practicers, charging them with engaging in immoral behavior such as inviting women to their places and forming groups in which people ate meat and drank wine.[97] The bakufu ordered them to be banned from Kamakura and their houses destroyed. The charge was not totally groundless, for among Shinran's communities there were actually some believers who deliberately committed immoral acts on the pretext that no evil act whatsoever was strong enough to obstruct the power of the Primal Vow that resolved to save evil persons. This was the so-called "licensed evil" that was based on a "presumption upon the Primal Vow" (*hongan bokori* 本願誇り). It is hard to deny that Shinran's teaching had in it an element that was open to such an antinomian distortion. For example,

> Thus, in the entrusting of oneself to the Primal Vow, other good [acts] are not essential; for there is no good [act] that can be better than the nenbutsu. And one should not fear evil; for there is no evil [act] so [great] that it obstructs Amida's Primal Vow.[98]

There were, however, deeper reasons for the persecution of the nenbutsu group than their alleged moral laxity. The more fundamental reason seems to be that Shinran's communities for the first time offered to the peasants an opportunity to organize themselves and emerge as a potential threat to the local authorities, including the established Buddhist and Shinto temples in the area. With their newly found religious freedom and the confidence instilled by the highly egalitarian gospel of Amida's grace, they were no longer blindly subservient to the authorities,

---

[97] I follow the view of Akamatsu and Kasahara on the time and reason of Shinran's return to Kyoto; see Akamatsu's discussion, *Shinran*, 251–54; See also Kasahara Kazuo, *Shinshū ni okeru itan no keifu*, 34–36.

[98] *Tannishō*, 53.

as can be seen from the lifestyle of a few nenbutsu followers who were not afraid to defy the moral restraints traditionally imposed upon them.[99]

If indeed Shinran's decision to leave Kantō was related to the persecution, it was not based so much on his fear of the persecutions as on his concern over some of his followers, who persisted in the perverse interpretation of his doctrine and continued lives addicted to immoral conduct. Shinran was in his early sixties, and his move to Kyoto may well have been a sort of retirement, in that he withdrew from active leadership of the rather flourishing community of faith with all its problems and potentialities. This does not mean that he had nothing to do afterwards with the Kantō community. On the contrary, the disciples from the Kantō region continued to visit him in order to consult with him on important matters of faith. For instance, Shinran said of the visit of his followers:

> Each of you has crossed the borders of more than ten provinces to come to see me, undeterred by concern for your bodily safety, solely to inquire about the way to birth in the land of bliss. But if you imagine in me some special knowledge of a way to birth other than the nenbutsu or a familiarity with writings that teach it, you are greatly mistaken. If that is the case, you would do better to visit the many eminent scholars in Nara or on Mt Hiei and inquire fully of them about the essentials for birth. I simply accept and entrust myself to what a good teacher [Hōnen] told me, "Just say the Name and be saved by Amida"; nothing else is involved.[100]

The Kantō disciples also communicated with Shinran through letters in which they showed their abiding affection for and loyalty to their revered master and sought his authoritative guidance on important doctrinal points. Shinran also wrote responses to them, in which his warm concern for them as well as his resolute position on doctrinal matters are clearly expressed. These extant letters of his, amounting to about forty-three, constitute an important source of our knowledge not only of Shinran the person and his faith, but also of the life of faith of his disciples. Akamatsu discusses the significance of the letters:

> The later thirty-seven letters were given to all the disciples. The leaders of the "place of practice" (Dōjō) who stood between Shinran and the disci-

---

[99] *Shinshūshi gaisetsu*, 60–63.
[100] *Tannishō*, 22–23.

ples inquired of him about unclear points of doctrine or reported the tense social relations. Shinran responded to their requests for instruction and taught them gently. These letters relate, clearly and concretely, the fundamental thought of Shinran's religion. Through them the nature of the faith of the leaders and the disciples was clarified as they desired. It is well to study the *Kyōgyōshinshō* in order to know Shinran's religion as doctrine or as a system and tradition. To get it in just a word, we can repeatedly read the *Tannishō*. However, in order to know what kind of counter-influences the gospel of absolute Tariki [Other Power] brought about in those who accepted it, and how that influenced Shinran's action and thought, in other words, when we try to make clear the constitution of Shinran's religion historically and socially, we must, above all, study his letters.[101]

Shinran's letters reveal some of the difficulty, and yet the remarkable success, his disciples, who had no training in Buddhist doctrines, had in understanding some of the key points in Shinran's teaching, which were often not merely subtle and profound but also bold and novel. For instance, Shinran taught that when their faith and birth (in the Pure Land) is settled—we will examine more closely this important concept later on—they are equal to none other than Maitreya Buddha himself in that they are certain to attain enlightenment in the next life. It is no wonder that this incredibly bold message caused a great deal of confusion in the minds of Shinran's followers, as can be seen by the fact that it is one of the most often discussed topics in the letters exchanged between them and him. The letters demonstrate to us that his message of salvation through faith in Amida's Vow was to a considerable degree successful in breaking the traditional barrier between monks and lay people, despite the fact that it also gave rise to serious misunderstandings and problems that he had not foreseen.

Shinran seems to have depended for a substantial portion of his livelihood upon whatever occasional donations of money his disciples in the Kantō area sent to him, and this must have been a practical reason for him to maintain a constant concern for the communities he had left behind. He was not only kept informed of the situation within the Kantō communities of faith; he also had to take concrete action when necessary. The most famous and the most tragic case of such action was the series of

---

[101] Quoted in Bloom, "The Life of Shinran," 39.

events that led to Shinran's disowning of his son Zenran in 1256.[102] This sad incident, which occurred during the very late years of his life, has to be understood in the light of several problems that were ailing the communities of faith in Kantō even while he was there. These problems seem to have grown more serious after he left—to the degree that the Kamakura bakufu had to intervene and hold a trial.

Two problems in particular troubled the communities: the antinomian tendency, and the defamation of traditional Shinto deities and other Buddhas by some of Shinran's followers. The former, as we have already seen, was based upon the theory that since one is saved through Amida's compassionate Vow regardless of one's moral effort and state, one can commit evil and yet be sure of salvation. Through his letters, Shinran warned against this perverse interpretation of the Pure Land gospel. He said that no one who genuinely aspires for the Pure Land would harbour the thought of indulging in immoral acts for sensual gratification, and that one does not take a poison simply because there is an antidote.

The defamation of traditional deities, also attributable to a certain degree to the exclusivistic faith and practice taught by Shinran, caused a serious conflict between the traditional religious bodies, which were closely allied with local authorities, and the new communities of faith. The "antisocial" tendencies among some of Shinran's followers grew serious enough to bring the Kamakura bakufu to intervene and hold a trial. According to Shinran's letters, one of Shinran's disciples, named Shōshin, had to defend the nenbutsu practicers with the argument that the nenbutsu was recited "for the sake of the court and for the sake of the people." Shinran praised Shōshin for this, saying that it is good to say nenbutsu "for the peace of society and for the spread of the Buddha-dharma" as a way of repaying one's gratitude to the Buddha.[103]

Although the trial ended in favor of Shinran's communities, the problems did not disappear and continued to hound them. This seems to have been what led Shinran to dispatch his son Zenran to Kantō, even though we do not know exactly when and how Zenran came to be there. Unfortunately, however, Zenran did not prove himself to be worthy of this important mission. Instead, he further aggravated the situation by the

---

[102] The following account of the event surrounding Zenran is largely based upon Akamatsu, *Shinran*, 281–306.

[103] Akamatsu, *Shinran*, 286–88.

high-handed manner in which he dealt with the problems and by his personal ambition to control the communities.[104] When Shinran discovered through the letters sent to him by other disciples in Kantō that Zenran had betrayed his mission, he sent letters to Zenran and Shōshin notifying them that he was disowning his son. Given his age of eighty-four at the time, it is not difficult to imagine the mental anguish he must have gone through before and after he took this drastic action. Such was the intensity and seriousness with which Shinran approached the problem of faith, and such was the zeal with which he cared for the communities of faith he had established. Once the storm was over, the Kantō communities seem to have enjoyed a degree of peace and prosperity, as the later letters of Shinran show.[105]

The antisocial behavior among Shinran's followers and the consequent intervention by the government raised a very sensitive and difficult issue for Shinran. On the whole, while critical of unjust charges by the authorities against the nenbutsu group, he was of the view that just punishment should be accepted by individuals responsible for wrongdoings. Even in the case of unjust persecution, he taught believers not to criticize the authorities but to have sympathy and to recite nenbutsu for them as a means to bring them to salvation.[106] He was also of the view that persecution was natural to expect in the age of *mappō* and thus to be endured, and that in case of severe persecution too hard to endure the believers should leave the place and go somewhere else.[107]

What occupied Shinran's time most after his return to Kyoto, however, was not so much his pastoral care for those left behind in the Kantō area as his tireless writing activity. Most of his writings, including the *Kyōgyōshinshō* in its present form, were composed during this period.[108]

---

[104] Kasahara Kazuo suggests that Zenran, in order to take charge of the communities, joined hands with the local authorities who, representing the interest of the established Buddhism and Shinto, used the "licensed evil" found among some of the followers of nenbutsu as an excuse to suppress the movement as a whole; *Shinshū ni okeru itan no keifu*, 34–36.

[105] Bloom, "The Life of Shinran," 53.

[106] *Shinshūshi gaisetsu*, 63–65; Bloom, 57.

[107] *Shinshūshi gaisetsu*, 65.

[108] The following list of Shinran's writings and their dates is from Ueda and Hirota, *Shinran*, 322–24.

1248   *Hymns on the Pure Land (Jōdo wasan)*
           Hymns on the Masters (Kōsō wasan)

1250   *Notes on "Essentials of Faith Alone" (Yuishinshō mon'i)*

1251   Earliest letter in *Letters of Shinran* (Lamp for the Latter Age,
           Mattōshō, compiled in 1333)

1252   *Passages on the Pure Land Way (Jōdo monrui jushō)*

1255   *Notes on the Inscriptions on Sacred Scrolls (Songō shinzō meimon)*
           *Passages on the Modes of Birth in the Three Pure Land Sūtras (Jōdo
           sangyō ōjō monrui)*
           Gutoku's Notes (Gutokushō)
           Hymns in Praise of Prince Shōtoku (Kōtaishi Shōtoku hōsan)

1256   *Hymn on the Two Gates of Entrance and Emergence (Nyūshutsu
           nimon geju)*

1257   *Collection Showing the Way to the West* (Words of Hōnen, *Saihō
           shinan shō)*
           Notes on Once-calling and Many-calling (Ichinen-tanen mon'i)
           *Hymns to Prince Shōtoku, Monarch of the Millet-Scattered Islands
           of Japan (Dai Nihon koku zokusan ō Shōtoku taishi hōsan)*
           *Passages on the Two Aspects of Amida's Directing of Virtue
           (Nyorai nishu ekō mon)*

1258   *Hymns on the Right, Semblance, and Last Dharma-Ages
           (Shōzōmatsu wasan)*
           On Jinen hōni (Jinen hōni shō)

1260   *On the Virtues of Amida Tathāgata's Name (Mida nyorai myōgō
           toku)*[109]

Shinran spent the last days of his life in the home of his brother
Kaneari, who was a Tendai monk. He was attended by his widowed
daughter Kakushinni. He showed a great deal of concern before his death
for this daughter, who was poor, and left letters in which he asked his disciples to take care of her after his death.[110] Eshinni, his wife, who for some
reason was living at this time in Echigo (the old place of Shinran's exile
and Eshinni's home area), was informed of Shinran's death by Kakushinni. After the cremation, his ashes were preserved in a tomb in the
Ōtani area in the Higashiyama section of Kyoto, which belonged to

---

[109] At this time Shinran was 88 years old.
[110] See Akamatsu's discussion of this matter, 328–45.

Kakushinni. It was eventually through Kakushinni's lineage that the Honganji sect was established to become the mainstay of Shinshū orthodoxy down to the present day. The *Shinran denne*, the illustrated biography of Shinran composed by Kakushinni's grandson Kakunyo in 1295, describes the last days of Shinran as follows:

> Towards the latter part of mid-winter in the second year of Kōchō (1262), the Shōnin showed the symptoms of a slight indisposition, and after that, his talk never referred to earthly things, dwelling only on how deeply grateful he was to the Buddha; he uttered nothing but the name of Amida, which he constantly repeated. On the twenty-eighth of the same month, at noon, he laid himself on his right side with his head toward the north and his face towards the west; and when at last recitation of the name of Amida was heard no more, he expired. He was then just completing his ninetieth year.[111]

Thus ended the life of a man who agonized throughout his life over his inability to be more than an ordinary being (*bonpu*) but, out of this despair, found a new way of salvation that accepted him as he was, i.e., as a "foolish being full of blind passions."

---

[111] D. T. Suzuki, trans., *The Life of Shinran Shōnin*, 181.

3

Faith

WE HAVE SEEN IN THE LAST CHAPTER that the most innovative aspect of Shinran's Pure Land soteriology vis-à-vis the tradition he had inherited was his view of nenbutsu as "non-practice," "not-good," and "non-directing" of merit. Through his profound awareness of human sinfulness Shinran came to the conclusion that there is really no practice, however easy it may be, that we can genuinely carry out to meet the requirement for our salvation or contribute to it. In Shinran's understanding, nenbutsu is not another requirement for our salvation. If it were, it would be just as difficult as any other practice, and we would be in just as desperate a situation as when we had to fulfill the difficult demands set by the Path of Sages. With his keen insight into the human mind, Shinran discerned the last remnant of the self-power attitude in the "easy practice" of nenbutsu. Salvation should never depend upon our unreliable practice and impure action.

Salvation is an unconditional gift, which we can only accept in faith and gratitude, not something that can be secured by our doubtful action, even if it be the easy practice of nenbutsu recommended by the Vow. What makes our salvation possible is not the act of nenbutsu as such but the infinite wisdom and compassion of Amida as manifested in his Primal Vow. All we need do is simply recognize this fact and entrust ourselves joyfully to the Primal Vow. Faith, therefore, is said by Shinran to be the "true cause" (*shōin* 正因) for our birth in the Pure Land.

To be sure, Shinran, as a faithful disciple of Hōnen, continues to talk about nenbutsu as the true cause for birth in the Pure Land as well, although it is never to be considered as our act of transferring merit. After quoting in his *Kyōgyōshinshō* a series of passages by the Pure Land masters on the importance of nenbutsu, Shinran concludes:

> Clearly we know, then, that the nenbutsu is not a self-power practice performed by foolish beings or sages; it is therefore called the practice of "not-directing virtue [on the part of beings]." Masters of the Mahāyanā

and Hīnayāna and people burdened with karmic evil, whether heavy or light, should all in the same way take refuge in the great treasure ocean of the selected Vow and attain Buddhahood through the nenbutsu.[1]

The fact is that, for Shinran, faith and nenbutsu are inseparable, and it is hard to think about one without the other. Both are grounded upon Amida's Vow. Thus, explaining their inseparability, Shinran writes as follows in his letters:

> The reason is that the practice of nenbutsu is to say it perhaps once, perhaps ten times, on hearing and realizing that birth into the Buddha Land is attained by saying the Name fulfilled in the Primal Vow. To hear this Vow and be completely without doubt is the one moment of faith. Thus, although faith and nenbutsu are two, since faith is to hear and not doubt that you are saved by only a single pronouncing, which is the fulfillment of practice, there is no faith separate from nenbutsu; this is the teaching I have received. You should know further that there can be no nenbutsu separate from faith. Both should be understood to be Amida's Vow. Nenbutsu and faith on our part are themselves the manifestations of the Vow.[2]

While this passage apparently emphasizes the inseparability, and even the equal importance, of faith and the practice of nenbutsu, in fact the last sentence of the statement, "Nenbutsu and faith on our part are themselves the manifestations of the Vow," already implies that it is after all faith that should be given precedence. For, apart from faith, how on earth are we on our part to take nenbutsu as the manifestation of the Vow, and how can we utter the nenbutsu as the Great Practice?

Nenbutsu without faith cannot be genuine nenbutsu for Shinran. Or we might even say that for Shinran, faith constitutes the essence of nenbutsu practice, meaning that nenbutsu is subsumed under faith, not the other way around. Thus, for instance, Shinran says: "To entrust oneself wholeheartedly to the Vow of birth through the nenbutsu and be single-hearted is called wholehearted single practice."[3] This, of course, does not suggest that nenbutsu as a visible practice is dispensable or unnecessary for Shinran. On the contrary, faith should always be followed by nenbutsu,

[1] *True Teaching*, I: 136; *SSZ*, II: 33.

[2] *Letters*, 39–40.

[3] *Letters*, 63.

only the latter is to be uttered out of the depth of faith as its natural expression or outflow. This is why Shinran says that faith is necessarily followed by nenbutsu, but nenbutsu is not necessarily accompanied by faith.[4]

It is very significant to note that Shinran, in his *Kyōgyōshinshō*, treats the eighteenth Vow, the most important and crucial among the forty-eight Vows, under the heading of faith, rather than under the heading of practice as Hōnen would have done. Among the five names given to the Vow by Shinran, two are the traditional ones he inherited from Hōnen and Shan-tao: "the Vow of attaining birth through the nenbutsu" (Shan-tao) and "the selected primal Vow" (Hōnen). For both of them, the point of the eighteenth Vow lies in the act of nenbutsu, which it prescribes as the condition for our birth in the Pure Land, although neither of them ignores the Vow and a person's faith in it. For Shinran, however, the entire focus falls on faith, i.e., the threefold mind mentioned in the Vow. Hence the three other names Shinran gives to the Vow: "the Vow of the threefold mind of the Primal Vow," "the Vow of sincere mind and entrusting," and "the Vow of faith, which is Amida's directing of virtue for our going forth."[5] By shifting the focus of attention from the visible external behavior of nenbutsu to the invisible inner state of mind, however, Shinran's soteriology, while gaining in depth and subtlety, gives rise to a host of problems that are very different from the ones encountered by Hōnen's teaching of nenbutsu. Now the important questions become: what faith is, how it arises in us, how it is confirmed, whether it itself is not another condition for our salvation, whether it alone is sufficient no matter what we do and how we live our life, and what the actual benefits are that faith can bring to our life here on earth. These are the problems that we will have to examine in this and the next chapters.

In discussing Shinran's concept of faith, we must above all bear in mind the fact that there are various aspects and dimensions of faith discussed by Shinran. Although these diverse aspects of faith are all interrelated and Shinran often talks about them in one breath without differentiating among them—hence, our usage of a single term "faith" is certainly valid[6] —it is nevertheless essential for an accurate understanding

---

[4] *Kyōgyōshinshō*, SSZ, II: 68.

[5] *True Teaching*, II: 204; SSZ, II: 48.

[6] "Faith," as we shall see, refers in Shinran to the state as well as act of believing and trusting; but all of these are mental phenomena that are sufficiently interconnected or unified to be designed by a single term, faith. When he refers to the state of mind, Shinran

of this vital concept in Shinran's thought to distinguish them carefully. Failure to do so can lead to a distorted and one-sided understanding of this concept or cause unnecessary confusion and mystification.

As we shall see, for Shinran faith is itself a gift from Amida; genuine faith cannot be the product of our impure and false minds, just as genuine practice of nenbutsu can only be given by Amida as the Great Practice. Both practice and faith are understood by Shinran to be "directed to us" by Amida. Faith is the consequence of Amida's transferring his "true and real" (*shinjitsu* 眞実) mind to our minds, which are so full of falsity and selfish desires. To this extent, therefore, faith is certainly a mystery for Shinran. By its transcendent origin and nature, it is something that lies beyond human possibility, contrivance, and understanding. To try to define it or pin down the method by which one is to acquire it does violence to its fundamental character as a free gift from Amida and turns it into another product of self-power. Thus Yoshifumi Ueda states:

> Shinran advises his followers, "Simply entrust yourself to the Tathāgata" or "Simply entrust yourself to the power of the Vow," yet in his writings there is no instruction concerning how one should do this and no

---

usually uses the word *shinjin* 信心; but there is no need to translate it as "the mind of faith" instead of "faith," because it is obvious to everyone that faith is, after all, a certain state of *mind*. Faith, at the same time, refers in English to a certain mental act as well, although the lack in English of a verb form related to the noun has caused serious problems in Western religious history, as Wilfred Cantwell Smith has pointed out (*The Meaning and End of Religion*, 1978 [1962]). Whether a mental state or an act, whether believing or trusting, I believe that the single word *faith* is flexible enough to cover all these diverse shades of meaning and be at the same time meaningful as a single term. Recently there have been debates concerning whether or not *shinjin* can legitimately be translated as "faith" in English; see Thomas Kasulis's review, "Letters of Shinran," *Philosophy East and West*, 31/2 (April, 1981), 246–48, and the response to it by the Translation Committee of the Shin Buddhism Translation Series, *Philosophy East and West*, 31/4 (October, 1981), 507–11. Luis O. Gomez has also joined the debate in his review article, "Shinran's Faith and the Sacred Name of Amida," *Monumenta Nipponica*, 38/1 (Spring 1983), 73–84; see also the "Correspondence" between Ueda, Hirota, and Gomez in the same journal, 38/4 (Winter 1983), 413–27. Also, Takeda Ryūsei has recently voiced his view in favor of translating *shinjin* by "faith." See his "Shinran's View of Faith," in Takeda Ryūsei, *Shinran jōdokyō to Nishida tetsugaku* (Kyoto: Nagata Bunshōdō, 1991), pp. 43–76. With Kasulis, Gomez, and Takeda, I also find no justification for not using "faith" as the translation for *shinjin* and other terms intimately related to it. Wherever the translation team of the Shin Buddhism Translation series has left *shinjin* untranslated, I have therefore invariably changed it to "faith" in my quotations from its otherwise magnificent translations of Shinran's works. My view will be made clearer as this chapter progresses.

description of a general process that results in realization of faith. This is to be expected; were there some course of action to be fulfilled in order to attain faith, it would become our own practice, subject to our deliberation and designs. "Faith and joy" would be another condition of awareness that we achieved, and not the mind of Amida.[7]

Does this, then, mean that all our discussion of the concept of faith in Shinran is futile and all our efforts to come to a clearer understanding of it should be abandoned from the outset? By no means. Despite the essential validity of the above statement, it harbors the danger of unnecessarily mystifying the concept of faith in Shinran.[8] That faith has a transcendent origin does not necessarily mean that it is not our mental phenomenon, something that occurs in *our* minds consciously or unconsciously. That faith is a gift of Amida does not necessarily imply that there is nothing we do on our part. If it did, Shinran would not have preached to and converted people. He would not have talked about the "conversion of mind" (*eshin* 廻心) at all. In fact, in one place, Shinran quite specifically refers to faith as "karmic-consciousness," i.e., a mental phenomenon belonging to us in this world of birth-and-death.[9] Yes, all the mental phenomena related to faith may ultimately be attributable to the transcendent power about which we can do nothing, but the fact remains that these phenomena still occur in our minds, and, to some extent at least, we can be aware of them. How else could Shinran have said so much about it? Just as Zen masters, while being emphatic about the ineffability of the experience of enlightenment, have produced abundant verbal discourses on it, so did Shinran end up saying many things about this vital aspect of his thought. On the basis of Shinran's own words, therefore, we can produce a certain "phenomenological" description of faith, of the kind of mental phenomenon it is in itself. This will be our first task.

[7] Ueda and Hirota, *Shinran*, 158.

[8] The authors of this statement are also involved in the Shin Buddhism Translation Series, and this fact is not unrelated to its decision not to translate *shinjin* as "faith," as if *shinjin* were something so unique and mystical that it cannot be comprised under the general concept of "faith." See Gomez's criticism of this particularistic view in the above-mentioned review article.

[9] *True Teaching*, I: 138; *SSZ*, II: 34. It is significant to note that the translators of the *Kyōgyōshinshō* in the Ryukoku Translation Series take this "karmic-consciousness" as merely a "metaphor." See *The Kyō Gyō Shin Shō: The Teaching, Practice, Faith, and Enlightenment* (Kyoto: Ryukoku University Translation Center, 1966; Ryukoku Translation Series V), 56 (note 2).

We can then go from there to examine how faith arises in us, again not merely in its transcendent origin but on its phenomenal level as it becomes a part of our consciousness. In so far as we can meaningfully say with regard to Shinran's conception of faith that a person comes to have faith where previously he did not have any, and that a person's faith grows stronger than before, there is clearly a "dynamics" of faith involved in its arising and settling, as we shall see later. Although it is questionable whether this interpretation will be acceptable to the Shinshū orthodoxy, a close examination of Shinran's writings on faith clearly reveals that, despite its transcendent dimension, faith comes to be our reality through a certain empirical "process" of which we can be aware, at least to the extent that Shinran can talk about it. Examining this dynamics of faith may therefore contribute considerably toward demystifying it and give to those who remain outside "the circle of faith" an access to the property of the mind that Shinran called faith.

The concern of Shinshū orthodoxy to safeguard the mystery of faith and its pure gratuitous character as Other Power should be duly respected. But Shinran would have been the last person to make faith an esoteric reality accessible to only a few people. It is likely that Shinran said nearly everything he could on faith so that all people may share the same joy and gratitude that he himself experienced. Let us then proceed to examine first the kind of mental phenomenon faith is.

THE PHENOMENON OF FAITH

There are many passages in the three Pure Land sūtras that mention faith or the essential mental attitude with which we are to respond to Amida's work of salvation as manifested in his Vow. First, the *Kanmuryōju kyō* (*Sūtra of contemplation on the Buddha of immeasurable life*; briefly, the *Contemplation Sūtra*) mentions sincere mind, deep mind, and aspiration (for enlightenment) by directing merit. The *Amida kyō* (*Smaller sūtra of immeasurable life*) mentions the single mind. The *Daimuryōju kyō* (*Larger sūtra of immeasurable life*), finally, mentions three kinds of three-fold mind, among which the one mentioned in the eighteenth Vow is considered by Shinran to reveal the highest truth and the real intent of Amida's salvific will.[10] It mentions sincere mind, entrusting or believing

[10] The nineteenth Vow mentions the awakening of thought to enlightenment, aspiration for birth (in the Pure Land) in sincere mind, and the desire to be born in Amida's

85

with joy (*shingyō* 心楽), and the aspiration for birth (in the Pure Land). The eighteenth Vow says:

> If, when I attain Buddhahood, the sentient beings of the ten quarters, with sincere mind entrusting themselves, aspiring to be born in my land, and saying my Name perhaps even ten times, should not be born there, may I not attain the supreme enlightenment. Excluded are those who commit the five grave offenses and those who slander the right dharma.[11]

Explaining the three mental attitudes mentioned here, Shinran states elsewhere:

> *With sincere mind entrusting themselves* : *Sincere* means true and real. "True and real" refers to the Vow of the Tathāgata being true and real; this is what *sincere mind* means. From the very beginning sentient beings, who are filled with blind passions, lack a mind true and real, a heart of purity, for they are possessed of defilements, evil, and wrong views. *Entrusting* is to be free of doubt, believing deeply and without any double-mindedness that the Tathāgata's Primal Vow is true and real. This *entrusting with sincere mind*, then, is that arising from the Vow in which Amida urges every being throughout the ten quarters, "Entrust yourself to my Vow, which is true and real"; it does not arise from the hearts and minds of foolish beings of self-power. *Aspiring to be born in my land*; "Out of the entrusting with sincere mind that is Other Power, aspire to be born in the Pure Land of happiness!"[12]

Let us examine these three minds more closely one by one.

1. SINCERE MIND (*shishin* 至心). Contrary to the plain meaning of the Vow, Shinran attributes the sincere mind to the mind of Amida with which he uttered the Vow and carried it out. "Sincere," which means "true and real" according to Shinran, is the quality of the Vow, not of the "sentient beings, who are filled with blind passions, lack a mind true and real, a heart of purity." Deeply aware of the incurable falsity and

---

land; the twentieth Vow mentions cherishing the thought of Amida's land, transferring the merit (toward birth) with sincere mind, and the desire to be born in Amida's land; *SSZ*, I: 9–10.

[11] *True Teaching*, II: 205; *SSZ*, II: 48–49.

[12] *Notes on the Inscriptions on Sacred Scrolls: A Translation of Shinran's Songō shinzō meimon* (Kyoto: Hongwanji International Center, 1981; Shin Buddhism Translation Series), 33–34; *SSZ*, II: 577. Hereafter, this will be referred to as *Inscriptions*.

impurity of the human mind, Shinran came to the conclusion that sincere mind cannot be the quality of our mind but something that comes into being by the power of the Vow. Hence, faith as the sincere mind, with which we are to respond to the Vow, is itself the product of the Vow. For Shinran, therefore, the subject and the object of faith agree in this sense. And this is a paradox of faith. Faith, which begins in Shinran with a clear awareness of the infinite distance between human beings and the Buddha, now becomes the link in which that distance is overcome because faith is no longer our act but something coming from the other side. How much of the distance and how much of the sense of "otherness" of Other Power still remains in Shinran despite this faith constitutes an important problem, to be discussed in chapter four, where the life of faith will be examined.

In this interpretation of sincere mind mentioned in the eighteenth Vow, Shinran was clearly influenced by Shan-tao's interpretation of the sincere mind (*shijōshin* 至誠心) mentioned in the *Contemplation Sūtra*. He contrasts the impure minds of sentient beings with the mind of Bodhisattva Dharmākara, the Amida Buddha in his causal state. Shinran quotes it:

> The sūtra states, *The first is sincere (shijō) mind. Shi* means truth, *jō* means reality. This shows that the understanding and practice of all sentient beings, cultivated through their bodily, verbal, and mental acts, unfailingly take as essential what was performed [by Amida] with a true and real mind. We should not outwardly express signs of wisdom, goodness, or diligence, for inwardly we are possessed of falsity. We are filled with all manner of greed, anger, perversity, deceit, wickedness, and cunning, and it is difficult to put an end to our evil nature. In this we are like poisonous snakes or scorpions. Though we perform practices in the three modes of action, they must be called poisoned good acts or false practices. They cannot be called true, real and sincere action.... To seek birth in the Buddha's Pure Land by directing the merit of such poisoned practice is completely wrong. Why? Because when, in his causal stage, Amida Buddha was performing practices as a bodhisattva, in every single moment—every single instant—he performed his practices in the three modes of action with a true and real mind.[13]

[13] *True Teaching*, II: 212; *SSZ*, II: 51–52.

The sinfulness of our minds becomes more clearly realized when they are set in contrast with the mind of Amida when he performed his practices and attained enlightenment and realized the Pure Land as the land of fulfillment. Thus Shan-tao urges us to "take as essential what was performed by Amida with a true and real mind." But nowhere does he suggest that the sincere mind that is Amida's is transferred to us from him. It was Shinran's "reason of heart" that compelled him to arrive at this conclusion. It is not merely the practice of nenbutsu but also faith that is given to us by Amida:

> Nevertheless, reflecting on this [threefold] mind for myself alone, I find that all beings, an ocean of multitudes, have since the beginningless past down to this day—this very moment—been evil and defiled, completely lacking the mind of purity. They have been false and deceitful, completely lacking the mind of truth and reality. Thus, when the Tathāgata, in profound compassion for the ocean of all sentient beings in pain and affliction, performed bodhisattva practices for inconceivable millions of measureless kalpas, there was not a moment—not an instant—when his practice in the three modes of action was not pure, or lacked the true mind. With this pure, true mind, the Tathāgata brought to fulfillment the perfect, unhindered, inconceivable, indescribable, and inexplicable supreme virtues. The Tathāgata gives this sincere mind to all living things, an ocean of beings possessed of blind passions, karmic evil, and false wisdom. This mind manifests the true mind of benefiting others. For this reason, it is completely untainted by the hindrance of doubt. This sincere mind takes as its essence the revered Name of supreme virtues.[14]

Three important things are said about the sincere mind: it is given by Amida to sentient beings; it is the mind completely untainted by the hindrance of doubt; its essence is the Name. The last item will be examined more closely later on. Suffice it here merely to sum up Shinran's view that sincere mind as the mind of truth and reality comes to us from Amida and that it is essentially characterized as "untainted by the hindrance of doubt."

2. ENTRUSTING WITH JOY (*shingyō* 信楽). Shinran uses the combined expression "entrusting with sincere mind" (*shishin shingyō*). The eighteenth Vow is called by him "the Vow of entrusting with sincere mind."

---

[14] *True Teaching*, II: 229–30; *SSZ*, II: 59–60.

This suggests that "sincere mind" adverbially modifies the act of entrusting; sincere mind is the mind that qualifies the act of entrusting. If sincere mind can be said to refer to the quality of the mind of faith—its formal characteristic, as it were—entrusting refers to the actual content of faith as an act, *what* it is as an act. If sincere mind negatively refers to the state of mind free from doubt, entrusting with joy positively refers to the act of believing without any doubt or double-mindedness. Shinran identifies it with the "deep mind" (*jinshin* 深心) mentioned in the *Contemplation Sūtra* as interpreted by Shan-tao.

The deep mind, according to Shan-tao, is "the deeply believing mind" (*jinshin no shin* 深信之心), "the mind that believes deeply without doubt and double-mindedness," to use Shinran's expression. What does it then believe? Shinran follows Shan-tao's exposition of the "deeply believing mind":

> *Deep mind* is the deeply entrusting [believing] mind. There are two aspects. One is to believe deeply and decidedly that you are a foolish being of karmic evil caught in birth-and-death, ever sinking and ever wandering in transmigration from innumerable kalpas in the past, with never a condition that would lead to emancipation. The second is to believe deeply and decidedly that Amida Buddha's Forty-eight Vows grasp sentient beings, and that allowing yourself to be carried by the power of the Vow without any doubt or apprehension, you will attain birth.[15]

This is the famous passage on the so-called "twofold deep believing" (*nishu jinshin* 二種深信). Several things need to be noted in particular. First of all, the verb "believe." Faith as the deep mind is the deeply believing mind; faith is believing. And it is "believe-that" rather than "believe-in." In this respect, faith as entrusting with joy definitely has a cognitive content contained in the objective clause that follows the verb "believe." "Entrusting," which translates the original word *shingyō* in the eighteenth Vow, could be misleading in that it does not clearly bring out the cognitive element in the "deeply believing mind." *Shingyō* consists of two Chinese characters, *shin* 信 and *gyō* 楽. *Shin* is a verb here that could mean "believe-that" as above, or it could mean "believe-in," as trusting or entrusting. Shinran uses the word in the latter sense too—hence, "believe in the Primal Vow," etc. In so far as Shinran follows Shan-tao's interpre-

---

[15] *True Teaching*, II: 213; *SSZ*, II: 52.

tation of the deep mind as the deeply believing mind and equates it with the *shingyō* of the eighteenth Vow, however, the former aspect should not be overlooked. Faith clearly involves a certain cognitive activity for Shinran, and a certain cognitive content as formulated in the twofold deep believing above. Faith is belief in this sense. *Gyō* means "rejoice, be joyful," and it is taken as modifying the act of entrusting or believing, hence "entrusting with joy."[16]

Secondly, the relationship between the two aspects of the deep belief should be correctly understood. In his explanation of the threefold mind of the eighteenth Vow, which we have quoted in the beginning of this discussion, Shinran only mentions the second aspect of the deep belief: "believing deeply and without any double-mindedness that the Tathāgata's Primal Vow is true and real." But there is no question that for Shinran this belief in the veracity of Amida's Primal Vow is inseparably interlocked with the deep realization of the incurable evil and falsity of one's own being and the utter failure of every self-powered attempt to escape from it.

The realization of the true state of one's being, however, is by no means a "natural" knowledge based upon self-reflection or self-consciousness. For a person thoroughly corrupt and false, such self-reflection can only be a mere camouflage and cannot reveal truth at all. Thus, for Shinran, the true realization of one's sinfulness paradoxically suggests that one is already under the light of grace and truth. To know the truth about oneself is already to be grasped by truth. The following words of Shinran are worth pondering over again:

> I know nothing of what is good or evil. For if I could know thoroughly, as is known in the mind of Amida, that an act was good, then I would know the meaning of "good." If I could know thoroughly, as Amida knows, that an act was evil, then I would know "evil." But in a foolish being full of blind passions, in this fleeting world—this burning house— all matters without exception are lies and gibberish, totally without truth and sincerity. The nenbutsu alone is true and real.[17]

[16] For some reason the translators of the Shin Buddhism Translation Series have left out the meaning of *gyō* by translating *shingyō* as merely "entrusting." I have followed them in many of the passages I have cited, for the sake of convenience, but strictly speaking, *shingyō* should be rendered as "entrusting with joy" or "joyful entrusting."

[17] *Tannishō*, 44.

Just as Socrates' search for knowledge began with his "knowledge" of ignorance, in Shinran's case, too, the consciousness of the ignorance of good and evil was truly a special form of "knowledge" that was possible only in the light of Amida's compassionate Vow. As far as Shinran is concerned, our ordinary moral self-reflection can never lead us to this confession of "ignorance," and our ordinary knowledge never reveals this deeply hidden truth of "ignorance" but only leads us to the false consciousness, hypocrisy, dogmatism, and deep egocentricity that usually characterize the world of conventional morality. This is why, for Shinran, mere brooding over one's wretchedness, however pious it may be, never leads to genuine faith.[18]

While the deepest self-knowledge cannot come from the self but becomes possible when confronted with Other Power, one does not, on the other hand, turn to Other Power without a deep realization of one's inability to extricate oneself from the karmic bondage to sin and evil. As Shinran says:

> A person who has been ignorant of the true significance of the Other Power of the Primal Vow comes to realize, through receiving Amida's wisdom, that he cannot attain birth by means of the thoughts and feelings he has harbored up to then, so he abandons [overturns] his former heart and mind and entrusts himself to the Primal Vow. This is "change of heart."[19]

Thus the twofold deep believing reveals nothing else than the structure of "change of heart" (eshin) or conversion of mind. Faith as entrusting, therefore, means conversion of our mind from self-power to Other Power, from the old mind that relies on self-power to the new mind that relies on Other Power, an act of overturning or turning about (hirugaesu) in one's attitude of mind, and not a mere cognitive act of believing. "Change of heart," says Shinran, "means to overturn and discard the mind of self-power."[20] "Faith alone" is "to be free of self-power, having

---

[18] In traditional Shinshū interpretation, the two aspects of the deep belief are considered to be inseparable, although not one. Thus, to regard the first aspect of deep belief (shinki 信機) as leading to—as an instrument to acquire—the second aspect (shinbō 信法) is considered to be a heretical view. See Kiritani Junnin, "Nishu jinshin," Kōza Shinshū no anjin rondai (Tokyo: Kyōiku Shinchōsha, 1983), 73–88.

[19] Tannishō, 39.

[20] SSZ, II: 628.

entrusted oneself to the Other Power of the Primal Vow."[21] And it is through this complete change of heart that one's birth in the Pure Land is secured:

> However, when a person overturns his heart of self-power and entrusts himself to Other Power, he will realize birth in the true fulfilled land.[22]

Or, for a more concrete explanation:

> By *jiriki* is meant that the devotees, each according to his karmic condition, think of a Buddha other [than Amida], recite his Name, and practise good deeds relying on their own judgments, that they plan out their own ideas as regards how properly and felicitously to adjust their activities of the body, mouth, and mind for the rebirth in the Pure Land. By *tariki* is meant wholeheartedly to accept and believe the Primal Vow of Amida whereby he assures those who pronounce his Name that they will be reborn in his Pure Land. As this is the Vow made by Amida, it has a sense which cannot be prescribed by any common measure of judgment—a sense which is beyond sense, as has been taught by my holy master. Sense is contrivance, that is, intention. The devotees have an intention to move in accordance with their own ideas, and thus their doings have sense.
>
> The *tariki* devotees, however, have placed their faith wholeheartedly in Amida's Primal Vow and are assured of their rebirth in the Pure Land—hence they are free from sense [or from intention of their own].[23]

To conclude, faith as entrusting (*shingyō*) is the act of a twofold deep believing that involves the conversion of the heart from self-power to Other Power.[24]

As in the case of faith as sincere mind, so faith as entrusting and deeply believing mind is also free from the hindrance of doubt and is entirely the work of Amida. It can never arise from our false and arrogant minds. Thus Shinran says:

---

[21] *Faith Alone*, 29; *SSZ*, II: 621.

[22] *Tannishō*, 61.

[23] Quoted in D. T. Suzuki, *Collected Writings on Shin Buddhism*, 55; *SSZ*, II: 658–59.

[24] Dennis Gira, who has carefully examined Shinran's concept of conversion (*eshin*) in his *Le Sens de la conversion dans l'enseignement de Shinran* (Paris: Editions Maisonneuve et Larose, 1985), calls conversion experience "the subjective appreciation and affirmation of a fundamental experience of faith" (p. 121).

Next, concerning entrusting, it is the ocean of faith, perfect and unhindered, that is the Tathāgata's consummately fulfilled great compassion. Hence, there is no mixture of doubt. It is therefore called "entrusting." The essence of entrusting is the sincere mind of benefiting others and directing virtues [by Amida].

However, since the beginningless past, the multitudes of beings have been transmigrating in the ocean of ignorance, sinking aimlessly in the cycle of all forms of existence and bound to the cycle of all forms of pain; accordingly, they lack the entrusting that is pure. In the manner of their existence, they have no entrusting that is true and real. Hence, it is difficult for them to encounter the unexcelled virtues, difficult to realize the supreme, pure faith.... The Tathāgata, turning with compassion toward the ocean of living beings in pain and affliction, has given unhindered and vast pure faith to the ocean of sentient beings. This is called the "true and real faith that is [Amida's] benefiting of others."[25]

Putting together sincere mind and entrusting, Shinran concludes:

This *entrusting with sincere mind,* then, is that arising from the Vow in which Amida urges every being throughout the ten quarters, "Entrust yourself to my Vow, which is true and real"; it does not arise from the hearts and minds of foolish beings of self-power.[26]

Amida's Vow, then, does not merely stipulate the "easy" condition for our birth in the Pure Land—that is, nenbutsu and faith—which we have to meet in order to attain the birth. It is a dynamic reality that calls everyone to faith and enables it to arise in the mind of sentient beings. Thus Shinran calls the eighteenth Vow "the Vow of faith, which is Amida's directing of virtue for our going forth."[27] Again, we must point out that, as far as the literal meaning is concerned, no passage in the *Larger Sūtra of Immeasurable Life* suggests the idea of faith being given by Amida. It was purely Shinran's "logic of faith" that compelled him to read that idea into the sūtra.[28]

---

[25] *True Teaching,* II: 234–35 (the first brackets mine); *SSZ,* II: 62.

[26] *Inscriptions,* 34; *SSZ,* II: 577.

[27] *True Teaching,* II: 204; *SSZ,* II: 48.

[28] In order to have scriptural support for his idea, Shinran often had to resort to a forced interpretation of the Chinese texts. The most famous example of this is the one concerning the interpretation of the passage in the *Larger Sūtra* that talks about the fulfillment of the eighteenth Vow by Amida Buddha; contrary to the plain meaning of the text, Shinran takes it as implying that faith is "transferred" to us by Amida Buddha. See *Once-calling,* 32; *SSZ,*

For Shinran, then, faith is not simply a movement from self-power to Other Power. Ultimately, it is a movement from Other Power to Other Power, the Vow being everything. The absolute can only be reached through the absolute. How much and in what sense faith is still "our" act and decision according to Shinran remains to be considered further. And, as we have already indicated, the question of the extent to which the distance and tension still hold between human beings and the Buddha also needs to be addressed.

3. ASPIRATION FOR BIRTH (*yokushō* 欲生). "Out of the entrusting with sincere mind that is Other Power, aspire to be born in the Pure Land of happiness." In this brief comment of Shinran's on the third element of the threefold mind of the eighteenth Vow, we find little explanation of it other than that it is based upon the previous two elements, that is, the entrusting with sincere mind that comes from Other Power. In the *Kyōgyōshinshō*, however, we find the following statement:

> Finally, "aspire for birth" is the command of the Tathāgata calling to and summoning the multitudes of all beings. That is, true and real entrusting is the essence of aspiration for birth. Truly, [aspiration for birth] is not the directing of merit through the self-power of meditative and non-meditative practices, whether performed by ordinary people or sages of the Mahāyāna or Hīnayāna. Therefore, it is called "not-directing."[29]

Contrary to the common meaning of the text, Shinran boldly asserts that aspiration for birth is the "command [or call] of the Tathāgata calling to and summoning the multitudes of all beings." In other words, it is not our act of religious piety but the work of Amida Buddha himself calling sentient beings through the entrusting with sincere mind that is also given to them by him.

Traditionally, before Shinran's time, the aspiration for birth was taken to mean that we bring our stock of merit—accrued through the performance of the meditative and non-meditative (moral) good acts or through the practice of nenbutsu—toward our birth in the Pure Land, expressing our desire for it. Shinran definitely rejects this idea here. For

---

II: 604; see what follows in this chapter, especially the part on the concept of hearing the Name of Amida Buddha; see also Bloom's discussion of this in his *Shinran's Gospel of Pure Grace* (Tucson, Arizona: The University of Arizona Press, 1965), 48–49.

[29] *True Teaching*, II: 242–43; *SSZ*, II: 65.

there is absolutely no stock of merit that we, the impure beings, can bring toward our birth; nor is there in us the true desire to direct the merit even if we may have it—true aspiration for birth and true compassion. Hence, the aspiration for birth is called by him "not-directing [of merit]." Like sincere mind and entrusting, the genuine aspiration for birth and the genuine directing of merit can only be the possession of Bodhisattva Dharmākara, which he directs to the sentient beings out of his great compassion. Thus Shinran continues:

> However, sentient beings of the countless worlds, floundering in the sea of blind passions and drifting and sinking in the ocean of birth-and-death, lack the true and real mind of directing virtue; they lack the pure mind of directing virtues. For this reason, when the Tathāgata was performing bodhisattva practices out of pity for the ocean of all sentient beings in pain and affliction, in every single moment—every single instant—of his endeavor in the three modes of action, he took the mind of directing virtues as foremost, and thus realized the mind of great compassion. Accordingly, he directs this other-benefiting, true and real mind of aspiration for birth to the ocean of all beings. Aspiration for birth is this mind of directing virtues. It is none other than the mind of great compassion; therefore, it is untainted by the hindrance of doubt.[30]

Thus far, we have examined Shinran's explanation of the threefold mind of the eighteenth Vow. This may give the impression that there are three separate elements, or even three separate minds, in faith. This is not the case. What we have seen is simply the fact that faith is in Shinran a complex mental phenomenon when seen from a phenomenological perspective. Essentially, however, faith is a single, perfectly integrated mind, the mind of faith (*shinjin*) for Shinran— the "true and real mind" (*shinjitsushin* 眞実心). Shinran also simply calls it "entrusting with joy" (*shingyō*), singling out the second aspect of the threefold mind as its essence and as a representation of the whole. All three aspects of faith have as their essence the freedom from the "hindrance of doubt." After examining the literal meanings of the Chinese terms for the threefold mind, Shinran concludes as follows:

> We see clearly that sincere mind is the mind that is the seed of truth, reality, and sincerity; hence, it is completely *untainted by the hindrance of doubt*. Entrusting with joy is the mind full of truth, reality, and sincerity;

---

[30] *True Teaching*, II: 243; *SSZ*, II: 65–66.

the mind of ultimacy, accomplishment, reliance, and reverence; the mind of discernment, distinctness, clarity, and faithfulness; the mind of aspiration, wish, desire, and exultation; the mind of delight, joy, gladness, and happiness; hence, it is completely *untainted by the hindrance of doubt.* Aspiration for birth is the mind of wish, desire, awakening, and awareness; the mind of accomplishment, fulfillment, performance, and establishment. It is the mind of great compassion directing itself to beings; hence, it is completely *untainted by the hindrance of doubt.*

Here, in considering the literal meanings of the terms for them, we find that the three minds are the mind of truth and reality, free of any taint of falsity; they are the mind right and straightforward, free of any taint of wrong and deceit. Truly we know, then, that *this is called entrusting with joy because it is untainted by the hindrance of doubt.* Entrusting with joy is the mind that is single. The mind that is single is *the mind of faith* that is true and real.[31]

Or,

Truly we know that although the terms "sincere mind," "entrusting," and "aspiration for birth" differ, their significance is the same. Why? Because these three minds are already completely untainted by the hindrance of doubt. They are therefore the true and real mind that is single. This is called the diamond-like true mind. The diamond-like true mind is true and real [mind of faith].[32]

Negatively defined, faith, therefore, is the mind free from doubt, the doubt in Amida's work of salvation as manifested in the Vow. For Shinran, this doubt is exemplified in two different types of people. Bloom correctly points out:

Behind Shinran's insistence on the seriousness of doubt lay concern for two types of individuals. He tried to appeal to the individual who did not believe that he was good enough to be saved, and to the individual who had confidence in his own good deeds.[33]

Thus, Shinran admonishes as follows:

Thus, on the one hand, you should not be anxious that Tathāgata will not receive you because you do wrong. A foolish being is by nature

---

[31] *True Teaching,* II: 228–29 (translation altered, italics mine); *SSZ,* II: 59.

[32] *True Teaching,* II: 248–49; *SSZ,* II: 68.

[33] *Shinran's Gospel of Pure Grace,* 41.

possessed of blind passion, so you must recognize yourself as a being of karmic evil. On the other hand, you should not think that you deserve to attain birth because you are good. You cannot be born into the true and real Buddha Land through such self-power calculation.[34]

In the one kind of people, doubt manifests itself in the form of despair, and in the other in the form of pride. Doubt, therefore, is not mere intellectual disbelieving; it touches the whole being of the person. Faith, then, overcoming despair in the one and overturning pride in the other, is the act of entrusting oneself to the power of the Vow.

THE DYNAMICS OF FAITH

We have thus far examined how Shinran describes faith as a mental phenomenon, and the kind of mental quality and act it is. In examining Shinran's explanation, however, we have seen again and again how Shinran attributes faith to the work of Other Power. For Shinran, who was constantly aware of the unbridgeable gap between himself and the Buddha, even faith cannot originate from our minds filled with impurities and falsities. It can only originate from Amida's mind in which he uttered the Vow and carried out the practice to fulfill it. Now, this Other Power, the transcendent ground of faith, is supposed to be a universal force, always available and working everywhere for all people. Why then does faith arise in some people and not in others? What occasions the actual awakening of faith in some people, and how do we account for the empirical differences in the faith experiences of people? In order to deal with, if not answer, these questions, we have to turn our attention to the other aspect of faith, what we call the "dynamics" of faith. Shinran is by no means silent on this aspect of faith despite his emphasis on its transcendent ground. Here we have to be very cautious and bold at the same time. For we are touching upon an area that is highly sensitive to the people who are personally involved in it, yet it has received relatively little attention from the scholars, whether within or outside of the Shinshū.

We have seen that, according to Shinran, faith is given to us by Amida. What does this mean more concretely, and how does faith arise in us as "our" mental state? Once again, we have to point out that, according to Shinran, the initiative comes from the Buddha's side in the forms

---

[34] *Letters*, 23; *SSZ*, II: 659.

of the Name and the Light. Amida's great Name and infinite Light are the forces that are constantly reaching down to us and already working within us to awaken faith. Shinran compares the Name and the Light to a compassionate father and mother who are working together to bring about our salvation:

> Truly we know that without the virtuous Name, our compassionate father, we would lack the direct cause of birth. Without the light, our compassionate mother, we would stand apart from the indirect cause of birth. Although direct and indirect causes may come together, if the karmic-consciousness of faith is lacking, one will not reach the land of light. The karmic-consciousness of true and real faith is the inner cause. The Name and light—our father and mother—are the outer cause. When the inner and outer causes are united, one realizes the true body in the fulfilled land.[35]

Yet, the question still remains. Why do some people see the Light and hear the Name so that faith arises in them, whereas others live completely oblivious of this cosmic reality? The outer cause, the Name and the Light, apparently works without discrimination for all; whence, then, the empirical difference in the inner cause, the "karmic-consciousness of faith"? While it is doubtful that we can find a satisfactory answer to this "mystery" of faith, let us nevertheless examine more closely the concept of the Name and "hearing" in Shinran to see if this helps us.

Faith arises through one's encounter with Other Power, and this enounter takes place empirically when one hears the Name of Amida Buddha. In other words, Other Power reaches us in the form of the Name. According to Shinran, the fact that faith arises through hearing is fundamentally based upon the following passage in the *Larger Sūtra of Immeasurable Life* on the fulfillment of the eighteenth Vow:

> When sentient beings hear the Name, say it even once in trust and joy, sincerely turn over their merits [toward the attainment of birth], and aspire to be born in that land, then they shall attain birth and dwell in the stage of non-retrogression.[36]

Shinran reads this text very differently, according to his highly creative interpretation:

---

[35] *True Teaching*, I: 137–38; *SSZ*, II: 33–34.

[36] Quoted in *Once-calling*, 32 (footnote).

All sentient beings, as they *hear the Name*, realize even *one thought-moment* of faith and joy, which is *directed to them* from Amida's sincere mind; and aspiring to be born in that land, they *then* attain birth and dwell in the stage of non-retrogression.[37]

Noteworthy points in the above interpretation have been italicized. The last point, "then," will be examined in our next chapter. The concept of faith being directed to us by Amida will be dealt with later on in this chapter under a separate heading, "Faith and Other Power." Here we shall examine the other two points more closely, looking at how Shinran explains them.

1. *Faith through hearing.* Shinran equates faith with hearing, or rather hearing with faith.[38] "Hear," says Shinran, "means to hear the Primal Vow and be free of doubt."[39] Or, a little more specifically, to hear means that "sentient beings, having heard how the Buddha's Vow arose—its origin and fulfillment—are altogether free of doubt."[40] And "faith," says Shinran, "is hearing the Vow of the Tathāgata and being free of doubt."[41] Hearing, therefore, brings one into faith in Other Power as manifested in the Vow and the Name.

The Name, for Shinran, is more than the physically audible name that human beings invoke in their nenbutsu; representing the Power of the Vow, it is a cosmic reality that has the power to awaken faith in sentient beings. This is based upon the fulfillment of the seventeenth Vow of Bodhisattva Dharmākara, "the Vow that all the Buddhas say the Name" as Shinran calls it:

If, when I attain Buddhahood, the countless Buddhas throughout the worlds in the ten quarters do not all praise and say my Name, may I not attain the supreme enlightenment.[42]

[37] *True Teaching*, II: 205–206 (italics mine); *SSZ*, II: 49, and *Once-calling*, 32; *SSZ*, II: 604.

[38] For an "orthodox" treatment of this tricky problem of the relationship between faith and hearing, see Kiritani Junnin, "Monshin gisō" 聞信義相 *Kōza Shinshū no anjin rondai*, 18–34.

[39] *Once-calling*, 32; *SSZ*, II: 604–05.

[40] *True Teaching*, II: 257; *SSZ*, II: 72.

[41] *Once-calling*, 32; *SSZ*, II: 605.

[42] *True Teaching*, I: 72; *SSZ*, II: 5.

Its fulfillment passage in the *Larger Sūtra* then says:

> The Buddha-tathāgatas throughout the ten quarters, countless as the sands of the Ganges, are one in praising the majestic power and the virtues, inconceivably profound, of the Buddha of immeasurable life.[43]

Further, the verse form of the same Vow, which Shinran also quotes, states:

> When I have fulfilled the Buddha-way,
> My Name will pervade the ten quarters;
> If there be any place it is not heard,
> I vow not to attain perfect enlightenment.[44]

It is this cosmic Name ever praised by Buddhas throughout the universe that is heard by human beings on earth and calls forth faith in them, bringing them to call upon the Name as well. Ueda Yoshifumi puts the relationship between Name, faith, and nenbutsu in the following way:

> For Shinran, genuine utterance of the Name and faith are not generated out of human will, but emerge together as manifestations of the Buddha's working. They are always interfused. Because the Name is given—is spread throughout the universe by all the Buddhas—sentient beings are able to hear it and come to know Amida's Primal Vow. Through hearing the Name—not just grasping it intellectually, but being penetrated by the dynamic reality of compassion that it embodies—faith is awakened in them. This faith is therefore also "given," and is itself the Buddha's wisdom-compassion turning itself over to beings. Further, this faith expresses itself in utterance of the Name, which is true practice, and which therefore results in attainment of birth.[45]

This must be why Shinran, as we have seen previously, says that the Name constitutes the essence of the sincere mind, which in turn is the essence of entrusting. The Name, as an embodiment of the power of the Vow and its fulfillment, is thus the link between the cosmic realm and the human hearing and faith here on earth. Bloom rightly points out:

> However, Shinran saw deep spiritual meaning in the Seventeenth Vow that escaped previous teachers. For him it revealed the link between the

---

[43] *True Teaching*, I: 72–73; SSZ, II: 5–6.

[44] *True Teaching*, I: 72; SSZ, II: 5.

[45] *Shinran*, 149–50.

effect of the fulfillment of Amida Buddha's Vows in the ideal realm and the historical appearance of that teaching in the time-space realm of sentient beings. It provided an absolute basis for the historical tradition.[46]

The hearing of the cosmic Name is concretely mediated by the historical tradition of nenbutsu practice as represented by the Pure Land masters. In Shinran's case, it was of course through Hōnen that he heard the Name in that true sense of "hearing." As Takeuchi Yoshinori points out, there is a sense of both fortuitousness and necessity in one's encounter with the Name through hearing, and hence surprise, wonder, thrill, and joy.[47] Shinran expresses it as follows:

> Ah, hard to encounter, even in many lifetimes, is the decisive cause of birth, Amida's universal Vow! Hard to realize, even in myriads of kalpas, is pure faith that is true and real! If you should come to realize this practice and faith, rejoice at the conditions from the distant past that have brought it about....
>
> How joyous I am, Gutoku Shinran, disciple of Śākyamuni! Rare is it to come upon the sacred scriptures from the westward land of India and the commentaries of the masters of China and Japan, but now I have been able to encounter them. Rare is it to hear them, but already I have been able to hear....[48]

2. *A single moment of faith.* This faith through hearing, according to Shinran, occurs in a single moment, in "one thought-moment" (*ichinen* 一念), abruptly and suddenly. The word *ichinen* in the text was originally taken by Pure Land masters before Shinran to mean a single act of nenbutsu.[49] For Shinran, for whom it did not matter at all whether one calls upon the Name once or many times, it assumed an entirely different meaning. It meant for him the decisive moment of the opening of faith, the moment when one enters into the stage of non-retrogression and is guaranteed birth in the Pure Land, as we shall see shortly. Shinran calls this decisive moment "time at its ultimate limit," the extreme brevity of the time when faith arises.[50] But "one thought-moment" does not merely

---

[46] *Shinran's Gospel of Pure Grace*, 52.

[47] See Takeuchi's analysis of "encounter" (*sōgū* 遭遇) in his *Kyōgyōshinshō no tetsugaku* (Tokyo: Ryūbunkan, 1987), 142–48.

[48] *True Teaching*, I: 58–59.

[49] *Once-calling*, 14–15 (Introduction).

[50] *Once-calling*, 32; SSZ, II: 605.

express the utter brevity of time span of faith arising; it also refers to the single mind (*isshin* 一心), that is, faith itself:

> ....because faith is free of doublemindedness, *one thought-moment* is used. It is the mind that is single. The mind that is single is the true cause of [birth in] the pure fulfilled land.[51]

Further,

> Thus, the term *one thought-moment* in the passage teaching the fulfillment of the Vow is wholehearted thought. Wholehearted thought is deep mind. Deep mind is deep entrusting. Deep entrusting is deep entrusting that is steadfast and firm. Deep entrusting that is steadfast and firm is decisive mind. Decisive mind is supreme mind. Supreme mind is true mind.... The true and real mind that is single is the mind of great joy. The mind of great joy is true and real faith. True and real faith is the diamond-like mind. The diamond-like mind is the mind that aspires for Buddhahood. The mind that aspires for Buddhahood is the mind that saves sentient beings.... This mind is the mind aspiring for great enlightenment. This mind is the mind of great compassion. For this mind arises from the wisdom of immeasurable light.[52]

Here, we come across various terms for the mind of faith. One of them, "the mind that aspires for Buddhahood" (or enlightenment; *bodhicitta*), needs special attention. Traditionally it has been considered the foundation, the starting point, for the Mahāyāna scheme of bodhisattva's practice. Thus it is a concept that belongs to the Path of Sages, and Hōnen was severely criticized by its followers for having rejected it as unnecessary in his sole-practice of nenbutsu. Now, Shinran boldly reintroduces it here in his discussion of faith—perhaps with an apologetic motive—giving it a totally different meaning. It now refers to the mind of faith as given by Amida. For Shinran, who could not endorse the idea that we have the power within us to awaken a genuine aspiration for enlightenment, faith was the only way to have hope for enlightenment. Shinran also identifies this mind of faith, the single mind, with the traditional notion of Buddha-nature.[53] Here again, the diamond-like mind of faith,

---

[51] *True Teaching*, II: 257; *SSZ*, II: 72.

[52] *True Teaching*, II: 258–59; *SSZ*, II: 72.

[53] *Kyōgyōshinshō*, *SSZ*, II: 62–63.

which is "directed to beings through the power of the Primal Vow,"[54] was the only form of Buddha-nature Shinran could recognize. Whatever potentiality we may possess within us for achieving Buddhahood comes from Other Power; it cannot be inherent in us, because we are ever afflicted by blind passions. Yet here we may once again raise the critical question of whether Shinran is not reverting by these concepts to the traditional Mahāyāna view of the identity between sentient beings and the Buddha, thereby weakening the sense of their infinite distance that compelled him to kneel down before the grace of Other Power in the first place. But let us leave this question for the moment and turn to another important aspect of Shinran's concept of faith, namely, what we call the "process" of faith.

According to the traditional view—certainly a common and "orthodox" view that finds strong support in Shinran's own texts—faith arises in us in a single moment; and, as soon as it arises, we are "being grasped, never to be abandoned" (*sesshu fusha* 攝取不捨) by Amida's light, so that we immediately belong to the group of people called the "truly settled" (*shōjōju* 正定聚) who are destined to attain enlightenment (birth in the Pure Land, for Shinran) without fail. In this view, therefore, the moment of the arising of faith coincides with the moment of being truly settled for the birth in the Pure Land. But there are many passages in Shinran's writings that are clearly suggestive of the idea of the settling of *faith* as distinct from its arising. The two may even occur in the same moment, but they seem to refer to two distinct aspects of faith experience in Shinran. It is this concept of the settling of faith in Shinran that, in our view, deserves more attention than has been accorded to it. Let us then turn to this matter.

Faith may arise in a single moment as a single mind. The actual experience of the faithful, however, tells us that faith is not always so secure and firm. Despite its transcendent origin, it is also subject to the influence of blind passions and doubts. This is why Shinran had to talk not only about the arising (*hokki* 発起) of faith but also about its settling (*sadamaru* 定まる). More than anybody else, Shinran was well aware that our faith, as a mental phenomenon belonging to sentient beings who are always under the sway of blind passions, is in reality not so reliable. It is also no exception to the general law of impermanence; it fluctuates.

---

[54] *True Teaching*, II: 257; *SSZ*, II: 72.

103

Unless it is settled, therefore, our birth in the Pure Land also becomes uncertain and not settled. Only when faith is settled can we abide in the "stage of the truly settled" who are destined to attain birth and enlightenment in the Pure Land. In one of his letters Shinran admonishes his disciples:

> Each of you should attain your birth without being misled by people and without faltering in faith. However, the practicer in whom faith has not been settled will continue to drift, even without being misled by anyone, for he does not abide among the truly settled.[55]

Unfortunately, however, this aspect of the settling of faith, which certainly adds a lively psychological dimension to Shinran's concept of faith, has often become completely overlooked or neglected in many discussions of Shinran's thought, which overemphasize the instantaneous, miraculous, and transcendent arising of faith.[56] It is no wonder that we find this idea of the settling of faith particularly prominent in Shinran's pastoral letters, in which he addressed the various spiritual problems and doubts occurring in the minds of his followers.[57] If we read these letters carefully, faith clearly needs the separate grace of Amida in order to become settled so that we can enter the stage of the non-retrogression or the truly settled. It is this connection between the settlement of faith and being truly settled (*shōjō* 正定) for birth that has not been given the amount of attention it deserves.

Just as the arising of faith comes from Amida, the settling of faith also comes from a special form of Amida's grace, the benefit of "being grasped, never to be abandoned" (*sesshu fusha*) by Amida's light. Although both of them, the arising and the settling, are equally the work of Amida and there may be little time interval between them, the settling of faith nevertheless constitutes for Shinran a facet of the faith experience that is clearly distinct from its arising. Thus, to put the whole matter in

---

[55] *Letters*, 31.

[56] For instance, neither Ueda's *Shinran* nor Bloom's *Shinran's Gospel of Pure Grace* pays any attention to this aspect of Shinran's doctrine of faith.

[57] I could ascertain at least twenty places in Shinran's writings where the concept of the settling (*sadamaru* or *ketsujō*) of faith occurs; among them seven occur in the *Mattōshō*, Shinran's pastoral letters, and four in the *Tannishō*. See "shinjin" and "ketsujō" in the *Shinran Shōnin chosaku yōgo sakuin: Wakan senjutsu no bu* (Kyoto: Ryūkoku Daigaku Shinshūgaku Kenkyūshitsu, 1971).

the proper order: First, faith arises, then we partake of the benefit of being grasped by Amida never to be abandoned, and our faith becomes settled thereby, so that we may abide in the stage of the truly settled who will unfailingly attain birth in the Pure Land. We can let Shinran speak for himself on this matter:

> You should understand that the settling of the mind that entrusts itself to Tathāgata's Primal Vow is none other than the settling into the stage of non-retrogression, because he receives the benefits of being grasped, never to be abandoned. Whether we speak of the settling of true faith or the settling of the diamond-like faith, both come about through being grasped, never to be abandoned. Thus is awakened the heart and mind that will attain the supreme enlightenment. This is called the stage of non-retrogression, the stage of the truly settled, and the stage equal to the supreme enlightenment.[58]

Or,

> You ask about "being grasped never to be abandoned." Shan-tao's *Hymn of Meditation on the Presence of the Buddha* states that Śākyamuni and Amida are our parents of great compassion; using many and various compassionate means, they awaken the supreme faith. Thus the settling of true faith is the working of Śākyamuni and Amida. A person becomes free of doubt about his birth because he has been grasped. Once grasped, there should be no calculation whatsoever. Since he dwells in the stage of non-retrogression until being born into the Buddha Land, he is said to be in the stage of the truly settled.
>
> Since true faith is awakened through the working of the two honored ones, Śākyamuni and Amida, it is when one is grasped that the settling of faith occurs. Thereafter he abides in the stage of the truly settled until he is born into the Buddha Land.[59]

It is clear from the above that "being grasped, never to be abandoned" and "settling of faith" and "being in the stage of the truly settled" are a series of events inseparably bound together. Note that in the first quotation Shinran even uses the expression "settling into the stage of non-retrogression," which means settling in the stage of the truly settled, which, in turn, occurs when faith becomes settled due to the benefit of being grasped, never to be abandoned by Amida. It is also clear that

[58] *Letters*, 33 (translation altered); *SSZ*, II: 666.
[59] *Letters*, 42; *SSZ*, II: 673–74.

Shinran distinguishes between the arising or awakening (*hokki, hiraki okoru*) of faith and the settling (*sadamaru*) of faith. The two are inseparable and may even occur at the same moment—Shinran does not discuss the time difference of the two—but they are distinguishable phenomena. Both of them are the work of Amida, but the settling of faith requires a separate act of grace on the part of Amida, called *sesshu fusha*, that is "being grasped, never to be abandoned."

The notion of *sesshu fusha* is based upon the promise given by Amida in the *Contemplation Sūtra*: "Each ray of Amida's light shines universally upon the worlds of the ten quarters, embracing and not forsaking those sentient beings who utter the nenbutsu."[60] It is when one partakes of this special benefit that one's faith becomes settled and "a person becomes free of doubt about his birth because he has been grasped."

Now, we must ask why Shinran had to use the concept of settling of faith as distinct from the arising of faith, and as distinct from the concept of being truly settled for the birth in the Pure Land. The answer is rather straightforward: Wavering faith cannot have the assurance of salvation. The settling of faith assures our settling of birth in the Pure Land; certainty of faith is for Shinran certainty of salvation. Salvation is secured without any doubt the moment faith is settled free from doubt. When faith is settled our birth is also settled and to that extent becomes the present reality here and now. Without the settling of faith, our settling of birth in the Pure Land becomes not only uncertain psychologically but also vague and abstract. Hence there was a good reason for Shinran to resort to this concept, although he did not use it too often. The person of settled faith does not fret over the future possibility of salvation; he has no anxiety about his future destiny. More specifically, for instance, he does not have to wait until the last moment of his life when, according to the traditional Pure Land belief before Shinran, he will be visited in his deathbed by Amida Buddha, surrounded by a host of bodhisattvas, coming to welcome him into the Pure Land, his birth thereby becoming settled, there being no settlement or assurance of his birth until then. By his concept of the settling of faith and birth, Shinran put a definite end to this futuristic soteriology of the traditional Pure Land Buddhism.

---

[60] Quoted in *The Tanni Shō* (Kyoto: Ryukoku University Translation Center, 1962; Ryukoku Translation Series II), 93; *SSZ*, I: 57. "Embracing" is a better translation for *sesshu* than "grasping," even though I have mostly retained the latter in accord with the Shin Buddhism Translation Series.

The futuristic soteriology, based upon the nineteenth Vow of Amida as well as upon a passage in the *Smaller Sūtra of Immeasurable Life*,[61] caused a great deal of anxiety among believers over the last moment of their lives; one may meet death unexpectedly and unprepared, and thus not be welcomed by Amida and his holy host. Moreover, according to another traditional view based upon the *Contemplation Sūtra*, believers can expiate by a single utterance of nenbutsu the sins that would involve them in birth-and-death for eighty millions of kalpas.[62] Thus, they have to be in the right frame of mind when they meet death so that they may be able to expiate whatever sins had been accumulated up to that moment. It is obvious that this belief also is the basis of another source of anxiety among believers over the last moment of their lives. Now Shinran was saying that all these worries are entirely meaningless once our faith is settled. For that is the moment when our birth is settled. In Shinran's words:

> The person who lives true faith, however, abides in the stage of the truly settled, for he has already been grasped, never to be abandoned. There is no need to wait in anticipation for the moment of death, no need to rely on Amida's coming. At the time faith becomes settled, birth too becomes settled; there is no need for the deathbed rites that prepare one for Amida's coming.[63]
>
> The person whose faith has become true and real—this being the benefit of the Vow—has been grasped, never to be abandoned; hence he does not depend on Amida's coming at the moment of death. The person whose faith has not become settled awaits the moment of death in anticipation of Amida's coming.[64]

The moment of death is not crucial, says Shinran. What is crucial is whether or not one has a settled faith. For those who have such a faith every moment is an "eschatological" moment, as it were. Even though such a person still remains in this world, he lives an ecstatic mode of life, his birth already secured and guaranteed. Instead of waiting in anxiety for the uncertain moment of Amida's coming, he is already "grasped, never to be abandoned," by Amida here and now. In a way, therefore, Shinran demythologized the traditional idea of Amida coming to welcome the

[61] *SSZ*, I: 69.

[62] *SSZ*, I: 65.

[63] *Letters*, 19–20; *SSZ*, II: 656.

[64] *Letters*, 55; *SSZ*, II: 684–85.

believer with a host of holy beings at the moment of death. It is made
entirely superfluous for the person of settled faith who has already been
embraced by Amida's light. Once faith is settled, every moment is the
eschatological moment, and ordinary time is special time. Thus Shinran
says:

> Grasped by the karmic power fulfilled through the great Vow, one is
> brought to the attainment of birth. This refers to the person who has
> already realized faith in ordinary times, not to one who becomes definite-
> ly settled in faith and who is blessed with Amida's compassionate grasp
> for the first time at the point of death. Since the person who has realized
> the diamond-like heart has been grasped and protected by the light of
> Amida's heart from ordinary times, he dwells in the stage of the truly set-
> tled. Thus the moment of death is not the crucial matter; from ordinary
> times he has been constantly grasped and protected, never to be aban-
> doned, and so is said to be *grasped by the power of the Vow and brought to
> attainment of birth.*... There may be people lacking true faith in ordinary
> times who, by the merit of having long engaged in saying the Name, first
> encounter the guidance of a true teacher and realize faith at the very end
> of their lives; at that moment, being grasped by the power of the Vow,
> they attain birth. But those who await Amida's coming at the end of life
> have yet to realize faith and so are filled with anxiety, anticipating the
> moment of death.[65]

Traditionally, the stage of non-retrogression (*avinivartinīya*) or the
stage of being truly settled (for enlightenment) was supposed to be
attained after one's birth in the Pure Land, where conditions are favorable
for the practice to achieve enlightenment. Thus it is promised in the
eleventh Vow that:

> If, when I attain Buddhahood, the human beings and devas in my land
> do not dwell among the settled and necessarily attain *nirvāṇa*, may I not
> attain the supreme enlightenment.[66]

Now, by moving forward this moment of being truly settled for birth and
enlightenment and making it coincidental with the moment of the settlement of faith, Shinran brought about a revolutionary change in the traditional Pure Land soteriology. Salvation, or birth in the Pure Land, is now

---

[65] Inscriptions, 53–54; *SSZ*, II: 589–90.

[66] Quoted in Ueda and Hirota, *Shinran*, 313; *SSZ*, I: 9.

made a present reality to the extent that it is settled or assured here and now when faith is settled. All that is now left to the person of faith is to wait in joyful expectation—this is regarded as the true meaning of "aspiration for birth"—until the time comes when the present existence, the outcome of the past karma, comes to an end. We should examine more closely this aspect of Shinran's notion of salvation, already secured but not yet realized, in the next chapter. Let it be simply noted here that, according to Shinran, the person of faith to a certain degree already enjoys here and now the life of a "realized eschatology."

Another significant corollary that follows from the above change in the traditional soteriology was that Shinran made birth into the Pure Land identical with the attainment of enlightenment itself. Enlightenment is now no longer considered something to be attained *after* the birth through which the stage of non-retrogression was supposed to be secured. The latter being already secured now through faith, the birth itself is consequently regarded as none other than the enlightenment—another profound reinterpretation of the traditional Pure Land soteriology. For it practically means a "demythologization" of the traditional concept of birth ($\bar{o}j\bar{o}$) as physical birth in the Pure Land. What made this reinterpretation possible was none other than Shinran's concept of faith, especially the notion of its settlement.

FAITH AND OTHER POWER

Thus far, we have examined Shinran's concept of faith from two angles. One was to examine, by focusing on the threefold mind of the eighteenth Vow, the kind of mental phenomenon faith is, and the other was to examine the dynamics of faith with reference to its arising and settling. To sum up what we have seen so far, faith refers to the act of entrusting oneself to (or deeply believing) Amida's Primal Vow without any doubt, an act that involves one's conversion from self-power to Other Power. It arises through one's encounter with Other Power when one hears the Buddha's Name, and it becomes settled by being "grasped, never to be abandoned" by Amida's light. This act of entrusting, whether in arising or in settling, is considered to be entirely the work of Other Power, being directed to us by the power of the Vow. In this respect, faith is ultimately a mystery to Shinran. We do not know why it arises in some people and not in others. Even if it is said to arise when we come into contact with the Vow through hearing the Name, we may still ask why it arises in some when they hear the Name while it does not in others when they hear the Name. It is indeed a gift.

Now, with regard to this idea of faith as a gift, another theoretical question arises: If faith is ultimately the gift of Amida, does not this fact itself require another act of faith to accept the gift? Thus, do we not have an infinite regress? Indeed, we are not surprised to find that there are some passages in Shinran's writings that seem to suggest this concept of a "faith of faith," so to speak. For example,

> Since we have been given this Vow by the Tathāgata, we can take any occasion in daily life for saying the Name and need not wait to recite it at the very end of life; we should simply *give ourselves up totally to the entrusting with sincere mind of the Tathāgata.* When a person realizes this true and real faith, he enters completely into the compassionate light that grasps, never to abandon, and hence becomes established in the stage of the truly settled. Thus it is written.[67]

> "Faith alone" is the heart that *aspires solely to this true and real entrusting.*[68]

In these passages, the expressions "should give ourselves up totally to" (*fukaku tanomu beshi*) and "aspire solely to" (*hito sujini toru*) are all equivalent expressions of the act of faith or entrusting. Literally, therefore, they take faith as their object, which seems to suggest the idea of double faith, i.e., faith of faith, or faith to accept faith.

To be fair to Shinran, however, we should probably not take these expressions too literally and charge Shinran with holding a position that he would obviously not accept, despite the loose expressions.[69] Clearly, for Shinran, the object of faith is Other Power, the power of the Vow, not faith itself. Nevertheless, it is not difficult to see why such a loose expression is possible in the first place. It is most likely due to the idea that faith is not based upon our decision but given by Amida, an idea that in itself

---

[67] *Inscriptions,* 34 (italics mine); *SSZ,* II: 578.

[68] *Inscriptions,* 34 (italics mine); *SSZ,* II: 578.

[69] It is rather surprising to see that Ueda and Hirota accept this "double faith" as an authentic aspect of Shinran's thought. Does this mean, then, that there are practically two kinds of faith in Shinran? But can this be true? See "Correspondence," *Monumenta Nipponica,* 38/4 (Winter 1983), 416–17.

seems to require another act of faith.

Why then, we might ask, does Shinran so persistently emphasize the givenness of faith? We have seen that, according to Shinran, given the thorough depravity of human nature, we are incapable not merely of the practice necessary for enlightenment but also of "the true and real faith." From nowhere in our hearts can such a faith arise, says Shinran. The very concept of faith, of the absolute reliance on Other Power, requires for Shinran that faith itself be given rather than be something we can generate. If we can generate faith through some practice or systematic cultivation, then it is turned into another act of self-power. Neither our deepest self-reflection nor even our most pious religious aspiration for birth, we have seen, can give rise to faith for Shinran. Faith is not something that begins from our consciousness or religious experience in the first place, however pure and sincere they may be. Nor should faith be made into another condition for our salvation, for there is absolutely no condition, however easy it may be, that human beings can meet—knowledge, wisdom, good and meritorious acts, precepts, meditation, nenbutsu, not even faith. Nor is any condition necessary at all, because Amida's compassionate Vow has made it entirely superfluous. All we need to do is to realize this fact, enter into the vast ocean of Amida's Primal Vow and ride on the "ship of the Vow." And this act of faith should not become another condition for our salvation, according to the very definition of faith; faith should not be turned into another "work" or another "good" karma. Otherwise, grace would not be grace, and Other Power would not be Other Power. Salvation, for Shinran, is simply given naturally (*jinen hōni* 自然法爾) without any effort or design (*hakarai*) on our part, including our act of faith. Faith itself demands that faith be given, rather than be the last act of our self-power.

Despite this profound logic of faith and grace that we can read in Shinran's thought, a lingering doubt remains. If faith is completely beyond our act, our control, and our decision, does this not indeed make faith very difficult to attain, turning it into a "difficult path" instead? Faith may not be something we can "attain," but it is certainly an essential element, the *sine qua non*, we need to possess in order to ride on the "ship of Vow" and enjoy salvation even if it is naturally (*jinen hōni*) given. Now, if faith is completely beyond our control, does it not constitute in practice a more difficult path than the so-called traditional Path of Sages, where there is at least some room for our action? Like the Calvinist doctrine of predestination, Shinran's deterministic doctrine of the givenness of faith seems to lead to a purely fortuitous conception of salvation (Amida saves whomever he wants to) and to put salvation completely beyond the reach of our effort and decision. In this sense, faith is a difficult path, and indeed Shinran repeatedly emphasizes—rhetorically, to be sure—that faith is truly very difficult to have, more difficult to attain than enlightenment! Shinran says:

> For the foolish and ignorant who are ever sinking in birth-and-death, the multitudes turning in transmigration, it is not attainment of the unexcelled, incomparable fruit of enlightenment that is difficult; the genuine difficulty is realizing true and real faith. Why? Because this realization takes place through the Tathāgata's supportive power, because it comes about wholly through the power of great compassion and all-embracing wisdom.[70]

According to Hōnen, nenbutsu is the easiest act that anybody can perform, and this is the reason that Amida chose it as the condition for our salvation, rather than any other conditions such as precepts, knowledge, good conduct, meditation, and other pious acts. Once the stress has been shifted, however, from this simple act of nenbutsu to the inner attitude of faith with which we are supposed to respond to Amida's salvific work, somehow salvation can appear to be more elusive than it was in Hōnen's teaching. Shinran himself was keenly aware of this. For he repeatedly emphasized that faith is extremely difficult to realize—in fact more so than the "perfect fruit of enlightenment"!—because our pride and our attachment to self-power are extremely hard to uproot.[71] The way of pure Other Power is difficult to follow for the sentient beings who are constantly engaged in their own designs (*hakarai*) as to how to attain salvation, despite the fact that Amida did and does everything for them.

The fact is, unlike Hōnen's concept of practice and faith, Shinran's concept, I want to point out, was from the beginning very puristic and perfectionistic. Behind it there is the presupposition that the pure can only be reached through the pure, the absolute only through the

---

[70] *True Teaching*, II: 204; *SSZ*, II: 48.

[71] See *Essentials of Passages on the Pure Land Way: A Translation of Shinran's Jōdo monrui jushō* (Kyoto: Hongwanji International Center, 1982; Shin Buddhism Translation Series), 34; *SSZ*, II: 445; *Faith Alone*, 46; *SSZ*, II: 633; *True Teaching*, II: 204; *SSZ*, II: 48. See also *SSZ*, II: 1, 44, 454, 494, 496, 650.

absolute. The following passage from the chapter on realization (*shō*) in the *Kyōgyōshinshō* neatly sums up the whole matter:

> As I contemplate the teaching, practice, faith, and realization of the true essence of the Pure Land way, I see that they are the benefit that the Tathagata directs to us in his great compassion.
>
> Therefore, whether with regard to the cause or to the fruition, there is nothing whatever that has not been fulfilled through Amida Tathāgata's directing of virtue to beings out of his pure Vow-mind. *Because the cause is pure, the fruit is also pure.* Reflect on this.[72]

It is no wonder that such a pure practice and faith is unattainable for "ordinary beings filled with blind passions," except when they are given it by Amida Buddha himself. But Hōnen does not start with such a puristic conception of practice and faith. Is it not precisely because we cannot come up with such a perfect practice and faith, he would say, that Amida Buddha uttered his compassionate Vow and set a very easy condition for our salvation? Hōnen, for instance, is reported to have said:

> When Shōkō-bō said he had not the least doubt about the *ōjō* [birth in the Pure Land], Hōnen said to him, "Do not imagine that a slight fault can prevent your attaining it. But I have a thing to say regarding outsiders, and that is that they may attain *ōjō* by saying the nenbutsu, even if their faith is not so ardent as to make them weep.[73]

In contrast to this, Shinran, having set the high puristic standard of practice and faith according to the logic that the absolute can only be reached through the absolute (or, some would perhaps say, he was "obsessed" with human sinfulness and the problem of the certainty of salvation), the only choice left for him was to resort to the view that both practice and faith are entirely given by Amida, and not something we can generate or do anything about.

But does this really solve the problem? Shinran, it appears, may have paid too high a price for this solution. It not only makes his concept of faith too abstract to be a concrete psychological experience for ordinary men and women and for it to be meaningful in their ordinary lives; it also creates other serious problems unforeseen by Shinran. First of all, it does not even seem to have solved the very problem it was meant to deal with,

[72] *True Teaching*, III: 364 (italics mine); *SSZ*, II:106; see also *SSZ*, II: 67, 111.
[73] Coates and Ishizuka, *Hōnen*, II: 449–50.

that is, the problem of the certainty of salvation. For, despite the transcendent grounding of faith, its arising and settling, does not the actual religious experience of the believers tell us that they still suffer from doubts and oscillations in their faith, making their salvation doubtful in their concrete experiences, no matter what they may believe in terms of the doctrine of faith? The ninth chapter of the *Tannishō*, which we have quoted previously, vividly illustrates how Shinran himself, as much as his disciples, suffered from weakness of faith despite all the doctrines he himself taught concerning the "true and real" "diamond-like" faith given by Amida.

Shinran's preoccupation with the givenness of faith seems to have created another difficult problem with regard to the propagation of faith. In addition to engendering uncertainty about whether or not one really has faith —and hence, whether one is saved or not—because of its invisible transcendent origin, it also completely shuts the door of salvation to those who feel that they are not gifted with faith and believe that there is nothing they can do about it. The following story about an important event that occurred in the evangelizing activity of Ippen, a nenbutsu holy man (*hijiri* 聖) of medieval Japan and the founder of the Jishū Sect of Pure Land Buddhism, dramatically illustrates this problem:

> There was a monk. Ippen said, "Please accept this slip, awakening one thought (*ichinen*) of faith and uttering Namu-amida-butsu."
>
> The monk refused, saying, "At present faith that is single-minded (*ichinen*) does not arise in me. If I accepted your slip, I would be breaking the precept against lying."
>
> Ippen said, "Don't you believe in the Buddha's teaching? Why can't you accept the slip?"
>
> The monk replied, "I do not doubt the teaching, but there is nothing I can do about faith not arising in me."[74]

Ippen was awfully embarrassed. By *ichinen* Ippen meant "even once"—even a single moment of faith and utterance. For the monk, however, it meant the single mind, a wholehearted and total entrusting. The story continues:

---

[74] Quoted in *No Abode: The Record of Ippen*, trans. by Dennis Hirota (Kyoto: Ryukoku University Translation Center, 1986), 18.

By that time, a large number of pilgrims had gathered. If the monk did not take the slip, neither would any of the others, so with great reluctance Ippen said, "Please accept it even if faith does not arise in you," and gave him the slip. Seeing this, the other pilgrims all took one, and the monk went on his way.[75]

For Ippen, who had rather taken faith for granted in nenbutsu, this was not merely an embarrassing experience but the cause of a serious crisis in his preaching activity as well. Would Shinran's idea that faith is given by Amida Buddha himself have helped Ippen? Should he have answered, "Yes, you are right that there is nothing you can do about faith not arising in you, because it only comes from Amida's Vow Power"? Probably not. Ippen agonized over this shocking experience and eventually came to draw an entirely different conclusion. The story continues:

Reflecting on this incident, Ippen decided that it was not without significance, and thinking that in the matter of propagation he should look to higher guidance, he prayed with this wish before the Hall of Witness (Shōjōden) in the main shrine at Kumano. When he had closed his eyes but not yet fallen asleep, the doors of the sacred hall were pushed open and a yamabushi with white hair and a long hood emerged. On the veranda three hundred other yamabushi touched their heads down in obeisance. At that moment Ippen realized that it was surely the Manifestation himself and entrusted himself completely. Then the yamabushi stepped before Ippen and said, "Hijiri spreading the nenbutsu of interpenetration, why do you go about it mistakenly? It is not through your propagation that sentient beings come to attain birth. In Amida Buddha's perfect enlightenment ten kalpas ago the birth of all sentient beings was decisively settled as Namu-amida-butsu. Distribute your slips regardless of whether there is faith or not, and without discriminating between purity and impurity."[76]

Later on, Ippen interpreted this experience in the following way:

While I was in retreat at Kumano, I received a revelation that declared:

Make no judgments about the nature of your heart and mind. Since this mind is illusory, both when it is good and when it is evil, it cannot be essential for emancipation. Namu-amida-butsu itself is born.

[75] *No Abode*, 19.
[76] *No Abode*, 19–20.

At that time I abandoned my own intentions and aspirations of self-power once and for all.[77]

Unlike Shinran, who emphasized the givenness of faith, Ippen changed the focus of attention from faith, the subjective state of mind, to the objective givenness of salvation itself, what he calls the Namu-amida-butsu. Ippen says:

> Everybody laments not awakening faith that their birth is decisively settled. This is completely absurd. No settledness is to be found in the hearts of foolish beings. Settledness is the Name. Thus, even though you lack faith that your birth is decisively settled, if you say the Name leaving all to your lips, you will be born. Birth, then, does not depend on the attitude of heart and mind; it is through the Name that you will be born....[78]

Or,

> I have come to believe that whatever spurious doctrine you may utter with your lips or accept in your mind, the Name is Dharma that does not depend on doctrine, nor on the mind, so if you say it, you will unfailingly attain birth. When something is set aflame, you may wish mentally, "Do not burn," and say this aloud, but fire does not depend on such words or on the power of thought; it simply burns out of its own inherent power. It is the same with water moistening things. In like manner, the Name possesses, by its own nature, the virtuous power to bring about birth, so when a person says it, he will be born, without any dependence on doctrine, without any dependence on the heart or mind, without any dependence on words. This is, I believe, the practice of Other Power that surpasses conceivability.[79]

I have quoted Ippen rather extensively, not because I believe that he solved the paradox of the "easy path" posed by the emphasis on the purity of faith—Ippen's emphasis on the Name, after all, is bound to start the problem all over again—but because it highlights the problem in great clarity. Shinran tried to solve the problem of the uncertainty and impurity of faith by stressing its transcendent origin, its givenness. But it appears that he did this at the expense of the believer's lively psychological

[77] *No Abode*, 38.

[78] *No Abode*, 141–42.

[79] *No Abode*, 169.

experience of faith. Is not real empirical faith, however imperfect and impure it may be, more tangible and meaningful for believers than the abstract concept of faith that Shinran taught? It is probably for this reason that the Shin Buddhists have had to search throughout their history for more tangible proof of their faith and salvation, something that has often led them to ways deviating from the path of the true faith envisaged by the founder. Stanley Weinstein makes the following keen observation on this matter:

> For the simpleminded monto [followers] the aspect of Shinran's teach-ings that was hardest to comprehend was the abstract concept that one's salvation was guaranteed the moment one accepted Amida's grace. In the other Jōdo schools, the devotee could derive some sense of self-sat-isfaction from the fact that he was contributing in tangible fashion toward his own salvation by reciting the nenbutsu, chanting a Pure Land text, or worshipping an image of Amida. In the Shinshū, however, recit-ing the nenbutsu or chanting sūtras were not regarded as means of enter-ing Pure Land, and the use of images of Amida as objects of worship was frowned upon. How, then, could unsophisticated believers in Pure Land be certain of their ultimate salvation, since the crucial "awakening of faith" (*shin no ichinen*) was something so intangible?[80]

Throughout Shinshū doctrinal history, there have been many attempts to pin down a certain religious experience as the unmistakable sign of faith, but such attempts have consistently been repudiated by the orthodox theologians, lest the attachment to such an experience should lead to an erroneous conception of faith as self-power, something we can generate by certain psychological preparation or training.[81] Faith, for Shinran, is not to be understood as an ordinary religious experience that occurs between a subject and the object of faith. So long as it is conceived of as something that is dependent upon our unreliable subjective state of mind, ever changing and fickle, salvation also remains uncertain. The dis-tance between us and Amida remains always far and wide, and our salva-tion far away too. Unless there is an absolute unconditional and

---

[80] Stanley Weinstein, "Rennyo and the Shinshū Revival," *Japan in the Muromachi Age,* ed. by John Whitney Hall and Toyoda Takeshi (Berkeley: University of California Press, 1977), 341–42.

[81] See, for instance, "shingan kōsai" 信願交際 and "kanki shogo" 歡喜初後 in Kiritani, *Kōza Shinshū no anjin rondai.*

unbreakable relationship established between us and Amida, unless, therefore, our relationship with Other Power is grounded upon Other Power itself, our salvation is always subject to doubt and uncertainty. Behind Shinran's insistence upon the givenness of faith lay this yearning for the absolute objectivity and givenness of salvation, its certainty. Thus the subject and the object of faith should not be separate but one, as is expressed by the Shinshū doctrine of "the identity of the person and the dharma" (*kihō ittai* 機法一體).

The *Anjin ketsujō shō*, which was originally a text belonging to the Seizan branch of the Jōdoshū but which greatly influenced Shinshū doctrinal thought after Shinran,[82] puts the logic of absolute Other Power in faith and practice in the following way:

> The nenbutsu of the person who relies on self-power puts the Buddha yonder in the west. Since such a person, considering himself to be just an ordinary being, occasionally thinks about Other Power in his mind and calls upon the Name, there is no intimacy between the Buddha and the sentient beings. Although the birth [in the Pure Land] is felt to be close at hand when the aspiration for enlightenment arises a little in his mind, the birth becomes extremely uncertain when the nenbutsu becomes languid and the aspiration for enlightenment withers. Since it is rare for the mind of an ordinary being to give rise to the aspiration for enlightenment, such a person always becomes uncertain of the birth. He may wait for this and that moment, but the birth is not settled for sure until death. Thus he may occasionally call upon the Name with his mouth, but the birth becomes hard to rely on. It is, for instance, like a person going to serve somebody. For, the more one thinks of pleasing the mind of the Buddha and follows him, counting on being granted the favor of the birth, the further the peace of the person's mind and the great compassion of the Buddha become separated from each other, always finding oneself alienated from the Buddha. In such a situation, the birth truly becomes extremely uncertain.[83]

These are not Shinran's words, but they express remarkably well the fundamental religious motivation behind his doctrine of the givenness of

---

[82] Dobbins, *Jōdo Shinshū*, 106–107. For the Pure Land thought of this book, see Winston L. King, "An Interpretation of the *Anjin Ketsujōshō*," *Japanese Journal of Religious Studies*, 13/4 (1986), 277–98.

[83] *Anjin ketsujō shō* in *SSZ*, III: 624; see D. T. Suzuki, *Collected Writings on Shin Buddhism*, 52, for a different translation.

practice and faith. In short, salvation should never be made dependent upon our subjective psychological conditions, not even upon our deepest and most pious religious experiences—unpredictable, unreliable, full of falsity, constantly under the attack of blind passions. It should entirely be left to the work of Other Power, the ever reliable and ever compassionate reality that constantly throws the light of wisdom and compassion upon sinful beings, calling them to Great Faith and Great Practice. Even the slightest vestige of self-power is a "revolt" against the purity of the absolute grace of Other Power, its sheer benevolence, jeopardizing the pure relationship between us and Other Power.

Yet, as Shinran himself is said to have confessed, is our infirmity of faith not all the more reason to believe in the compassionate Vow of Amida? Can we not simply allow our faith to be a *human* faith with all its infirmities and impurities? Did Shinran not pay too high a price by letting human subjectivity in faith be completely eclipsed by Other Power? Would we be terribly wrong if we find in Shinran a sort of "faith legalism," from which his master Hōnen seems to have been remarkably free?

Besides the problem of "double faith" and the preoccupation with the abstract purity of faith, Shinran's concept of faith as a gift of Amida raises another serious issue, namely, the question of whether it might completely dissolve the infinite distance that Shinran's faith initially posited between sentient beings and the Buddha. How much of the element of transcendence and tension is still left in his concept of faith when its subject, human beings, and its object, the Other Power, are made to coincide? Are we already saved when we are given that pure diamond-like faith, the gift of Buddha-nature, by Amida Buddha? Is Shinran really reverting to the traditional Path of Sages (*shōdōmon*) of Mahāyāna? It is to these questions that we are going to turn in the next chapter.

4

The Life of Faith

MOST RELIGIOUS TRADITIONS promise salvation, the ideal world where the fundamental problems of human existence are completely overcome and life is transformed into a qualitatively higher form. The salvation promised by the religious message is a transcendent reality, in the sense that it is not empirically evident to all people; it is epistemologically transcendent. It may also be conceived of as ontologically transcendent, in the sense that the ideal world or realm may be viewed as lying completely beyond the present world, an ontological order entirely separate from the world in which we live and die. It is axiomatic that in this case salvation is never fully attainable in the present world, although we may somehow be able to have a foretaste of it. When transcendence is primarily conceived of in epistemological terms, it is theoretically fully possible to experience salvation here and now, if only we can remove the epistemic obstacle that prevents us from seeing the reality deeply hidden behind our ignorance— although here, too, the knowledge of salvation is seldom fully attainable in practice, because of human finitude. Whether epistemological or ontological, therefore, the transcendent world of salvation is never an unambiguous reality. It remains forever elusive for us despite the dogmatic assertions and pious rhetoric of the religious professionals. Herein lies one of the central problems with which all religious traditions have to deal. While they promise a complete overcoming of the present human situation, marked as it is by sin and evil and ignorance, this overcoming rarely becomes for common mortals an immediate reality as obvious as the everyday world. While the high ideal of salvation appears to us forever unreachable, it does not, nevertheless, cease to beckon to us in our longing for a perfect world in which the problems that make human life ultimately meaningless and tragic are completely absent.

The Mahāyāna Buddhist traditions, especially Kegon (Hua-yen 華嚴) and Zen in particular, teach the complete identity of *saṃsāra* and *nirvāṇa*—Form is Emptiness, Emptiness is Form—as well as of sentient

120

beings and Buddha. Seen with the wisdom of *śūnyatā*, all the dualities and conflicts characterizing human life lose their ultimacy and become dissolved into the non-dual reality of peace and serenity. For Shinran, a *bonpu* heavily laden with karmic hindrances, one who lived in constant awareness of the enormous gap between himself and Buddhahood, there was no human potential for realizing such an immediate identity, unmediated by the experience of evil and sinfulness. The traditional rhetoric about a Buddha-nature inherent in every sentient being, the absolute identity of *saṃsāra* and *nirvāṇa*, the realization of the Pure Land as Mind-only, the realization of Buddhahood in this very body—all these doctrines sounded to Shinran, who was constantly aware of his own ineradicable sinfulness, like so much empty talk, too good and too easy to be true. He found himself unable even to evoke a genuine aspiration for enlightenment and found in himself no genuine disposition to confess his own sinfulness; instead, what he found was only the stubborn will to adhere to self-power even in the disguise of piety. For him the only possible avenue to salvation was to find something that was effective in spite of his sinfulness and evil, or even because of his evil, and subsequently he came to realize that it was precisely for the sake of such an evil person as himself that Amida uttered his compassionate Vow. How to be saved despite one's sinfulness was the cardinal concern for Shinran. The salvation that he had to seek was, therefore, one that recognized human depravity as it is without denying or covering up its stark reality, and yet made human liberation possible, one that allowed us to "attain *nirvāṇa* without severing blind passions." In short, what Shinran sought and found was a paradoxical form of salvation. And, as far as the present life is concerned, it is precisely this paradoxical form of salvation that, according to Shinran, is made possible by faith in Amida's salvific work as manifested in his compassionate Vow.

THE PARADOX OF SALVATION

Shinran's writings provide us with plenty of witnesses to this paradoxical state of salvation, which is characterized by the simultaneous presence of the two opposite poles of salvation experience and the resulting dialectical tension. His writings also reveal that the delicate balance between the two was often difficult to maintain even for him, not to mention for his followers, who struggled, some even unsuccessfully, to understand and appreciate such a subtle form of salvation experience. Thus we find Shinran emphasizing one aspect of it at one time, and the other at another, oscillating between the two according to the mood in which he found himself when he wrote a particular passage. We have already seen that the two aspects of the "twofold deeply believing"—one about oneself and the other about the Vow—are inseparably bound up with each other and that we cannot have one without the other. This structure of faith already contains within it the structure of the life of faith. In the actual manifestation of faith in the life of the believers, including Shinran himself, the two aspects, although structurally bound, are not necessarily simultaneously present with equal strength. Sometimes one falls into the bottomless pit of deep despair, while at another moment one rejoices over the salvation freely given by Amida's Primal Vow in spite of one's wretchedness. Our picture of the life of faith in Shinran should therefore not be distorted by certain passages in which only one side of the salvation experience comes to the fore. It is not that Shinran found himself at one moment saved and at another lost, nor that he felt himself partly saved and partly lost. Rather, in faith Shinran found himself *totally* saved and yet totally lost, *simultaneously* and *always*—hence, the true paradoxicality of his salvation experience. What Steven Ozment says about Luther's concept of *simul justus et peccator* (being simultaneously justified and sinner) holds equally well for Shinran's experience of salvation:

> The *semper* [always] and *nondum* [not yet] lay the foundation for a *simul.* He who is always in sin and always "not yet" righteous can only be righteous as one who is simultaneously sinful. He cannot be "partly righteous and partly sinful," nor can he be either righteous or sinful. He must be righteous and sinful simultaneously.[1]

This paradoxicality, as we shall see later, ultimately derives from the temporal paradoxicality of salvation being *already* secured and *not yet* realized. In other words, in Shinran salvation is, as far as the present life of the believer is concerned, only given in the form of a firm assurance for the future, an assurance that is secured in faith. Thus, in one sense, salvation is already here in the lives of the believers, but in another sense, it is not yet here. The crux of the whole matter then lies in the question of what

---

[1] Quoted in John Ishihara, "Luther and Shinran: *Simul justus et peccator* and *nishu jin-shin*," *Japanese Religions*, 14/4 (1987), 38.

kind of *nirvāṇa* it is that we can enter "without cutting the blind passions," and of when it is attained: now, or in the future? If now, in what sense? It is to these questions, therefore, that we must turn our attention.

We have already seen that Shinran's concept of faith brought about a profound change in the futuristic soteriology of traditional Pure Land Buddhism. The traditional soteriology emphasized the last moment of one's life—the moment when one should utter the nenbutsu and thereby wipe away all the evil karma one has committed up to that moment, and meet Amida Buddha, surrounded by his holy retinue, coming to welcome one into the Pure Land. By stressing the crucial importance of the moment of the arising and settling of faith, Shinran made this traditional piety entirely superfluous, and the normal anxiety arising from the thought of an unprepared death was completely done away with. The *Tannishō* says:

> To believe that each time you say the Name your karmic evil is eradicated is nothing but to strive to attain birth by eliminating your karmic evil yourself. In that case, you can attain birth only by remaining diligent in the nenbutsu to the very point of death, for every thought a person has throughout the course of his life forms one more fetter binding him to birth-and-death. But since there is a limit to the karmic recompense by which our present life is maintained, we may meet with a variety of totally unforeseen accidents, or, tormented by sickness, reach the end of our lives without abiding in right-mindedness; in such circumstances, saying the Name is difficult. How then is the karmic evil committed in that final interval to be eliminated? And if it is not eliminated, is not birth unattainable?
>
> If we entrust ourselves to Amida's Vow to grasp and never abandon us, then even though, through unforeseen circumstances, we commit an evil act at the very end or die without the nenbutsu emerging from our lips, we will immediately realize birth into the Pure Land. Moreover, even if we do spontaneously say the Name at the point of death, it is nothing other than our expression of gratitude for Amida's benevolence, entrusting to the Buddha more and more as the time of enlightenment draws near.[2]

The most decisive moment in one's life is, according to Shinran, the moment when faith arises and becomes settled by one's being embraced,

---

[2] *Tannishō*, 36–37.

never to be abandoned, by Amida.[3] In that very moment, and not later on at the uncertain moment of one's death, you are one of the truly settled who are destined to attain birth no matter what occurs to you thereafter. In that very moment, you already enjoy an ecstatic life; the last moment, the *eschaton*, is already here in the midst of your life. Shinran is never tired of repeating this doctrine throughout his writings, showing how much importance he attached to it in his soteriological thinking. With this re-interpretation of the traditional Pure Land soteriology, however, it is hard to deny that Shinran came dangerously close to the classic Mahāyāna doctrine teaching the possibility of attaining Buddhahood in this very life. No wonder that his bold assertion—that believers attain a status equal to Maitreya, who is destined to become the Buddha in the next life—caused such a sensation as well as confusion among his followers. Is Shinran then betraying his own teaching about the necessity of faith by which alone we can be saved, and that clearly presupposes the infinite transcendence of Buddhahood, the distance between sentient beings and the Buddha?

Entering the stage of the truly settled by being embraced by Amida is one of the ten benefits that Shinran says the person of faith "unfailingly gains in the present life." The other nine benefits are also worth listing here:

> First, the benefit of being protected and sustained by unseen powers.
>
> Second, the benefit of being possessed of supreme virtues.
>
> Third, the benefit of our karmic evil being transformed into good.
>
> Fourth, the benefit of being protected and cared for by all the Buddhas.
>
> Fifth, the benefit of being praised by all the Buddhas.
>
> Sixth, the benefit of being constantly protected by the light of the Buddha's heart.
>
> Seventh, the benefit of having great joy in our hearts.
>
> Eighth, the benefit of being aware of Amida's benevolence and of responding in gratitude to his virtue.

[3] Despite what we have seen in our previous chapter, I follow the traditional interpretation in treating the arising of faith and its settling as occurring in the same moment, distinguishable as they are.

Ninth, the benefit of constantly practicing great compassion.[4]

While these benefits do not include any concrete material benefits, they are certainly "this-worldly" benefits in the sense that through faith they are made available to believers in the present life. Because of faith, believers' lives are now lived in a different spirit and attitude from the lives of those without faith. Faith brings about a transformed life that is lived in joy, gratitude, compassion, and freedom from fear. Most importantly, however, it is a life lived in the firm assurance of salvation as the consequence of the benefit of entering the stage of the truly settled.

Despite the radical change brought about by Shinran in the traditional futuristic soteriology, however, it should be made clear that this stage of the truly settled, or the stage of non-retrogression, which is attained by faith settled, is by no means identical to the attainment of enlightenment itself. The latter, according to Shinran, comes only after, or along with, one's birth in the Pure Land, and this birth is for Shinran clearly a future event occurring at the moment of the believer's death. Shinran did not differentiate the moment of great enlightenment from birth in the Pure Land; the birth itself is the enlightenment. This, as we have pointed out earlier, constitutes one of the most profound transformations in traditional Pure Land soteriology. Yet this birth, although by faith assured in the present, occurs in a separate moment from the settling of faith; it occurs only when the present karmic body dissolves. It is a grave mistake to equate faith with enlightenment. The *Tannishō*, for instance, rejects in unmistakable terms the idea of attaining enlightenment with the present body, as contrary to the Pure Land teaching of Other Power:

> The assertion that one actually realizes enlightenment while possessing a bodily existence full of blind passions is absurd. The attainment of Buddhahood with this very body is the fundamental import of the esoteric teaching of Shingon, the realization [achieved] through the three mystic acts. The purification of the six sense organs is the teaching of the One Vehicle expounded in the *Lotus Sūtra*, the virtue [attained] through the four practices of repose. These are all difficult practices, the endeavor of those of superior capacity; they are enlightenment fulfilled through meditation. The realization of enlightenment in the coming life is the essential intent of the Pure Land [teaching] of Other Power, the way of

[4] *True Teaching*, II: 257–58; *SSZ*, II: 72.

the settlement of faith. It is the easy practice, the endeavor of those of inferior capacity; it is the dharma that does not discriminate between the good and the evil. Generally speaking, to sever one's blind passions and obstructing evil in this life is extremely difficult; hence even the pure monks who practice Shingon and *Lotus Sūtra* [teachings]... aspire for enlightenment in the next life. What need be said [concerning foolish beings like ourselves]? Although we lack both the practice of observing precepts and wisdom, once we have reached the shore of the fulfilled land, riding in the ship of Amida's Vow and crossing this painful ocean of birth-and-death, the dark clouds of blind passion will clear immediately and the moon of enlightenment that sees things as they are will swiftly appear. Becoming one taste with the unhindered light filling the ten quarters, we will bring benefit to all sentient beings: at that moment [there] is enlightenment.[5]

Certainly, there are passages in Shinran's writings that seem to suggest the idea of immediate liberation from the world of birth-and-death when faith is settled. The following hymn, for instance, is typical:

Looking to and encountering the moment
When faith, firm and diamondlike, becomes settled:
In that instant Amida's compassionate light grasps and protects us,
So that we part forever from birth-and-death.[6]

Taken literally, this hymn suggests that the moment faith is settled we transcend the world of birth-and-death for good, i.e., attain *nirvāṇa*. Yet it is precisely in order to dispel this misunderstanding that the author of the *Tannishō* quotes this hymn and explains its meaning as follows:

At the moment faith becomes settled, a person is immediately grasped, never to be abandoned, and therefore he will not transmigrate further in the six paths; thus, "We part forever from birth-and-death." Should realizing this be confusedly labeled "enlightenment"? Such misunderstanding is indeed pitiful.

The late master said, "According to the true essence of the Pure Land way, one entrusts oneself to the Primal Vow in this life and realizes enlightenment in the Pure Land; this is the teaching I received."[7]

---

[5] *Tannishō*, 107–09 (translation altered).

[6] *Kōsō wasan, SSZ*, II: 510. The present translation is quoted from the *Tannishō*, 38.

[7] *Tannishō*, 38–39.

Here, "part forever from birth-and-death" is taken as meaning "*will not* transmigrate further." Psychologically viewed, for Shinran, the assurance of the future birth, given by faith, was just as good as the present reality, for the assurance itself is the "present reality" experienced here and now. Thus there was no need for him to distinguish carefully the future reality from the present reality, nor the present tense from the future tense in his expressions. Perhaps we can also surmise that the "confusion" may have been aggravated by the absence of a clear future tense in the Japanese language. At any rate, for Shinran, the future was in faith already the present reality in the proleptic sense. We have to agree with Suzuki when he says:

> The objection that the assurance is a kind of promise and must not be identified with the fact of enlightenment, is not a serious one. For we can for all practical purposes regard this assurance as the fact itself as long as the assurance implies the spiritual recognition of Amida's grace on our part while this grace grows operative only as the outcome of Amida's Enlightenment. There is a process indeed, logically stated, between the two notions, assurance and enlightenment, but psychologically the assurance on the part of sentient beings as the objects of the Primal Vows is identical with Enlightenment on the part of Amida.[8]

Let us examine another example. In one of the best known passages often adduced in support of the theory of immediate realization of salvation (or birth) by faith, Shinran says as follows:

> *Then they attain birth* means that when a person realizes faith, he is born immediately. "To be born immediately" is to dwell in the stage of non-retrogression. To dwell in the stage of non-retrogression is to become established in the stage of the truly settled. This is also called the attainment of the equal of perfect enlightenment. Such is the meaning of *then they attain birth*. *Then* means "immediately"; "immediately" means without any passage of time and without any passage of days.[9]

Here again, "to be born immediately" is identified with none other than the stage of non-retrogression, the stage of the truly settled who are sure to attain birth—and enlightenment—after the present existence has come to an end. We may be able to put the matter in the following way: For Shinran, to be born in the Pure Land is to attain the stage of the truly

---

[8] D. T. Suzuki, *Collected Writings on Shin Buddhism*, 27.

[9] *Faith Alone*, 34–35; *SSZ*, II: 625. See also *Once-calling*, 32–34; *SSZ*, II: 604–606.

settled, but not *vice versa*; for the only form of birth Shinran knew of in the present world was the one given in the form of a firm assurance and promise for the future, the assurance obtained by faith. Yet this assurance is not the reality itself. It is only in psychological impact that the truly settled are already in the Pure Land. The certainty of birth is in this sense just as good as "immediate birth," and Shinran's faith and conviction did not find it necessary at all to distinguish them sharply. What Shinran is speaking is a language of the heart, not the head. As the author of the *Epistle to the Hebrews* puts it, "faith is the reality of things hoped for." Yet, for Shinran, sentient beings are not yet Buddhas, nor is this world the Pure Land. In spite of faith, the gap still remains.

In another example, right before mentioning the ten benefits acquired by faith in the present life, which we have quoted previously, Shinran says:

> When we realize the diamond-like true mind, we transcend crosswise the paths of the five courses and eight hindered existences and unfailingly gain ten benefits in the present life.[10]

Taken in itself, "transcend crosswise the paths of the five courses and eight hindered existences" seems to refer to the immediate result of faith here and now, that is, the present *nirvāṇa*. Carefully examined, however, it is actually put in contrast with the "ten benefits" to be gained in the present life. The most we can hope for in the present life by faith is not enlightenment itself but the stage of the truly settled, which is accompanied by joy, gratitude, love, and the sense of security, the "fruits" of faith in the present life. The meaning is clearly that we *will* transcend crosswise birth-and-death *in the Pure Land*, but not here on earth. Shinran says:

> *Transcending crosswise* is the true teaching based on the fulfillment of the Vow, which embodies the perfectly consummate true reality. This indeed is the true essence of the Pure Land way....
>
> In the pure fulfilled land of the Great Vow, grade and level are irrelevant; in the space of an instant, one swiftly transcends and realizes the supreme, perfect, true enlightenment. Hence, *transcending crosswise*.[11]

Or, commenting on a passage from his *Shōshinge* (The Hymn of True Faith) that says, "when one realizes faith, seeing and revering and attaining

[10] *True Teaching*, II: 257; *SSZ*, II: 72.
[11] *True Teaching*, II: 261–62; *SSZ*, II: 73.

great joy, one immediately leaps crosswise, severing the five evil courses," Shinran explains:

> *Immediately* means that the person who realizes faith becomes settled in the stage of the truly settled without any lapse of time or passage of days. *Crosswise* means laterally or transcendently; it indicates the power of the Tathāgata's Vow. It refers to the working of Other Power. *Leaps* means to go beyond. It means easily going crosswise beyond the vast ocean of birth-and-death and realizing the enlightenment of supreme *nirvāṇa*. Know that faith is the true intent of the Pure Land teaching.[12]

It is clear from these explanations that Shinran meant by "immediately" the immediate settlement of the person of faith in the stage of the truly settled who are destined to attain enlightenment in the Pure Land. The concept of "crosswise transcendence [or leap]" (*ōchō* 横超), which represents the quick way of liberation by Other Power in contrast with other gradual and difficult ways of salvation in Mahāyāna, and which strongly reminds us of the sudden-enlightenment in Zen, actually refers to the liberation realized in the Pure Land, and faith is no more than its assurance here and now. Zen, which teaches sudden-enlightenment here and now, belongs to the path of "lengthwise transcendence" (*shuchō* 堅超) that, fast as it is, belongs to the difficult Path of Sages.

Finally, we should examine in this context the celebrated concept of *jinen hōni* 自然法爾 in Shinran, and its implication as an experience of salvation. For the idea of natural spontaneity and carefreeness this term suggests might be interpreted as referring to the enlightened mode of life here on earth that is made possible by faith. Suzuki beautifully describes such a life:

> To begin with, according to Shinran, Amida's Primal Vow is a mysterious deed altogether beyond human comprehension, and now that you have awakened faith in it, what worries could ever harass you? What contrivances could ever save you from sinfulness so completely that you would be worthy residents of the Pure Land? You just give yourselves up absolutely to the mysterious workings of the Primal Vow and, instead of growing anxious about or being vexed by anything of this world, be satisfied with yourselves, be free as the wind blows, as the flowers blossom, in the unimpeded light of Amida. Shinran frequently advises not to think of good, nor of evil, but just to give oneself up into the mysterious

---

[12] *Inscriptions*, 73; *SSZ*, II: 602.

Primal Vow and be "natural."[13]

The concept *jinen* is used in Shinran's writings in many different ways and with different nuances and shades of meaning. But basically two meanings can be distinguished. On the one hand, it refers to ultimate reality, the supreme formless Buddha: "The supreme Buddha is formless, and because of being formless is called *jinen*."[14] On the other hand, it also refers to the way this supreme formless Buddha appears in the form of Amida Buddha in order to save sentient beings, specifically the way the Primal Vow works to make sentient beings realize supreme Buddhahood: "In order to make us realize that the true Buddha is formless, it is expressly called Amida Buddha; so I have been taught. Amida Buddha is the medium through which we are made to realize *jinen*."[15] In other words, *jinen* refers to ultimate reality itself as well as the way in which this reality works for our salvation, i.e., enlightenment. To be precise, one is a noun and the other an adverb. And it is the latter that is used uniquely in Shinran with its soteriological implication. Shinran explains it as follows:

> As for *jinen*, *ji* means "of itself"—it is not through the practicer's calculation [*hakarai*]; one is made to become so. *Nen* means "one is made to become so"—it is not through the practicer's calculation; it is through the working of the Vow of Tathāgata. As for *hōni*, it means "one is made to become so through the working of the Vow of Tathāgata." *Hōni* means that one is made to become so (*ni*) by the virtue of this dharma (*hō*), being the working of the Vow where there is no calculation on the part of the practicer. In short, there is no place at all for the practicer's calculation. We are taught, therefore, that in Other Power no self-working is true working.[16]

Jinen hōni, therefore, refers to the natural, spontaneous, and inevitable (in accordance with the law, *dōri* 道理) way in which the Primal Vow as Other Power works for our salvation without any room for human calculation or self-powered intervention.

The subjective counterpart of *jinen hōni* is, therefore, none other than faith, which lets go of self-power and simply lets Other Power be

---

[13] D. T. Suzuki, *Collected Writings on Shin Buddhism*, 55–56.

[14] *Letters*, 30; *SSZ*, II: 664.

[15] *Letters*, 30; *SSZ*, II: 664.

[16] *Letters*, 29; *SSZ*, II: 663.

Other Power without any intervention on our part. Our salvation being already secured by faith, there is absolutely no need for our religious toil and "work," our calculative designs (*hakarai*); faith simply leaves everything to Amida's Vow Power, which works *jinen hōni*. To have realized this marvelous natural world of Amida's Vow Power, its pure grace, was perhaps the highest form of wisdom and insight, or even "enlightenment," that Shinran was able to, or was made to, arrive at in his life. Yet it is important not to forget the fact that *jinen hōni* by no means describes the state of Shinran's own mind, but the marvelous working of Amida's Vow to save sinful beings like him. *Jinen hōni* does not describe Shinran's *nirvāṇa*, and to have realized it did by no means constitute his enlightenment. In other words, Shinran discovered the world of *jinen* not through enlightenment but through faith. This is why, despite this simple and yet profound insight into the wonder of the pure grace of Other Power, Shinran the *bonpu* still remained as ever before, and faith still remained the only way he could be saved—although even this faith was a gift of *jinen hōni*. In the wonderful world of *jinen hōni* realized by faith, our evil karma is transformed immediately, but "without being nullified or eradicated":

> *Ji* also means "of itself." "Of itself" is a synonym for *jinen*, which means "to be made to become so." "To be made to become so" means that without the practicer's calculating in any way whatsoever, all his past, present, and future evil karma is transformed into the highest good. To be transformed means that evil karma, without being nullified or eradicated, is made into the highest good, just as all waters, upon entering the great ocean, immediately become ocean water. We are made to acquire the Tathāgata's virtues through entrusting ourselves to his Vowpower; hence the expression, "made to become so." Since there is no contriving in any way to gain such virtues, it is called *jinen*.[17]

For Shinran, it was perhaps in this wisdom of *jinen hōni* that faith came the closest to the experience of realization (*shō*), or enlightenment. Yet faith was not realization for Shinran. Despite faith, we are still sinners heavily laden with karmic evils. The transformation experienced in faith is not yet the *existential* transformation but the *essential* (or ideal) transformation by Amida's grace, which accepts sinners as they are, transferring all *his* virtues to them as "their" virtues. Thus we *will* enter *nirvāṇa*, not

---

[17] *Faith Alone*, 32–33; *SSZ*, II: 623.

by our effort but effortlessly by *jinen hōni*. The following words from the *Anjin ketsujō shō* are perhaps helpful in explaining what we mean by "essential" transformation:

> The purport of all the three sūtras of the Jōdo school is to manifest the significance of the Primal Vow. To understand the Vow means to understand the Name, and to understand the Name is to understand that Amida, by bringing to maturity his Vow and Virtue (or Deed) in the stead of all beings, effected their rebirth even prior to their actual attainment. What made up the substance of his Enlightenment was no other than the rebirth of all beings in the ten quarters of the world. For this reason, devotees of the nenbutsu, that is, of the *tariki*, are to realise this truth each time they hear Amida's Name pronounced, that their rebirth is indeed already effected, because the Name stands for the Enlightenment attained by Hōzō [Dharmākara] the Bodhisattva who vowed that he would not attain enlightenment until all beings in the ten quarters of the world were assured of their rebirth in his Pure Land.... As far as the devotees themselves are concerned they have nothing in their nature which will enable them to practise any form of good either worldly or unworldly since they only know how to commit evil deeds; but because of Amida's having completed an immeasurable amount of meritorious deeds, which constitutes the substance of Buddhahood, even we who are ignorant and addicted to wrong views are now destined for the Land of Purity and Happiness. What a blessing it is then for us all![18]

In other words, in our faith in Amida's Vow and Name, we are not what we are anymore, because our birth in the Pure Land has already been essentially effected by Amida's merit transferred to us. As far as our faith directed to Amida is concerned, we are already in the Pure Land, there being no doubt about it at all in our diamond-like faith. Yet, when we look at our own conditions, we have yet to be liberated from what we are existentially.

This paradoxical transformation, a transformation without transformation, is the true miracle occurring in the world of faith in Amida's Vow. This is what is meant by Shinran when he said:

> When such shackled foolish beings—the lowly who are hunters and peddlers—thus wholly entrust themselves to the Name embodying great wisdom, the inconceivable Vow of the Buddha of unhindered light, then

---

[18] Quoted in Suzuki, *Collected Writings on Shin Buddhism*, 53.

while burdened as they are with blind passion, they attain the supreme *nirvāṇa....* When we entrust ourselves to the Tathāgata's Primal Vow, we, who are like bits of tile and pebbles, are turned into gold.[19]

In the world of grace and faith, the more evil passions we have the more virtues we will be endowed with. Amida's grace defies our commonsense moralistic calculation; it is a world of moral paradox:

By the benefit of the Unhindered Light,
The virtuous, great Faith is obtained;
Assuredly does our evil passion turn into Enlightenment
As ice melts to water.

Hindrances of evil become the substance of virtue.
As with the example of ice and water:
The greater the ice, the greater the water;
The greater the hindrance, the greater the virtue.[20]

Shinran even goes so far as to say that in the perfect instantaneous One Vehicle of the Primal Vow, passions and enlightenment are not two in essence—which certainly sounds like the well-known Mahāyāna statement of non-duality.[21] But we are now in the right position to understand correctly what Shinran really meant by it and what it meant for him to say that "they attain the supreme *nirvāṇa*, while burdened as they are with blind passion,"or that "*nirvāṇa* is attained without severing blind passions." In T'an-luan 曇鸞 (Donran, 476–542), from whom this latter expression comes, the words originally referred to the *nirvāṇa* to be realized after one's birth in the Pure Land.[22] If this were the case with Shinran's expression here too, then we would have no problem with it at all, for Shinran also believes that we will attain *nirvāṇa* in the future despite our lives being full of blind passions here in this impure land. But

[19] *Faith Alone*, 40–41; SSZ, II: 628–29.

[20] *The Kōsō Wasan: The Hymns on the Patriarchs* (Kyoto: Ryukoku University Translation Center, 1974; Ryukoku Translation Series VI), 62–63; SSZ, II: 505–506.

[21] *Kōsō Wasan*, 52; SSZ, II: 505.

[22] In this plain sense, the passage does not pose any problem because all Pure Land Buddhists believe that they will be able to attain *nirvāṇa* in the Pure Land, where they will be born despite the blind passions from which they are now suffering in this world. T'an-luan says in his *Wang-sheng-lun chu* (Jpn. *Ōjōronchū*): "When foolish beings possessed of blind passions attain birth in the Pure Land, they are not bound by the karmic fetters of the three realms. That is, without severing blind passions, they realize *nirvāṇa* itself. How can this be conceived?" Quoted in *True Teaching*, III: 360; SSZ, II: 105.

this purely futuristic interpretation is too simplistic and does not capture the subtlety of the expression, which was clearly meant by Shinran to be paradoxical—hence, surprising; he could not have been unaware of such an apparent contradiction. If, on the other hand, we take *nirvāṇa* as referring to present reality, it means that Shinran flatly committed a logical contradiction. There is no *nirvāṇa* that coexists with blind passions, no half-*nirvāṇa* that shares the other half with blind passions! If this *nirvāṇa* is then neither present nor future reality, it should somehow be understood as both present and future reality at the same time. And this is exactly the way Shinran understood it in his faith experience and the way he wanted it to be understood. It is "already here, but not yet," to use the Christian theological language used to interpret Jesus' understanding of the kingdom of God. When we look at ourselves, we ever remain sinful beings. When we look at Amida's compassionate Vow in faith, however, sins and evil have no power and we will certainly be in the Pure Land. Our blind passions are like non-being as far as our faith in Amida is concerned, and we are beings already transformed in Amida's Vow and Name, not in ourselves; in Amida's eyes, not in our eyes. In the language typical of him, D. T. Suzuki expresses this mystery with a bit of comparative remark as follows:

> Amida, according to the teaching of Shin, has no intention to interfere with the working of karma, for it has to run its course in this world, the debt incurred by one person is to be paid by him and not by another. But the mysterious power of Amida's Name and Vow—which is the mystery of life to be simply accepted as such, all the logical contradictions notwithstanding—lifts the offender from the curse of karma and carries him to the Land of Purity and Happiness, where he attains his supreme enlightenment. While karma is left to itself, what is beyond the reach of karma which may be termed the akarmic power of Buddha, is working quite unknowingly to the karma-bearer himself. But he begins to realise this fact as soon as faith in Amida is awakened in him. Faith works this miracle in his consciousness. Although he knows that he is subject to the law of karma and may have to go on in spite of himself, committing deeds of karma, his inmost consciousness, once his faith is established, tells him that he is bound for Amida's Land at the end of his karmic life on this earth. It is by this inmost consciousness in the Shin devotee that the truth of merit-transference (*pariṇāmana*) is demonstrated. In a similar way Christians feel assured of vicarious atonement when their faith is confirmed in Christ. Whatever theological and ethical interpretation may

be given to this, the truth or fact, psychologically speaking, remains the same with Christians and Buddhists: it is the experience of a leap from the relative plane of consciousness to the Unconscious.[23]

While Zen promises a complete freedom from karma and the life of a perfect *jinen* here and now, Shinran, the *bonpu*, would not recognize such a miracle, not as far as the present life is concerned. Only Amida is completely beyond karma, and only by faith in his Vow and Name can we be free from the power of karma—essentially, though not existentially; as the present certainty of salvation but not as present reality. For the moment, all we have is this firm assurance for the future that we will surely attain birth in the Pure Land and be enlightened. Then only will we be existentially transformed and able to enjoy the unambiguous form of salvation. As far as the present existence is concerned, the person of faith has to be satisfied with an ambiguous form of salvation, the paradoxicality of "already, and not yet." Already saved when we look at Amida's Vow of compassion—or, rather, when we are seen by it—in faith, we are at the same time not yet saved when we look at our wretched condition. Salvation by faith is in Shinran never an unambiguous salvation. For faith is not realization. Not yet.

Frequently the above words of Shinran that we have discussed have been interpreted by modern Shinshū scholars more or less along the line of the classical Mahāyāna doctrine of the identity of *saṃsāra* and *nirvāṇa*, passions and enlightenment, sentient beings and Buddhas.[24] Indeed, in appearance, it would seem that this wisdom of *śūnyatā* may be able to provide the key to solving the enigma of the paradox. But this, we 'believe, is a gross misunderstanding and misrepresentation of Shinran's thought. For it dissolves the very paradoxicality of Shinran's salvation by faith. Faith, for Shinran, has nothing to do with the ontological insight

---

[23] *Collected Writings on Shin Buddhism*, 60.

[24] Ueda and Hirota's *Shinran* shows this tendency on the whole; see 56, 83–89, 167–73, for examples. Hoshino Genpō is certainly right in interpreting "attaining *nirvāṇa* without severing blind passions" as referring to the "reality of faith" (*kakushin no jitai*), and not to the "future benefit" to be obtained in the Pure Land. But he interprets this "reality of faith" along the line of traditional Mahāyāna ontology and Nishida Kitarō's philosophy. Consequently, the sense of the "otherness" of Other Power is *aufgehoben*, and faith, which presupposes the distance between Amida and the believers, is ultimately rendered meaningless. See his "Fudan bonnō toku nehan no ronri," *Shinran to jōdo* (Tokyo: San'ichi Shobō, 1984), 75–90. Hoshino even extends the same logic to the reality of the Pure Land itself; see his *Jōdo no tetsugaku. Zoku—Jōdo* (Kyoto: Hōzōkan, 1975), 42–44.

into the nature of reality as emptiness (*śūnyatā*), upon which the doctrine of identity (*soku*) is based. On the contrary, faith is only real when the "otherness" or transcendence of Other Power is preserved and the distance between the two poles reaches its utmost limit, so that there is no other way out than grace. The knowledge of the "identity" between *saṃsāra* and *nirvāṇa* comes from faith, not from the transcendent insight of *prajñā*:

> When faith arises in a deluded and defiled ordinary being,
> he realizes that birth-and-death is none other than *nirvāṇa*.
> Unfailingly he will reach the Land of Immeasurable Light;
> He will save universally all sentient beings.[25]

The logic of grace, which accepts our evil passions as they are without dissolving them in the slightest degree, has nothing to do with the so-called "dialectical" logic of identity *sive* difference (*sokuhi*), which can never take the reality of evil seriously in its raw force, and hence not the wonder of grace either. The logic of *sokuhi*— "A" is "A" because it is not "A"—destroys the realistic sense of the irreducible gap between *saṃsāra* and *nirvāṇa*, the sense of the tension and the crisis upon which faith rests; it renders the whole Pure Land faith meaningless, depriving it of its seriousness, such as we find in Shinran. The dualistic confrontation of sinful sentient beings and the Buddha of infinite wisdom and compassion, the world of karmic bondage and the land of absolute freedom is overcome in Shinran, as far as the present life is concerned, only by faith with all its paradoxical tension, not by the transcendent wisdom of emptiness. While faith leaves the future open, there is no room for it in the wisdom of emptiness. For the moment, whatever transcendent insight, whatever enlightenment there is, all belong to Amida Buddha, not to us still bound by blind passions. Faith, for Shinran, is not enlightenment. Enlightened beings we will be in the Pure Land, not here in this defiled world:

> Tathāgata is *nirvāṇa*;
> Nirvāṇa is called Buddha-nature.

[25] This translation is based on the one found in *The Shōshin Ge: The Gāthā of True Faith in the Nembutsu* (Kyoto: Ryukoku University Translation Center, 1962; Ryukoku Translation Series I), 36. The *Shōshin ge*, or the *Shōshin nenbutsu ge* (Hymn of True Faith and Nenbutsu), which also contains the phrase "attaining *nirvāṇa* without severing blind passions," is originally a part of the *Kyōgyōshinshō*; see *SSZ*, II: 45 for the present verse.

One cannot realize it in the state of an ordinary man,
But is to realize it in the Land of Serene Sustenance.[26]

From this perspective, it is also very significant to note that even when Shinran composed the chapter on realization (*shō*; the True Realization of the Pure Land Way) in his *Kyōgyōshinshō*, he had to start with numerous scriptural passages that, in reality, set forth the certainty of attaining *nirvāṇa* in the future rather than its reality as experienced here and now. Thus, for instance, the central Vow upon which the truth of the whole chapter rests is called by Shinran "the Vow of necessary attainment of *nirvāṇa*." For Shinran, as yet an unenlightened person, this was practically all he could really say on the matter—on the basis of his faith, not on the basis of his realization.

Shinshū orthodoxy has certainly been right in repudiating the view that believers can attain enlightenment in the present life and that the Pure Land can be realized in this world.[27] Despite this, however, there has been a noticeable tendency among some modern interpreters of Shinran, perhaps under the influence of Zen as well as of modern secular thought, to emphasize that the Pure Land is not to be understood merely as something to be attained after death but as something already realizable here and now. Otherwise, they argue, the Pure Land has no meaning and relevance for us living here on this earth. When conceived of purely as a future reality, the Pure Land is out of touch with the present life we have to live here in this defiled world. But is this view really true? Is a future reality simply no more than a future reality without any bearing on the present? Maybe so for those who have no certainty about the future reality. But not so for Shinran, who tirelessly stressed the believers' privilege of belonging to the truly settled. And this was not a small matter for Shinran.

One of the most rewarding achievements of contemporary Christian theology has been the rediscovery of the meaning of eschatology. As in Christian faith, the dimension of futurity and transcendence can only be ignored in Shinran at the cost of a genuine faith. The future is always in the present, impinging upon it and giving it a new meaning, even a new

[26] *The Jōdo Wasan: The Hymns on the Pure Land* (Kyoto: Ryukoku University Translation Center, 1965; Ryukoku Translation Series IV), 127; *SSZ*, II: 497.

[27] See article 23, "sokutoku ōjō" 即得往生 and 25, "shōjō metsudo" 正定滅度 in *Kōza Shinshū no anjin rondai*.

"reality." Takeuchi Yoshinori, clearly recognizing the dialectic between faith (*shin*) and realization (*shō*) in Shinran, correctly observes as follows:

> The immanence-oriented position of the Zen people who, by their [doctrine] of one's own self as Amida and Pure Land as Mind-only, ignore the absolute discontinuity between faith and realization, is fundamentally unable to reveal the true purport of the Pure Land teaching. Neither, however, can the view of the Pure Land scholars who, in opposition to this, point to a direction and establish forms [with regard to the Pure Land], be said to exhaust the true purport of the Pure Land teaching, if they cause the mistaken view that sees the other shore and this shore as existing in mere separation. The direction pointed to in their pointing and establishing forms is the future. Even if the future cannot [yet] be realized (*shōsuru*), should we not think that it is already coming in the present of faith?[28]

For Shinran, faith clearly brings about a profound transformation in one's life. It brings with it the wisdom to transform our ignorance into insight on the true reality of ourselves as well as of the "true and real" world of Amida Buddha's infinite wisdom and compassion. As an experience of conversion from an attachment to self-power and self-centeredness to the Other Power, faith brings us the wisdom to let salvation be worked out by itself (*jinen hōni*) without our intervention, despite all our persisting blind passions. Faith brings with it the joy, gratitude, and confidence that derive from being truly settled to inherit the Land of Purity. For it assures us that the blind passions tormenting us in this life can no longer hinder us from entering *nirvāṇa*. Nay, faith may even make us realize that birth-and-death is none other than *nirvāṇa*. All in all, however, we must conclude that the transformation brought about by faith is in Shinran more noetic than ontic, more emotional than moral. For the distance between ourselves and the Buddha, *saṃsāra* and *nirvāṇa*, and this world and the Pure Land still remains as ever before. Nay, we should say that it remains even greater than when we had no faith and did not realize Amida's grace. Salvation is secured, but not yet attained. The decisive battle has been won, but the final victory still awaits us ahead. This is the situation of the faithful, those who are saved "already, and not yet," and this is what is portrayed in the following famous passage of the

---

[28] Takeuchi, *Kyōgyōshinshō no tetsugaku*, 159.

Shōshinge:

> When the one thought-moment of joy arises,
> *Nirvāṇa* is attained without severing blind passions;
> When ignorant and wise, even grave offenders and slander[er]s of the
>   dharma, all alike turn and enter faith,
> They are like waters that, on entering the ocean, become one in taste
>   with it.
>
> The light of compassion that grasps us illumines and protects us always;
> The darkness of our ignorance is already broken through;
> Still the clouds and mists of greed and desire, anger, and hatred,
> Cover as always the sky of true and real faith.
>
> But though light of the sun is veiled by clouds and mists,
> Beneath the clouds and mists there is brightness, not dark.
> When one realizes faith, seeing and revering and attaining great joy,
> One immediately leaps crosswise, closing off the five evil courses.[29]

In the sky of faith, the sun of Amida's compassionate Vow and the clouds of our blind passions coexist: *simul justus et peccator*, already saved and not yet. This is the situation of the faithful in this world according to Shinran. To use D. T. Suzuki's expression on the life of *myōkōnin*, the ideal people of faith in Shinshū, "Though bound, yet they are free."[30]

FAITH AND MORAL RESPONSIBILITY

Now, if it is true that faith does not necessarily bring about moral transformation in the believer and that salvation is possible for sinful beings as they are without moral change, this raises one of the most serious problems in Shinran's soteriological teaching, one that has troubled the nenbutsu movement from its inception in Hōnen. This is the problem of faith and moral responsibility. If moral transformation is not necessary for our salvation, does this mean that the believer is free to act in any way he likes without jeopardizing his chance of salvation? That this was not

---

[29] *True Teaching*, I: 161–62; *SSZ*, II: 44.

[30] *Shin Buddhism* (New York: Harper & Row, 1970), 87. Everything Suzuki says about *myōkōnin* ("wonderfully good men"), the most pious and devoted followers of Shin Buddhism, provides an excellent witness to the paradoxical nature of the life of faith in Shinran that I have tried to analyze thus far. See also Suzuki, *Collected Writings on Shin Buddhism*, 78–91.

merely a theoretical issue among the nenbutsu practicers is indicated by
the fact that, as we have already seen, there were people who actually
drew this antinomian conclusion from Shinran's doctrine of faith and carried it out in their lives, causing a serious social problem and inviting
harsh measures upon the nenbutsu movement. They are the ones who
practiced "committing unbridled evil" (*zōaku muge* 造悪無礙) or
"licensed evil."

Although the problem of antinomianism had arisen already from
Hōnen's time, it appears to have become more acute among some of
Shinran's followers because of the clear emphasis placed by him on faith
rather than practice. Hōnen not only faithfully upheld the precepts and
administered them to those who wanted them, he also encouraged the
diligent practice of nenbutsu throughout the rest of the believer's life. But
none of these things was true for Shinran. The distinction between the
monks and the lay people was essentially meaningless for him, and the
practice of nenbutsu was basically regarded as an expression—important
and inevitable, to be sure—of faith rather than its indispensable requirement. From the following letter of Shinran, we can see that his emphasis
on faith alone was misunderstood by some of his followers as a rejection
of nenbutsu altogether, so that they even despised those who practiced
nenbutsu:

> In answer to your question about the nenbutsu: it is completely mistaken
> to look down upon people who believe in birth through the nenbutsu,
> saying that they are destined for birth in the borderland [of the Pure
> Land]. For Amida vowed to take into Perfect Bliss those who say the
> Name, and thus to entrust oneself deeply and to say the Name is to be in
> perfect accord with the Primal Vow. Though a person may have faith, if
> he does not say the Name it is of no avail. And conversely, even though
> he fervently says the Name, if his faith is shallow he cannot attain birth.
> Thus, it is the person who both deeply entrusts himself to birth through
> the nenbutsu and undertakes to say the Name who is certain to be born
> in the true Buddha Land.[31]

There seems to be hardly any doubt that Shinran's teaching of ideas
such as "One should not fear evil; for there is no evil [act] so [great] that
it obstructs Amida's Primal Vow,"[32] or "Even the good person realizes

[31] *Letters*, 40–41.
[32] *Tannishō*, 53.

140

birth [in the Pure Land]—what need is there to speak of the evil person!"[33] strengthened the antinomian tendency that was already there among some of the nenbutsu practicers. Taken at face value, would not these remarks have the danger of leading some to boast of their evil in order to praise the merits of the Primal Vow (*hongan bokori* 本願誇り)? Indeed, it was not merely some malicious misinterpreters of Shinran's teaching who drew such conclusions from it. The author of the *Tannishō* is quite bold and frank in admitting the antinomian implication, if not conclusion, of his master's teaching. For him, there is no such thing as boasting of, or "presuming" on, the Primal Vow (*hongan bokori*). Those who admit such a thing, he argues, not only doubt the Primal Vow, but also do not understand the karmic nature of good and evil acts. The argument is that our evil acts are not only unable to deter the power of the Primal Vow; they are also inexorably unavoidable, being the karmic consequence of our past acts. It was precisely in order to rescue us from such inescapable evils, including the very act of presuming upon the Primal Vow, that Amida uttered his compassionate Vow. Thus the author says:

> Even the evil we commit "presuming" upon Amida's Vow to save us has its cause in the action of past karma. Thus, it is when a person leaves both good and evil to karmic recompense and entrusts wholly to the Primal Vow that he is one with Other Power. *The Essentials of Faith Alone* states:
>
>> Do you know the extent of Amida's power, that you suppose yourself hard to save because your existence is one of karmic evil?
>
> Through your having a heart that presumes upon the Primal Vow, the faith by which you entrust yourself to Other Power also becomes firmly settled.[34]

Would it be an exaggeration to call this the "triumph of grace" in Shinran and his disciple? Yet, this does not mean that they condoned the deliberate committing of evils. Just as St. Paul, another champion of the doctrine of grace, was aware of the antinomian danger of his doctrine when he asked rhetorically, "What are we to say, then? Shall we persist in sin, so that there may be all the more grace?" (Romans 6: 1), so were Shinran and his disciple, the author of the *Tannishō*. And they clearly rejected the antinomian interpretation as a perverse attachment and a per-

[33] *Tannishō*, 59.
[34] *Tannishō*, 34–35.

verse view. The *Tannishō* records the following story as an example:

> There was, in those days, a person who had fallen into a mistaken under-
> standing. He asserted that since the Vow was made to save the evil per-
> son, one should purposely choose to do evil, taking it as the cause of
> birth. When rumors of misdeed gradually reached Shinran, to end adher-
> ence to that wrong understanding he wrote in a letter: "Do not take a
> liking to poison just because there is an antidote."[35]

Certainly, evil does not constitute an obstacle to our salvation in the
world of Amida's grace, nor does good work constitute any ground for
salvation in that world. The hard and fast law of moral causality is completely dissolved in the vast ocean of Amida's compassionate Vow, and
karmic power is rendered utterly powerless before Other Power. This is
indeed a gospel, a joyful message of liberation. Yet, the question remains:
How do you mend, or reestablish, if you have to, this severance of faith
and ethics, religious experience and moral responsibility? More concretely,
if evil does not hinder our salvation, what religious reason can we provide
for avoiding evil? And if good acts do not contribute to our salvation,
what kind of religious motivation can we find for the moral life? If,
according to Shinran, salvation is not contingent upon our ethical behavior, and the traditional belief in the law of moral causality has no validity
in the order of grace, what kind of moral reason can Shinran's teaching
provide for the life of the believers?

Shinran's response to these questions is basically as follows: If you
have a genuine faith, and if you truly feel grateful for the Vow of Amida
that saves you, moral life is bound to follow naturally. Moral life is not to
be lived in a legalistic way out of a sense of duty or any external compul-
sion; it should arise spontaneously, just as nenbutsu arises as a natural
outflow of faith. Thus the *Tannishō* states:

> If faith has become settled, birth will be brought about by Amida; hence
> there must not be any of one's own efforts and designs (*hakarai*). If we
> turn more and more to the power of the Vow even when we [find that
> our acts] are evil, through the reality of *jinen* the mind of gentlehearted-
> ness and forbearance will surely emerge [in us]. With everything we do,
> whatever it may be, as far as [attainment of] birth is concerned, we
> should simply recall constantly and unselfconsciously, without any con-

---

[35] *Tannishō*, 33–34.

triving thoughts, the profundity and immensity of Amida's benevolence. Then the nenbutsu will be uttered of itself. This is *jinen*. Our not designing is called *jinen*. This is none other than Other Power.[36]

Here a parallel is drawn between nenbutsu and moral life; both of them are to flow naturally (*jinen*) out of our faith. In this sense, faith brings about a change of heart and of our attitude toward life and the world. On the basis of this change, ethical life should be lived in freedom and natural spontaneity rather than in law and duty. After all, having great joy of heart, being aware of Amida's benevolence and responding in gratitude to his virtue, and constantly practicing great compassion, are among the ten benefits to be gained by the believers in the present life.

According to Shinran, one who has genuine faith and aspiration for nenbutsu cannot continue to indulge in an immoral life:

> You must not do what should not be done, think what should not be thought, or say what should not be said, thinking that you can be born in the Buddha Land regardless of it. Human beings are such that, maddened by the passions of greed, we desire to possess; maddened by the passions of anger, we hate that which should not be hated, seeking to go against the law of cause and effect; led astray by the passions of ignorance, we do what should not even be thought. But the person who purposely thinks and does what he should not, saying that it is permissible because of the Buddha's wondrous Vow to save the foolish being, does not truly desire to reject the world, nor does he consciously feel that he himself is a being of karmic evil. Hence he has no aspiration for the nenbutsu nor for the Buddha's Vow; thus, however diligently he engages in nenbutsu with such an attitude, it is difficult for him to attain birth in the next life. Please transmit this point fully to the people.[37]

Shinran here stresses to his followers the incompatibility of genuine faith and an immoral life lest they should fall victim to the antinomian temptation. According to him, those who call upon the Name aspiring for the Pure Land undergo a "change of heart":

> If a person, justifying himself by saying he is a foolish being, can do anything he wants, then is he able to steal or to murder? Even that person who has been inclined to steal will naturally undergo a change of heart if he comes to say the nenbutsu aspiring for the Buddha Land. Yet people

[36] *Tannishō*, 115–17.
[37] *Letters*, 57.

who show no such sign are being told that it is permissible to do wrong; this should never occur under any circumstances.[38]

Shinran distinguishes between a deliberate wrongdoing and one that is committed by our being "maddened beyond control by blind passion," that is, by our unavoidable karmic influence:

> Maddened beyond control by blind passion, we do things we should not and say things we should not and think things we should not. But if a person is deceitful in his relations with others, doing what he should not and saying what he should not because he thinks it will not hinder his birth, then it is not an instance of being maddened by passion. Since he purposely does these things, they are simply misdeeds which should never have been done.[39]

A subtle form of moral reasoning is going on here in Shinran's words. What he is saying is that when we commit a wrongdoing with conscious thought, it is no longer an act committed in uncontrollable blind passion (major premise); karmic determination, when aware, is no longer a determination; it is a deliberate wrongdoing. Being aware means being controllable and hence being responsible. Now, the antinomian excuse is certainly a form of consciousness or awareness (minor premise)—that evil action does not hinder birth in the Pure Land. Therefore, it follows (conclusion) that the antinomian excuse is incompatible with a genuine karmic determination, i.e., being "maddened beyond control by blind passion." Hence, it is invalid as an excuse for immoral action. We are responsible for our immoral acts, so long as they are done with an antinomian "excuse."

It is, incidentally, extremely significant that Shinran shows his concern for the antinomian danger most clearly and strongly in the pastoral letters sent to his followers. Understandably so, because whatever he may have taught about faith, he could not simply disregard its consequence in the actual life of the believers; he had to be responsible for his own teaching. Thus we find the voice of Shinran the pastor assuming a different tone from that of Shinran the theologian. Now we find him more attentive to the *visible* signs of the invisible faith he taught, and to the concrete process of *gradual* moral transformation in the lives of his followers

---

[38] *Letters*, 51–52.

[39] *Letters*, 52.

as well as to their moral responsibility. The following illustrates this pastoral spirit very well:

> It has not been uncommon for people like yourselves, who do not read or know the scriptures, to distort the teaching, having heard that no evil interferes with the attainment of birth. It seems that this is still the case....Formerly you were drunk with the wine of ignorance and had a taste only for the three poisons of greed, anger, and folly, but since you have begun to hear the Buddha's Vow you have gradually awakened from the drunkenness of ignorance, gradually rejected the three poisons, and come to prefer at all times the medicine of Amida Buddha.... It is indeed sorrowful to give way to impulses with the excuse that one is by nature possessed of blind passions—excusing acts that should not be committed, words that should not be said, and thoughts that should not be harbored—and to say that one may follow one's desires in any way whatever. It is like offering more wine before the person has become sober or urging him to take even more poison before the poison has abated. "Here's some medicine, so drink all the poison you like"—words like these should never be said.
>
> In people who have long heard the Buddha's Name and said the nenbutsu, surely there are signs of rejecting the evil of this world and signs of their desire to cast off the evil in themselves. When people first begin to hear the Buddha's Vow, they wonder, having become thoroughly aware of the karmic evil in their hearts and minds, how they will ever attain birth as they are. To such people we teach that since we are possessed of blind passion, the Buddha receives us without judging whether our hearts are good or bad.
>
> When, upon hearing this, a person's trust in the Buddha has grown deep, he comes to abhor such a self and to lament his continued existence in birth-and-death; and he then joyfully says the Name of Amida Buddha deeply entrusting himself to the Vow. That he seeks to stop doing wrong as his heart moves him, although earlier he gave thought to such things and committed them as his mind dictated, is surely a sign of his having rejected the world. Moreover, since faith which aspires for attainment of birth arises through the encouragement of Śākyamuni and Amida, once the true and real mind is made to arise in us, how can we remain as we were, possessed of blind passion?[40]

Thus, it is fair to conclude that, for Shinran, faith (and nenbutsu) is followed by a gradual change in one's moral life; faith, in this sense,

---

[40] *Letters*, 60–62.

provides believers with the psychological force for moral transformation.

Moral life, however, is a matter too weighty to be based merely upon subjective psychological attitude, too serious to be left to the natural spontaneity of the believers. If this is true, are we then able to find in Shinran other ways of conceptualizing the relationship between faith and ethics, ways that ensure a tighter link between the two? In fact, this is not just our concern, nor merely a problem confined to the ethical realm only. The relationship between the inner invisible faith and its outer manifestation in the visible forms of the believer's life has always been the problem at the heart of Shinshū orthodoxy in its continuous efforts to define more clearly, as it had to, the institutional framework of its faith. As Dobbins points out:

> The tie between these two [the internal faith and the external forms of life] has been the central question in the emergence of the Shinshū, resulting in its formulation of ceremony, doctrine, ethics, and sectarian organization. In this sense, all Shinshū history can be construed to be an attempt to explicate the meaning of faith as manifested in thought and action.[41]

To go back to the question of moral responsibility in Shinran's thought: the world of Amida's grace, like the Zen world of *satori*, is fundamentally beyond good and evil; both belong to a supramoral dimension of human experience. Not that they are human creations, but they clearly answer one of the deepest needs of the human spirit, which simply cannot remain bound to the world of ethical distinctions, often oppressive and full of hypocrisy and bigotry. If human beings cannot live by bread alone, they cannot live by morality alone, either—hence the liberating messages of Zen and Amida's grace. Unlike Zen, however, the discovery of Amida's grace starts from a painful awareness of one's moral inadequacy and the despair to which it ultimately leads. To use H. Tanabe's expression, Shinran's concept of faith is mediated by moral despair as its *kōan*.[42] To the extent that this is true, the way of Other Power differs in its ethical implication from Zen, which is not necessarily, in fact is mostly not at all, mediated by ethical predicament but by the aporia posed by our

[41] Dobbins, *Jōdo Shinshū*, 62.

[42] See Tanabe Hajime, *Philosophy as Metanoetics*, trans. by Takeuchi Yoshinori with Valdo Viglielmo and James W. Heisig (Berkeley: University of California Press, 1986), 125–28; Tanabe says that his metanoetics treats *zange* (repentance) as a *kōan*.

discriminating intellect, as in the *kōan* meditation. The ethical tension arising from the unbridgeable gap between the absolute and the relative, the Buddha and sentient beings, is intrinsic to Shinran's concept of faith. In this sense, faith is grounded upon—or at least mediated by—moral consciousness. But the crucial question is: Can we say the reverse too? Is moral consciousness grounded upon faith experience in Shinran?

Moral experience, the ultimate agony and despair it produces, may lead us to faith in Other Power, but in Shinran's teaching this faith does not necessarily seem to lead to moral consciousness and commitment. In fact, quite the opposite. Faith has the potential danger of dissolving the ethical tension with which it initially began. This is probably why Tanabe emphasizes the act of repentance and self-negation as the indispensable element in the concept of faith in Other Power and in the world of naturalness (*jinen hōni*):

> Thus, the standpoint of naturalness wherein everything is allowed to be just as it is does not mean "naturalness" or "as such" in the ordinary sense. For us, it means the sweat and blood of religious discipline. Only one who has really attempted to "be just as one is" truly knows how difficult a task that is. Many of a mind so shameless and indolent as never to have exerted themselves to seek the good and avoid evil, many who have not wrestled with moral torment employ the terms "absolute non-differentiation" or "naturalness" in order to justify themselves in staying just as they are and attributing their state to the grace of Other Power. They misuse the terms to defend an indolent, tranquil life by displacing the notion of "naturalness" from its rightful locus in the realm of absolute nothingness, where it is understood as being *beyond* ethics, to a new location *beneath* ethics. And that is surely the most frightful damage that can be inflicted on religion. "Naturalness" or the state of things "just as they are" is not a simple fact but a goal toward which one must strive through the mediation of self-negation.[43]

It was also out of a similar concern that Ienaga Saburō proposed *nenzai* 念罪 (consciousness of sin; or, meditation on sin) instead of *nenbutsu* as the essential religious practice, which he thinks is more in agreement with the concept of faith in Shinran.[44] Both Tanabe and Ienaga are legitimately concerned lest faith in Other Power may destroy the ethical

---

[43] Tanabe, *Philosophy as Metanoetics*, 154.

[44] Ienaga, "Shinran no nenbutsu," in *Chūsei bukkyō shisōshi kenkyū*, 238–46.

tension and be converted into a "cheap grace" that ignores human moral responsibility. With due respect for their sincere concern, the question still seems to remain open as to whether or not, how and in what sense, faith experience in Shinran entails a moral sense of responsibility.

The profound awareness of one's moral inadequacy and powerlessness may indeed mediate one's taking refuge in the liberation freely granted by Other Power, but this liberation may not necessarily motivate one to commit oneself to a life of strenuous moral struggle. On the contrary, the very feeling of moral helplessness, often easily exaggerated, and the extreme emphasis on Other Power in Shinran may easily render us morally impotent even before the fight has begun. Is Shinran's thought truly free from the temptation to adopt a deterministic resignation in moral life, despite the warnings he issued to his followers in the letters that we have cited? The fact is that just as the Zen enlightenment of no-self may not necessarily involve moral self-denial, the denial of self-power (*jiriki*) in Shinran may also not necessarily lead to a continuous denial of selfish desires in individual moral life, not to mention in the public realm of social life. Religious self-denial, that is, the giving up of self-power— mediated as it is by moral predicament—is by no means the same as moral self-denial. Nay, the two may even run in opposite directions, the former hindering the latter. For the one begins when our moral fight is given up, while the other constitutes its essence. Ippen, for instance, was aware of this danger when he said:

> Deep mind [of the *Contemplation Sūtra*] is interpreted as "realizing deeply and decidedly that you are in actuality a foolish being of karmic evil caught in birth-and-death, from vast kalpas ago ever plunged and ever driven in transmigration with never any condition that would lead to emancipation." Most people take this to mean that for a person to rush about in pursuit of sundry treasures and to gird himself with wife and children—all to enhance his own existence—is simply the usual weakness of ordinary human beings, and because abandoning these things is impossible, it is said that one is a "foolish being of karmic evil caught in birth-and-death" whose existence answers no purpose whatever.
>
> Such is not the meaning of this passage. It is precisely because this self, being evil, is vain and useless for attaining emancipation that it must be abandoned.[45]

---

[45] *No Abode*, 132.

This is a criticism of those who use the sense of inescapable human sinfulness in Pure Land faith as an excuse for worldly attachment. Yet, on the other hand, if one should—and can—abandon one's evil self as Ippen urges in this passage, what is the point then of having faith in Other Power? How is it different from the Path of Sages, the path of self-power? Hence the dilemma remains. Is there any way, then, to have both faith and ethics at the same time, to take them equally seriously without sacrificing one at the expense of the other—apart from the rather ambiguous psychological language in which Shinran talks about the moral life as a natural expression of faith?

In this connection, it is also important to turn to another concept in Shinran's thought for its ethical implication. It is the concept of the bodhisattvaic activity of the believers. For Shinran, birth in the Pure Land is not the end of one's religious aspiration. If we aspire for the birth and the enlightenment that come after our deaths, it is for the sake of returning to this world in order to save others who are still suffering. There is not only a "going forth" (ōsō 往相) but also a "coming back" (gensō 還相) in the life of the believers. Both of these are the work of Amida's directing (ekō 廻向) of his virtue for us.

Originally ekō was one of the five practices for Pure Land aspirants in Vasubandhu's *Treatise on the Pure Land* (*Jōdoron* 浄土論): worship, praise, aspiration, contemplation, and transference of merit (ekō). The first four are for our attainment of Buddhahood, that is, for self-benefit, whereas the fifth stands for our returning to this world of birth-and-death in order to carry out bodhisattvaic activities for the benefit of others. In Shinran's Other Power–oriented interpretation of these concepts, however, none of them can be our work or accomplishment. Whether self-benefit or other-benefit, whether it is our "going forth" or our "coming back," everything is the result of Amida's directing of his virtue that he, as Bodhisattva Dharmākara, accomplished by perfectly practicing these "five gates of mindfulness" (as they are called in Vasubandhu's treatise). Following T'an-luan's distinction of the two kinds of directing of virtue, one for our going forth and the other for our return to this world, but differing from his concept of these, Shinran attributes both of these directings of virtue purely to Amida Buddha. In short, Amida is the only subject and source of ekō according to Shinran. Thus Shinran says:

> As I contemplate the teaching, practice, faith, and realization of the true essence of the Pure Land way, I see that they are the benefit that the

Tathāgata directs to us in his great compassion.

Therefore, whether with regard to the cause or to the fruition, there is nothing whatever that has not been fulfilled through Amida Tathāgata's directing of virtue to beings out of his pure Vow-mind. Because the cause is pure, the fruit is also pure. Reflect on this.

Second is Amida's directing of virtue for our return to this world. This is the benefit we receive, the state of benefiting and guiding others. It arises from the Vow of necessary attainment of the rank next to Buddhahood, also known as "the Vow of attainment of Buddhahood after one lifetime." It may further be called "the Vow of directing virtue for our return to this world."[46]

Thus, the teaching (*kyō* 教), practice (nenbutsu, *gyō* 行), faith (*shin* 信), and realization (*shō* 證) constitute Amida's directing of virtue for our going forth (*ōsō ekō*), whereas our return to this world in order to carry out bodhisattvaic activities after our enlightenment in the Pure Land comprises Amida's directing of virtue for our return (*gensō ekō*). Now, our concern here is whether or not this concept of "return" in Shinran's soteriology can indeed lay a ground, fruitful and solid, for our ethical engagement in this world.

As soon as we raise this question, however, it becomes apparent that one factor fundamentally limits the ethical potentiality of this concept. It is clear that for Shinran the "return" is something that occurs in our next life, i.e., after we have attained the Pure Land and enlightenment. Thus it seems unable to provide a powerful ethical motivation for believers in the present life. Shinran seems to be of the view that compassion is hard for ordinary beings like us to practice in this world; our capacity for love is fairly limited and therefore the best we can do in this world is to say the nenbutsu as a possible way to benefit other beings. Shinran says:

> In the matter of compassion, the Path of Sages and the Pure Land path differ. Compassion in the Path of Sages is to pity, sympathize with, and care for beings. But the desire to save others from suffering is vastly difficult to fulfill.
>
> Compassion in the Pure Land path lies in saying the Name, quickly attaining Buddhahood, and freely benefiting sentient beings with a heart of great love and great compassion. In our present lives, it is hard to carry out the desire to aid others however much love and tenderness we may feel; hence such compassion always falls short of fulfillment. Only the

[46] *True Teaching*, III: 364; *SSZ*, II: 106–107.

saying of the Name manifests the heart of great compassion that is replete and thoroughgoing.[47]

Here we see Shinran's pessimistic view of human nature affecting his view on the human moral capacity. One has to perfect oneself, i.e., achieve Buddhahood through Other Power first, before one is able to really practice bodhisattvaic activities for others. In other words, it is primarily in the stage of the "return" that one can practice compassion. This by no means suggests that Shinran fell back into the so-called Hīnayāna spiritual egoism and forgot the Mahāyāna way, which lays equal stress on wisdom and compassion. For Shinran, the very aspiration for birth is none other than the aspiration to save suffering sentient beings: "The diamond-like mind is the mind that aspires for Buddhahood. The mind that aspires for Buddhahood is the mind that saves sentient beings.... This mind is the mind of great compassion."[48] The mind of faith, the true and real mind given by Amida, is the mind that aspires for Buddhahood as well as the mind that desires to save other beings. Faith, therefore, is clearly accompanied by compassion for others. Yet, in practice, Shinran seems to admit that "it is extremely difficult to save others as one wishes," our compassion not being strong or consistent enough. Nenbutsu, therefore, is practically the only activity that manifests consistent great compassion, Shinran concludes. Should we be wrong if we see in this conclusion a fundamental limitation of Shinran's moral thought that stems partly from his psychological approach and partly from the otherworldly orientation of his faith? Bloom is certainly right when he says:

> The difficulty with Shinran's view of altruism is that it tends to make compassionate action a matter of the future and not of this world. Hence the egolessness which Shinran inculcated often took the form of a passive quietism, and when it was linked to Rennyo's ethical theory of the two forms of truth, it became an acquiescence to the reigning social mores.[49]

What seems to be lacking in Shinran is the continuous sense of moral "ought to" despite the despair it may lead us into, and the positive ethical will to reduce the sufferings of the world—if not to change the world—despite its impermanence and ultimate "worthlessness." If we still

---

[47] *Tannishō*, 24.

[48] *True Teaching*, II: 259; *SSZ*, II: 72.

[49] Bloom, *Shinran's Gospel of Pure Grace*, 84.

have to continue the moral fight even after we have given it up and sur-rendered ourselves to the mercy of Amida's Primal Vow, where does this sense of "have to" come from in Shinran?

No human thought can transcend the basic limitations imposed upon it by the times in which it was conceived. Shinran's clear other-worldly faith had the virtue of being able to overcome the predominantly this-worldly orientation of the traditional Buddhism of his time; its ideal of transcendent salvation could relativize the value of the present world and its systems. Its doctrine of pure grace sharpened human conscience and deepened moral consciousness beyond the conventional moralism of the world. Overall, however, we cannot avoid the impression that it is difficult, if not impossible, to find in the life of faith that Shinran envisaged the ethical will and vision to shape the affairs of the world to improve it. In this respect, we have to agree with the following assessment of Shinran's thought by Katō Shūichi, despite its "modern" outlook:

> In the beginning of the thirteenth century, Yoritomo dealt a fatal blow to the ancient aristocratic society, which was disintegrating internally. Around the same time, and in the same Kantō region, the religion of Shinran finally succeeded in smashing the wall of this-worldliness that had been preserved in ancient Buddhism. The enormous spiritual energy spent for it was without parallel…. Shinran's logic of negation was sharp, whereas his logic of affirmation in the realm of the present world seems to have been nearly absent rather than being weak…. Perhaps, in order to break decisively the traditional this-worldliness…a transcendental thought was necessary that negated the externalistic conception of good and evil. Up to this point, Shinran's accomplishment was splendid. Yet, the internalization of ethics does not occur merely with this. In order for it to develop, in addition to the transcendent absolute being there has to be [human] free will, and ethical value has to be determined in a rela-tionship of tension between the two. This was something Shinran did not do. In his system, karmic retribution is emphasized and the element of free will is lacking…. In this sense, it was natural that, although there was the logic of religious denial of the present world, the internalization of ethics in the human world did not develop…. This has to be regarded as the deepest reason why transcendental thought did not appear again in the history of Japanese thought after the thirteenth century.[50]

[50] Quoted in Ienaga Saburō's "Rekishijō no jinbutsu to shite no Shinran," in Hoshino Genpō et al., eds., *Shinran*. Nihon Shisō Taikei 11 (Tokyo: Iwanami Shoten, 1971), 493–94.

Indeed, the deterministic view of karmic evil, like the Christian doctrine of original sin, may explain the deep-rooted nature of sin and evil in human beings and lead one to surrender oneself thoroughly before the "supernatural" grace of Other Power, but this religious self-surrendering often seems incompatible with the sense of moral freedom and responsibility that is required by an ethical will to grapple with the massive presence of evil in ourselves as well as in society.

5

Form and Formlessness

THE ULTIMATE GOAL of Pure Land faith is enlightenment and *nirvāṇa*, and in this it does not differ at all from the other forms of Buddhism. What differentiates it from other forms of Buddhism is that it promises enlightenment in the future in the Pure Land, whereas all the other sects of Buddhism teach the possibility of attaining the enlightenment here and now in this world. Whether in the future or in the present, whether in the Pure Land or in this world, enlightenment is enlightenment. It is the realization of truth by the light of wisdom that dispels the darkness of delusory thought and falsity. Following the traditional Mahāyāna vocabulary, Shinran calls it the world of Suchness (*tathatā*), Buddha-nature, Dharma-nature, Dharma-body, Supreme *Nirvāṇa*, and True Reality.

A more crucial difference between Pure Land Buddhism and other forms of Mahāyāna, however, comes from the question of whether or not one can attain enlightenment by one's own effort, i.e., through "self-power." It is here that the Pure Land Buddhism shows its most distinctive characteristic with its faith in Other Power, through which alone enlightenment is said to be possible. Thus, at the outset of his chapter on "The True Realization of the Pure Land Way" of the *Kyōgyōshinshō*, Shinran declares:

> To reveal, with reverence, the true realization: It is the wondrous state attained through Amida's perfect benefiting of others; it is the ultimate fruition of supreme *nirvāṇa*. It arises from the Vow of necessary attainment of *nirvāṇa*, also known as the "Vow of realization of great *nirvāṇa*."
>
> When foolish beings possessed of blind passions, the multitudes caught in birth-and-death and defiled by evil karma, realize the mind and practice that Amida directs to them for their going forth, they immediately join the truly settled of the Mahāyāna. Because they dwell among the truly settled, they necessarily attain *nirvāṇa*. To necessarily attain

nirvāṇa is [to attain] eternal bliss. Eternal bliss is ultimate tranquility. Tranquility is supreme *nirvāṇa*. Supreme *nirvāṇa* is uncreated dharma-body. Uncreated dharma-body is true reality. True reality is dharma-nature. Dharma-nature is suchness. Suchness is oneness. Amida Tathāgata comes forth from suchness and manifests various bodies—fulfilled, accommodated, and transformed.[1]

Whether by self-power or by Other Power, enlightenment is the same. Once it is realized, all the differences that characterize our ordinary world become dissolved and lose ultimate meaning; all the discriminations of dualities that lie behind our world of conflicts and confrontations are deprived of their power. More importantly for our concern here, all the forms and names that appear in the story of the Pure Land as told in the scriptures, and even the distinction between the Pure Land and the impure land, Amida Buddha and sentient beings, Other Power and self-power, *nirvāṇa* and *saṃsāra*, enlightenment and blind passions, are all rendered void of ultimate significance. Faith is then not merely unnecessary but also rendered meaningless and impossible, at least as understood by us: faith as a gift coming from Other Power. For we will be none other than the Buddha.

The Pure Land faith is based upon a story. Like the Christian story of the birth, deeds, crucifixion, and resurrection of Jesus, which constitutes the foundation of the Christian faith, the Pure Land faith is also grounded upon the story of the bodhisattva named Dharmākara, who made the forty-eight Vows of compassion in order to save sentient beings suffering in the world of birth-and-death. As related in the *Larger Sūtra of Immeasurable Life*, the story goes as follows:

Śākyamuni Buddha relates that aeons ago in the remote past, when a Buddha named Lokeśvararāja appeared in the world, there was a certain king who, upon hearing that Buddha's teaching, awakened the profound aspiration for enlightenment. He abandoned his throne and became a mendicant monk with the name Dharmākara ("Treasury of Dharma").

Dharmākara went to Lokeśvararāja Buddha and requested instruction in how to attain enlightenment and thereby establish the most excellent of Buddha lands. Lokeśvararāja enabled Dharmākara to see myriads of Buddha lands throughout the cosmos and explained to him their qualities and the natures of the beings in them. These Dharmākara

---

[1] *True Teaching*, III: 355–56; SSZ, II: 103.

contemplated for five kalpas, and then declared his aspiration in bodhisattva vows which, upon fulfillment, would result in the establishment
of a Buddha land that embraced the finest aspects of all the various
Buddha fields. His Vows are therefore said to be supreme and unexcelled.

Dharmākara made forty-eight Vows defining modes in which his
enlightenment would manifest itself. In a narrow sense, only three treat
specifically the characteristics of the Buddha that he resolved to become
(Amida), and another two the features of the Land of Bliss. All the
remaining Vows express ways in which the beings of his Buddha field,
and indeed those throughout the cosmos, will be benefited. In fact, the
Buddha and his land have as their essence the functioning of enlightenment to awaken all beings; the Buddha is Buddha as the benefiting of
beings. In each of his Vows, Dharmākara declares that he will attain
highest, perfect enlightenment only on condition that the content of the
Vow—that is, the benefiting of beings—is realized. Thus, the form of
the Vows itself reveals the basic bodhisattva vision, in which self-benefit
(attainment of enlightenment) is inseparable from the benefiting of
others.

The story continues:

When Dharmākara finished declaring his Vows before Lokeśvararāja
Buddha and a multitude of beings, the universe trembled, flowers show-
ered down, and the prophesy that he would indeed realize highest
enlightenment sounded from the skies. Thus he embarked on a career of
practice that extended for countless aeons. Though reborn many times,
he dwelled constantly in equanimity and tranquility, completely free of
ill-will, greed, pride, or any form of falsity. Practicing the *pāramitā*s and
guiding others to practice through kind and gentle words, he amassed an
immeasurable store of virtue. In his practice he was unrivaled among
gods and human beings, and all the Buddhas revered him, rejoicing in
his attainments.

Finally, ten kalpas ago, he attained Buddhahood and is now dwelling
in his Buddha field, the Land of Bliss, trillions of Buddha lands west of
this world.[2]

Whether we take this as a "real" historical story or a myth, the one
obvious fact that stands out is that Pure Land Buddhism is a religion

---

[2] Quoted from Ueda and Hirota, *Shinran*, 106–108.

based on a story, and that it seems to stand or fall with this story. Without this story, Pure Land faith not merely loses its most distinctive characteristic, it is also unthinkable. And this constitutes its most essential difference from the rest of Buddhism, which does not depend upon such a story as an indispensable element. Other Buddhism is primarily based upon what it regards as the eternal truth, the dharma that the Buddha preached. This dharma is considered to be eternally true in itself whether or not the Buddha preached it, and whether or not we realize it; it is said to reveal the way things always are, i.e., Suchness (*tathatā*). This Suchness is essentially timeless and storyless. All we need in order to realize it is a special form of intuitive knowledge or insight called *prajñā*, which depends on the development (*bhāvanā*) of the power of our mental concentration and contemplation rather than on a particular story or narrative of events. Yet, here is a form of Buddhism that proclaims a story as the basis of its faith, and that says that faith arises when one hears the story.

How should we then take this? How are the two contrasting forms of Buddhism to be reconciled, if they need to be? More specifically, is the story really essential to Pure Land faith, or is it merely an educative device to illustrate for the foolish and ignorant a universal timeless truth, and in this sense is thus ultimately dispensable? The difficult question concerning the relationship between the contingent truth of history and the necessary truth of reason raised by Lessing with regard to the Christian Gospel, seems to find a Buddhist parallel here—with a very different doctrinal and philosophical background, to be sure.[3]

This question has been raised by Buddhists themselves, not only by Buddhists of a philosophical bent for whom the Pure Land faith, with its attachment to the forms that adorn its story, appeared extremely crude and childish and incompatible with the highest philosophical vision of Mahāyāna, but also by Pure Land Buddhists themselves, who were aware of this problem and wanted to defend their faith. Among the Chinese Pure Land masters, it was above all T'an-luan (Donran, 476–542) who first took up this problem seriously in order to reconcile the popular faith of the story-based Pure Land Buddhism with the general Mahāyāna understanding of reality. He tried to secure an ontological basis for the

---

[3] What vexed Lessing's mind was the connection between history (particularly the miracle stories) and reason, whereas what is at stake in the case of Pure Land Buddhism is the relationship between "form" and "formlessness," as we shall see soon.

Pure Land story in view of the Mahāyāna doctrine of emptiness (*śūnyatā*).[4]

In the world of emptiness, indeed, all forms and names disappear and there is no place for a story such as we find in the Pure Land sūtras. All the distinctions we make in our lives lose their meaning and validity. Emptiness, however, is not mere nothingness, the absolute non-existence of anything; it is at the same time a world full of forms and names in their purity and rich variety. Form is emptiness; emptiness is form. Emptiness is a dynamic reality of diversity teeming with names and concepts, forms and characteristics. Neither being nor nonbeing, these forms are called wondrous beings (*myōu* 妙有), "forms without form." According to T'an-luan, it is in this world of wondrous beings that the Pure Land story, with its magnificent forms and features of Amida Buddha and his Land, finds its legitimate ontological place. The forms of the Pure Land story are not to be taken as real forms but as "forms without form," wondrous beings.

That Shinran too was clearly aware of this philosophical problem and that he shared T'an-luan's view of it can be seen in the following words that Shinran quotes from T'an-luan in his *Kyōgyōshinshō*:

> Because true reality is formless, true wisdom is no-knowing. Uncreated dharma-body is the body of dharma-nature. Because dharma-nature is tranquility, dharma-body is formless. Because it is formless, it never fails to manifest every kind of form. Therefore, the adornment of the Buddha's features and marks is itself dharma-body.[5]

Here, the formless Dharma-body (*dharmakāya*; *śūnyatā*) is said to manifest all the wonderful forms of Amida Buddha and his Pure Land. Likewise, our birth in the Pure Land is not to be taken as ordinary birth;

---

[4] On this philosophical aspect of T'an-luan's Pure Land thought, see Ishida Mitsuyuki, "Donran kyōgaku no haikei to sono kihonteki rinen," *Shinran kyōgaku no kisoteki kenkyū* (Kyoto: Nagata Bunshōdō, 1970), 96–112. Concerning the various views of Chinese Buddhist thinkers, especially Tao-ch'o (562–645), on this fundamental problem of the Pure Land faith, see David W. Chappell, "Chinese Buddhist Interpretations of the Pure Lands," *Buddhist and Taoist Studies*, ed. by Michael Saso and David W. Chappell (Honolulu: The University Press of Hawaii, 1977), 23–53. As far as this philosophical aspect of the Pure Land thought is concerned, however, it was above all T'an-luan who influenced Shinran most, as we shall see.

[5] *True Teaching*, III: 376–77; *SSZ*, II: 112. Shinran is quoting from T'an-luan's *Ōjōronchū*, which is the commentary on Vasubandhu's *Treatise on the Pure Land* (*Jōdoron*). How much Shinran relies on T'an-luan in his interpretation of the world of realization (*shō*) is demonstrated by an extremely long quotation he makes from the *Ōjōronchū*; see *True Teaching*, III: 365–91.

it is a birth without birth, a "birthless birth":

> Question: In the Mahāyāna sutras and treatises it is frequently taught that sentient beings are in the final analysis unborn, like empty space. Why does Bodhisattva Vasubandhu express aspiration for "birth"?
>
> Answer: The statement, "Sentient beings are unborn, like empty space," is open to two interpretations. First, what ordinary people see—such as sentient beings, which they conceive as real, or the acts of being born and dying, which they view as real—is ultimately non-existent, like imaginary "tortoise fur," or like empty space. Second, since all things are "born" from causal conditions, they are actually unborn; that is, they are non-existent, like empty space. The "birth" to which Bodhisattva Vasubandhu aspires refers to being born through causal conditions. Hence it is provisionally termed "birth." This does not mean that there are real beings or that being born and dying is real, as ordinary people imagine.[6]

The colorful forms of the Buddha and his land, and the idea of birth in that land, therefore, are not childish and crude "impure" objects of sensual attachment but, instead, the marvelous features of the "pure" land. And Amida Buddha and Bodhisattva Dharmākara are none other than manifestations of the nameless and formless reality, the Dharmabody, for T'an-luan and Shinran.

Despite T'an-luan's philosophical attempt to reconcile the form-oriented Pure Land faith with Mahāyāna ontology, which denies form (at least in its ordinary sense), subsequent Pure Land thinkers became bolder and bolder in their "realistic" understanding of the Pure Land faith, and less and less interested in the philosophical issue. Shan-tao (Zendō, 613–681) marks a period in this respect.[7] In defense of the Pure Land faith against those who regarded it as a lower form of truth to accommodate people of inferior spiritual capacity, he made two important points. While some argued that the Pure Land, with all its colorful forms and characteristics, is merely a "transformed land" (*kedo* 化土), a sort of fictitious means designed to induce ignorant people to higher truth and thus not the end in itself, Shan-tao asserted that the Pure Land is a true land of recompense (*hōdo* 報土) because it was realized as the result of Bodhisattva Dharmākara's long and heroic practice to fulfill his Vows. Others contended that, if the Pure Land is indeed the land of recom-

---

[6] *True Teaching*, I: 94–95; SSZ, II: 15.

[7] On Shan-tao's Pure Land thought, see Mochizuki, *Chūgoku jōdo kyōrishi*, 180–96.

pense, then it cannot be entered by ordinary beings like us but only by bodhisattvas in high stages, because it is the realm of true enlightenment. Against this view, Shan-tao argued that it is precisely for the sake of saving ignorant beings with blind passions that Amida Buddha uttered his Vows and established the Pure Land. For Shan-tao, therefore, the Pure Land faith is grounded upon the highest truth and is not an inferior form of Buddhism designed as a device to lead ignorant beings to higher truth. And the Pure Land practice *par excellence* was for Shan-tao the vocal recitation of the name of Amida Buddha—the nenbutsu in the common sense of the term, not the contemplative visualization of the Buddha and his Land. Yet it should be noted at the same time that there were still some elements left in Shan-tao's Pure Land thought that seemed to belong to, or smack of, the traditional Path of Sages.

Shan-tao's Pure Land thought was inherited in Japan by Hōnen. Hōnen, however, completely removed any vestiges of traditional Buddhism still remaining in Shan-tao's thought and boldly proclaimed nenbutsu based on the Primal Vow as the only path of salvation that is suitable for sentient beings living in the age of Last Dharma. With Shinran, however, we see a reverse in this trend toward a popular conception of Pure Land faith. We have already pointed out that Shinran heavily relies on T'an-luan's philosophical attempt to reconcile the two worlds of form and formlessness. We have also seen how Shinran "demythologized" certain conceptions in the traditional Pure Land faith, such as the idea of Amida's coming to welcome the faithful into the Pure Land at their deathbeds, and the idea of birth in the Land as the necessary step toward attaining enlightenment. We have also seen how he reintroduced some of the key concepts of traditional Mahāyāna thought by radicalizing the concept of faith as the gift of Amida. Thus the mind of faith, which is "directed" to us by Amida's Vow Power, is considered by Shinran to be none other than the Buddha-nature, and the arising of faith none other than the aspiration for enlightenment in the traditional bodhisattva's course of practice.

It is above all in his conception of the Pure Land, however, that Shinran's demythologization is most revolutionary in comparison with the traditional view. The Pure Land is no longer considered by Shinran a "place" or "land" to go after death, the preliminary step toward enlightenment and *nirvāṇa*. For him, just as it was realized as the consequence of Amida's enlightenment, so it is also the "land" of our enlightenment.

The land and the people dwelling there being inseparable—a general principle in Buddhism—the land cannot be conceived of apart from the enlightened beings whose object of experience or enjoyment it is, just as it is inconceivable without Amida Buddha who realized it in the first place by his enlightenment. Birth in the Pure Land therefore means for Shinran none other than enlightenment itself. Thus, in the Pure Land we all partake of the same enlightenment as Amida Buddha himself, there being no difference whatsoever not only among the faithful born there but also between them and the Buddha.

The implication of this demythologizing approach of Shinran is to be clearly recognized. While the way of faith that Shinran taught is obviously impossible without a clear distinction between sentient beings and the Buddha, impure land and pure land, this shore and the other shore, *saṃsāra* and *nirvāṇa*, self-power and Other Power, and the believer and the believed—this, despite the essential identity of the subject and object of faith in Shinran—all these distinctions become meaningless once we realize (*shō*) the Pure Land and the enlightenment. In this sense, there exists a clear disparity, epistemological as well as ontological, between the world of faith and that of realization. Faith in Other Power has ultimately no place once the the Pure Land is realized.

Not merely that, in that "land" there is no place for the Pure Land story either, the very foundation of faith. The multitudes of resplendent forms and figures that adorn the Pure Land story are nothing more than the products of our ignorance attached to forms and distinctions. Nor is there really any room in the world of realization for the story of Bodhisattva Dharmākara, who aeons ago gave rise to the aspiration for enlightenment with his forty-eight Vows and through the exemplary practice of the bodhisattva's course finally realized his goal and thereby established the Pure Land "ten kalpas ago." In this sense, there definitely exists an ontological disparity between the world of the Pure Land story and the world of realization (*shō*). The latter cancels out the former. Or, to put the matter more paradoxically, the Pure Land renders the Pure Land story itself meaningless. From the enlightened perspective, therefore, the story is nothing more than an expedient or temporary means (*hōben* 方便) to lead ignorant and sinful beings to an enlightenment that, once realized, has no use for the expedient. The Pure Land story is for the enlightened of the Pure Land an "unreal" means for realizing "reality." It is no more than a dream, except that it has within it the power to wake people up

161

from it! It is a dream from which one has to wake up, but nonetheless a necessary dream!

Why, then, is this faith and its story necessary in the first place? Why do we need the dream at all? Can we really take it seriously, knowing that it will turn out to be nothing but a dream? Or is there some way for Shinran to take the Pure Land story and faith more seriously while retaining his "demythologized" understanding of the Pure Land, the world of realization? His writings indicate that he was clearly aware of this ontological disparity and pondered deeply over the matter until he found the way to relate or mediate between the two worlds—essentially along the line followed by T'an-luan. Before we examine this important aspect of his thought, however, we have to dwell more on how he actually demythologized the popular conception of the Pure Land. Let us see how he actually treated the colorful luxuriant forms attributed to the Buddha and his Land in the sūtras.

According to the *Larger Sūtra of Immeasurable Life*, Dharmākara expressed the following wish in his Vow (the thirty-first among the forty-eight) concerning the land he wanted to establish through his practice and enlightenment:

> When I attain Buddhahood, all the myriad things of my land—palaces, towers, ponds and streams, flowers and trees—from the ground to the sky, will be formed of innumerable and diverse precious substances possessing a hundred thousand fragrances. Their grace and excellence will surpass those of human beings and devas, and their fragrances will imbue the worlds of the ten quarters. Bodhisattvas, hearing of this, will perform practices for Buddhahood. If it not be so, may I not attain the supreme enlightenment.[8]

Yet all these "forms," it is important to note, do not find any significant position in Shinran's understanding of the reality of the world of realization, that is, of the Pure Land. The only significant "form" that Shinran recognizes and attributes to the land and the Buddha—the two being inseparable—is infinite light (or life, though less often and perhaps less importantly). Shinran opens the chapter on the True Buddha and Land of the Pure Land Way of his *Kyōgyōshinshō* with the following statement:

> Reverently contemplating the true Buddha and the true land, I find that the Buddha is the Tathāgata of inconceivable light and that the land also

---

[8] Quoted from *True Teaching*, III: xxvii-xxviii (Introduction).

is the land of immeasurable light. Because they have arisen through the fulfillment of Vow of great compassion, they are called true fulfilled Buddha and land. There are relevant Vows that were made: the Vows of light and of life.[9]

The relevant Vow of light is the twelfth:

> If, upon my obtaining Buddhahood, my light should be limited and not be able at least to illumine hundreds of thousands of koṭis of Buddha-countries, may I not attain the Highest Enlightenment.[10]

But even the "light," it should be noted, is not really taken literally at all; it is a symbol representing Amida's infinite wisdom-compassion, its universal and unimpeded power to penetrate everywhere and benefit all sentient beings. The light stands for Amida's unobstructable saving activity:

> The Light of His wisdom is measureless,
> All conditional forms without exception
> Are enveloped in the dawning Light;
> Therefore take refuge in the True Light.[11]

> Far-reaching is the Light of Compassion.
> Wheresoever the Light reaches,
> Will Joy of Dharma arise, says the Buddha.
> Take refuge in the Great Consoler.[12]

> The Name of the Tathāgata of Unhindered Light and
> His Light, the manifestation of His Wisdom,
> Destroy the darkness of the long night of ignorance.
> And fulfill the aspirations of sentient beings.[13]

> Although my eyes, blinded by passions,
> Do not see the brilliant light which embraces me,
> The Great Compassion never tires,
> Always casting light upon me.[14]

[9] *True Teaching*, III: 395; *SSZ*, II: 120.

[10] Quoted from D. T. Suzuki, *Collected Writings on Shin Buddhism*, 44.

[11] D. T. Suzuki, tr., *Collected Writings on Shin Buddhism*, 111.

[12] *The Jōdo Wasan*, 38.

[13] *The Kōsō Wasan*, 70.

[14] *The Kōsō Wasan*, 120.

It is not difficult to figure out why Shinran particularly focused on light as the symbol of Amida's tireless salvific activity. Beyond the fact that Amida's very name is the Buddha of Infinite Light (Amitābha), light, among all the physical things in the world, is the least physical; among all the forms the least form-like; among all the objects with limits the most limitless. It is a symbol *par excellence* for the formless form, the world of Amida and his activity and his Land. But even light is inadequate as a symbol. For one thing, light is still obstructable by physical objects; it cannot penetrate three-dimensional objects. Amida's true light, however, knows no obstruction or impediment. Hence it is called not merely "immeasurable light" but also "unimpeded (or unobstructable) light" as well. Shinran says: "With the light of the sun or moon, when something has come between, the light does not reach us. Amida's light, however, being unobstructed by things, shines on all sentient beings; hence, he is named Buddha of Unhindered Light."[15] That is, Amida's invisible light can illumine even the darkest recesses of sentient beings' minds and dispel the darkness of their ignorance; it penetrates even the coldest mass of blind passions and melts it down into a heart of warm compassion. Overall, we have to agree with the following remark on Shinran's conception of Amida and the Pure Land:

> We find that, characteristic of Shinran's grasp of the reality of Amida and the Pure Land, he emphasizes their transcendence of human conceptualization and intellectual understanding. Amida is infinite light, transcending the spacial parameters of human consciousness, and further is infinite life, transcending conceptions of time. If we]objectify Amida as possessing particular features, or locate the Pure Land or give it a particular topography, our conceptions serve only to project our own idealizations and to isolate the reality of the Buddha's working as objects apart from us. Amida and the Pure Land, as the realm and the activity of enlightened wisdom-compassion, transcend time and space, and precisely because of this, they possess the power to become present to all sentient beings throughout the history of samsāric time.[16]

If all forms are ultimately meaningless in the Pure Land, the world of enlightenment, we then have to ask why Shinran still holds on to the

---

[15] Quoted from Ueda and Hirota, *Shinran*, 115; *Mida nyorai myōgō toku*, SSZ, II: 733.
[16] *True Teaching*, III: xxviii (Introduction).

forms of light and life, and why he, in the first place, has to name the nameless reality Amitābha Buddha, the Buddha of Immeasurable Light? Are not these forms and the name equally dispensable, like the other forms that adorn the Pure Land?

For Shinran, the forms appearing in the Pure Land story and faith are by no means dispensable; something vital is at stake here for the Pure Land faith. And it is in this regard that it differs crucially from the other traditions of Buddhism, which do not have to rely on such forms. For Shinran, forms and characteristics, at least those that comprise the Pure Land story, are grounded in the very nature of reality and are thus inseparable from it. Hence there is ultimately no ontological disparity between the Pure Land story and the world of realization (enlightenment). The forms of the Pure Land story arise from the activity of the nameless reality, the Dharma-body (*dharmakāya*) or Suchness; they are none other than the manifestations of the formless Buddha who reaches out (or, down) to the world of forms and names where sentient beings dwell. In short, they are consequences arising from the compassionate activities of the nameless and formless Buddha. Compassion is therefore the link that connects the two worlds, form and formlessness, mediating one for the other. Let us examine this problem more closely.

Following T'an-luan, Shinran distinguishes between two kinds of Dharma-body, or the Body of Truth. One is the Dharma-body as the Nature of Things (*dharmatā*) or Suchness, what he calls the *hosshō hosshin* 法性法身, and the other the Dharma-body as Expedient Means or Compassionate Means, the *hōben hosshin* 方便法身. Thus Shinran states:

> For this reason there are two kinds of dharmakāya in regard to the Buddha. The first is called dharmakāya-as-suchness and the second, dharmakāya-as-compassionate means. Dharmakāya-as-suchness has neither color nor form; thus, the mind cannot grasp it nor words describe it. From this oneness was manifested form, called dharmakāya-as-compassionate means. Taking this form, the Buddha proclaimed his name as Bhiksu Dharmākara and established the forty-eight great Vows that surpass conceptual understanding. Among these Vows are the primal Vow of immeasurable light and the universal Vow of immeasurable life, and to the form manifesting these two Vows Bodhisattva Vasubandhu gave the title, "Tathāgata of unhindered light filling the ten quarters." This Tathāgata has fulfilled the Vows, which are the cause of his Buddhahood, and thus is called "Tathāgata of the fulfilled body." This is

none other than Amida Tathāgata. "Fulfilled" means that the cause for enlightenment has been fulfilled.[17]

Essentially, what this means is that out of the formless, nameless, and story-less Buddha, the Dharmakāya-as-suchness, Amida Buddha who has immeasurable light as his essential form appeared as the Dharmakāya-as-compassionate-means. Initially appearing in the form of Bodhisattva Dharmākara, he uttered the forty-eight Vows of great compassion; and having fulfilled the Vows, he became the Buddha of Immeasurable Light and Life. Emphasizing the key concept of "expedient means" (*hōben*) or "compassionate means," Shinran makes the same concept clearer in the following text:

> From this treasure ocean of oneness form was manifested, taking the name of Bodhisattva Dharmākara, who, through establishing the unhindered Vow as the cause, became Amida Buddha. For this reason Amida is the "Tathāgata of fulfilled body."....This Tathāgata is also known as *Namu-fukashigikō-butsu* (namu-Buddha of inconceivable light) and is the "Dharmakāya as compassionate means." "Compassionate means" refers to manifesting form, revealing a name, and making itself known to sentient beings. It refers to Amida Buddha. This Tathāgata is light.[18]

In short, according to Shinran, Amida Buddha appeared with a form from the ultimate formless realm in order to save sentient beings wandering in the world of birth-and-death; hence, he is the Dharmakāya-as-compassionate-means (or expedient means). From a formless world into our world of forms, Amida Buddha is therefore the "medium" between the two worlds. Shinran says:

> This Vow is the Vow to make us all attain the supreme Buddhahood. The supreme Buddha is formless, and because of being formless is called *jinen*. When this Buddha is shown as being with form, it is not called the supreme *nirvāna* (Buddha)). In order to make us realize that the true Buddha is formless, it is expressly called Amida Buddha; so I have been taught. Amida Buddha is the medium through which we are made to realize *jinen*.[19]

---

[17] *Faith Alone*, 42–43; *SSZ*, II: 630–31. "Dharmakāya-as-compassion" in the translation has been changed to "Dharmakāya-as-compassionate-means."

[18] *Once-calling*, 46; *SSZ*, II: 617.

[19] *Letters*, 29–30; *SSZ*, II: 664.

Amida Buddha is the medium—or, even "mediator" if we may use a Christian term—between the formless Buddhahood and the sentient beings living in the world of forms and discriminations, between supreme *nirvāṇa* or *jinen* and *saṃsāra*, and between the world of enlightenment and the world of sentient beings with blind passions. Suzuki may be right in seeing a parallel here between this internal development within the Dharmakāya, i.e., the emergence of Amida's Vow from it, and Śākyamuni Buddha's emergence from his deep meditation in order to preach what he had realized, despite his initial hesitation. In both cases, it is compassion that impels the movement from the formless world to the sentient beings' world of forms.[20]

The heart of the mediating activity of Amida Buddha as the Dharma-kāya-as-compassionate-means is, needless to say, the Vow of compassion that he uttered as Bodhisattva Dharmākara, and the Name that he established as the result of the Vow. As the manifestation of the salvific will of the compassionate Amida Buddha, the Vow constitutes the central mediating link between sentient beings and the Buddha. D. T. Suzuki writes:

> The Primal Vow (*hongwan* in Japanese and *pūrvapraṇidhāna* in Sanskrit) is the expression of Amida's Will or Karuṇā ("love" or "compassion") which he cherishes over all beings. Karuṇā constitutes with Prajñā the personality of every Buddha; with Prajñā, "transcendental wisdom," he contemplates the world and perceives that it is of Suchness; while by Karuṇā he comes out of his meditation to live among us, and this coming out is the utterance of his vows known as the Primal Vow.... So the Primal Vow is Amida's Will-power, in this case Amida's compassionate heart, which is with him from the beginningless past; in other words, the Primal Vow is Amida himself expressed in human terms. As long as Amida abides in his meditation, as long as he is with himself as Prajñā, he is not at all accessible to beings or to the plane of relativity. But he is also the embodiment of Karuṇā by which he feels for beings other than himself and knows how to express this feeling in terms of the Primal Vow. In the Primal Vow, therefore, Amida communicates with us karma-bound beings and we in turn come thereby in touch with Amida.[21]

---

[20] D. T. Suzuki, *Collected Writings on Shin Buddhism*, 18. Suzuki's discussion of the internal connection between the *jiriki* (self-power)-oriented Buddhism and the *tariki* (Other Power)-oriented Pure Land Buddhism is very illuminating; see pp. 15–28 of the same work.

[21] *Collected Works on Shin Buddhism*, 68–69; "Original Vow" in the text has been changed to "Primal Vow."

In a comparative note, Suzuki earlier had said:

> In Shin, Amida performs in a sense the office of God and also that of Christ. Amida with Amidists is Light (*ābha*) and Life (*āyus*) and Love (*karuṇā*), and from his Love and Life issue his vows, and it is through these vows that Amida is connected with us. The Vow is mediator, and as it emanates from Amida's Love, it is just as efficient as Christ in its office of mediatorship.[22]

Representing the salvific will and power of Amida Buddha, the Vow is a cosmic power grounded in the very nature of reality, the Dharmakāya-as-suchness. Although no more than a particular form taken by the ultimate reality, it is nonetheless the universal reality to which all sentient beings in the world are made to respond. Although, according to the story, no more than an expression of the will of a particular being, called Dharmākara, at a particular moment of time, it is nonetheless an embodiment of the eternal truth that has always been with sentient beings despite their blindness. Although presented in the story in the form of cause and effect, it is really beyond cause and effect, time and space. It is the eternal reality without a story; it is "at the foundation of all reality."[23]

Shinran does not neglect to emphasize that Amida Buddha is, therefore, none other than the Dharmakāya-as-suchness—something that Buddhists of other schools would not recognize, and in fact, something that even Pure Land Buddhists themselves have not necessarily recognized. Although appearing in form and with a name, he is in reality beyond form and name. Although presented in the story as the Body of Fulfillment (*hōjin* 報身; or the Body of Recompense), and thus as the effect of the cause, i.e., the practice of Dharmākara, he is the eternal Buddha beyond time and causality. Shinran says:

> Thus appearing in the form of light called "Tathāgata of unhindered light filling the ten quarters," it is without color and without form, that is, identical with the Dharmakāya-as-suchness, dispelling the darkness of ignorance and unobstructed by karmic evil. For this reason it is called "unhindered light." Unhindered means that it is not obstructed by the karmic evil and blind passion of beings. Know, therefore, that Amida Buddha is light, and that light is the form taken by wisdom.[24]

[22] *Collected Works on Shin Buddhism*, 58.

[23] D. T. Suzuki, *Shin Buddhism*, 20.

[24] *Faith Alone*, 43–44; *SSZ*, II: 631.

In his *Hymns on the Pure Land* (*Jōdo wasan*), Shinran sings his praise:

> Since Amida became a Buddha,
> Ten kalpas is said to have elapsed till now.
> But He seems to be a Buddha
> Older than the innumerable mote-dot kalpas.[25]

> Pitying the long night of ignorance,
> [He] appeared in the Land of Serene Sustenance,
> As the Buddha of Unhindered Light,
> With the boundless Light-wheel of the Dharmakāya.[26]

In short, although appearing in forms, Bodhisattva Dharmākara, the Vow, and Amida Buddha and his Land are none other than ultimate reality itself, the Dharmakāya-as-suchness. They are its manifestations, appearing in order to reach us as we dwell in the world of forms, and to liberate us from our pitiable attachment to forms and distinctions. They are formless forms appearing to us as expedient or compassionate means to deliver us from the world of birth-and-death in which we have been wandering aimlessly, with "never a condition that would lead to emancipation."

Yet, for Shinran, this is not enough. Still another step of mediation is necessary if these formless forms are to reach us so that we may have faith in the Vow and be saved. For how do we, or did we, come to know this marvelous world of the Pure Land story and its truth? How does it actually reach us so that we can "hear" the story and take refuge with the Other Power? Yes, the power of the compassionate Vow is constantly at work, and the cosmic Name is always calling sentient beings. Yes, Amida's wisdom and compassion is shedding its boundless light over every corner of this impure land and every heart of sentient beings. Yet, how do we know this truth, unless somebody reminds us of it? In other words, we need concrete historical mediation by which we, sentient beings dwelling in the historical world of time and causality, may know the "metaphysical" or ontological mediation occurring within the Dharmakāya. Otherwise, this internal drama within the Dharmakāya would be of no use at all for us ignorant beings.

---

[25] *The Jōdo Wasan*, 87 (translation altered).

[26] *The Jōdo Wasan*, 121 (translation altered).

We have already seen in our chapter on faith that, according to Shinran, faith arises from hearing, and that he even equates faith with hearing. Faith arises when we come into contact with the cosmic reality of the Vow and the Name through hearing. The cosmic truth should be mediated to us by our actual hearing of the story of Bodhisattva Dharmākara who uttered his Vows of compassion and became Amida Buddha through his exemplary practice of the bodhisattva's course. For Shinran, the initiator of this historical mediation is none other than Śākyamuni Buddha himself, who "revealed" this whole story about the Pure Land in the three sūtras he preached, especially in the *Larger Sūtra of Immeasurable Life*. Shinran explains the relationship between Śākyamuni Buddha and the *Larger Sūtra*, on the one hand, and the cosmic truth of the Vow and the Name:

> To reveal the true teaching: It is the *Larger Sūtra of Immeasurable Life*. The central purport of this sūtra is that Amida, by establishing his incomparable Vows, has opened wide the dharma-storehouse, and full of compassion for small, foolish beings, he selects and bestows his treasure of virtues. [The sūtra further reveals that] Śākyamuni appeared in this world and expounded the teachings of the way to enlightenment, seeking to save the multitudes of living beings by blessing them with this benefit that is true and real. Thus, to teach the Tathāgata's Primal Vow is the true intent of the sūtra; the Name of the Buddha is its essence.[27]

To translate this into our philosophical terms, what Shinran is saying is that the metaphysical mediation of the Vow and the Name has become available to us as our "benefit" and "blessing" by the historical mediation of Śākyamuni Buddha and the *Larger Sūtra*.

This historical mediation, however, does not stop with Śākyamuni. It is continued in the commentarial ("hermeneutical") tradition of Pure Land masters who appeared after Śākyamuni and expounded the true meaning of the scriptures preached by the Buddha. Thus Shinran says:

> If Amida's Primal Vow is true and real, Śākyamuni's teaching cannot be lies. If the Buddha's teaching is true and real, Shan-tao's commentaries cannot be lies. If Shan-tao's commentaries are true and real, can what Hōnen said be a lie? If what Hōnen said is true and real, then surely my words cannot be empty.[28]

---

[27] *True Teaching*, I: 63–64; *SSZ*, II: 2–3.

[28] *Tannishō*, 23.

Shinran is not boasting about himself here, trying to bolster up his authority by the name of tradition. He is telling us how the "true and real" world of Amida's Primal Vow has been historically mediated by Śākyamuni Buddha and has come to reach even a *bonpu* like him through the gracious tradition, especially through the teaching of his master Hōnen. For Shinran, this was not a small matter, something that could be taken for granted. As we have pointed out earlier, there is in Shinran, on the one hand, a sense of sheer fortuitousness or of "being lucky" for having been able to hear the story of Amida's Vow and his Name, and on the other hand a sense of necessity or of having been destined to encounter it. Hence the deep feeling of indebtedness and gratitude as well as the continuing sense of marvel and wonder at his "good fortune":

> The benevolence of the Tathāgata's great compassion,
> Even if we must crush our bodies, should be returned in gratitude.
> The benevolence of the masters and teachers,
> Even if we must break our bones, should be returned in gratitude.[29]

Or, at the end of his major work, Shinran confesses:

> I am deeply aware of the Tathāgata's immense compassion, and I sincerely revere the benevolent care behind the masters' teaching activity. My joy grows ever fuller, my gratitude and indebtedness ever more compelling.[30]

Shinran's two Japanese hymns, the *Hymns on the Pure Land* (*Jōdo wasan*) and the *Hymns on the Masters* (*Kōsō wasan*) were also manifestations of Shinran's deep gratitude for the tradition of historical mediation of which he became a fortunate beneficiary. His famous *Shōshin nenbutsu ge* [Hymns on true faith and the nenbutsu] was composed out of similar gratitude and reverence for the masters, especially the seven patriarchs: "Thus, taking refuge in the true words of the Great Sage and turning to the commentaries of the revered patriarchs, I realize the depth and vastness of the Buddha's benevolence and compose the following hymn."[31]

---

[29] *Shōzōmatsu Wasan: Shinran's Hymns on the Last Age* (Kyoto: Ryukoku University Translation Center, 1980; Ryukoku Translation Series VII), 59.

[30] *True Teaching*, IV: 616–17; *SSZ*, II: 203.

[31] *True Teaching*, I: 160; *SSZ*, II: 43. The seven patriarchs are Nāgārjuna, Vasubandhu, T'an-luan (Donran), Tao-ch'o (Dōshaku), Shan-tao (Zendō), Genshin, and Genkū (Hōnen).

In Shinran's eyes, all these transmitters of the tradition, despite their historical differences, were only concerned with a single theme, i.e., the eternal truth of Amida's Vow, which alone constitutes the foundation of our salvation.

It is not surprising at all then that Shinran regards earthly human mediators as participants in ultimate reality itself. Like Bodhisattva Dharmākara, the Vow, and Amida, they are also manifestations of the ultimate reality. Or, to be more precise, Shinran considers them to be manifestations of Amida, from whose "Fulfilled Body" (*hōjin*) "innumerable personified and accommodated bodies are manifested, radiating the unhindered light of wisdom throughout the countless worlds."[32] Not merely is Amida Buddha, the Dharmakāya-as-compassionate-means, himself the manifestation of the Dharmakāya-as-suchness, he also manifests numerous forms and bodies (*ōjin* 應身 and *keshin* 化身). Śākyamuni Buddha, needless to say, is for Shinran the most important one of such manifestations. The very purpose of Śākyamuni's appearance on earth, says Shinran, was none other than to reveal the truth and reality of the Primal Vow (*hongan shinjitsu* 本願眞実). Shinran says:

> Truly we know, then, that the crucial matter for which the Great Sage, the world-honored one, appeared in this world was to reveal the true benefit of the compassionate Vow and to declare it to be the direct teaching of the Tathāgatas. The essential purport of this great compassion is to teach the immediate attainment of birth by foolish beings. Thus, looking into the essence of the teachings of the Buddhas, we find that the true and fundamental intent for which all the Tathagatas, past, present, and future, appear in this world, is solely to teach the inconceivable Vow of Amida.[33]

Śākyamuni Buddha is none other than the manifestation of Amida Buddha, who uttered the Vow and fulfilled it:

> Amida, the Buddha existing from the eternal past,
> Pitying the common fools (in the world) of the five defilements,
> Appeared in the Castle of Gayā
> Manifesting Himself as Śākyamuni Buddha.[34]

---

[32] *Faith Alone*, 43; SSZ, II: 631.

[33] *Essentials of Passages on the Pure Land Way: A Translation of Shinran's Jōdo monrui jushō* (Kyoto: Hongwanji International Center, 1982), 57; SSZ, II: 454.

[34] *The Jōdo Wasan*, 122.

How could Śākyamuni Buddha have told the wonderful story of the Vow unless he possessed the same mind as Amida and felt deeply the same compassion that was in Amida's Vow? Unless he himself came from the same reality from which the Vow originated, he could not possibly have known such a profound truth—a reasoning of this sort must have led Shinran to believe Śākyamuni to be Amida's manifestation on earth. And similar reasoning must have been behind Shinran's view of other transmitters of the Pure Land tradition, the other historical mediators of the eternal truth of the Vow.

What this means, therefore, is that, ontologically, Amida Buddha and the Vow precede Śākyamuni Buddha and the sūtras he preached. The former, we might say, is more "real" than the latter. Śākyamuni and the sūtras, which historically mediate the Vow and the Name to sentient beings, are themselves ontologically grounded upon the original ontological mediation that occurs within the Dharmakāya. The historico-epistemological mediation, in other words, is grounded upon the ontological mediation.

Perhaps I may be able to point out in this context that the traditional Shinshū piety, the feeling of indebtedness and gratitude (*on* 恩) to the founder as well as to the transmitters of its traditions, has its roots in the precedent Shinran himself had set. Also, the traditional Mahāyāna doctrine of "manifestation" that is essential for the salvific process of mediation, historical as well as metaphysical, may have worked as an important factor stimulating a "personality cult" in Shinshū—something that Shinran probably would not have endorsed despite his doctrine of mediation.

Despite the obvious importance for Shinran of the historical mediation starting with Śākyamuni Buddha, it should nevertheless be emphasized that after all it is the metaphysical mediation, the internal drama within the Dharmakāya itself, that constitutes the "true and real" foundation for our salvation. Without this prior movement on the part of the nameless Buddha to reach down to the world of forms, no historical mediation would have begun in the first place. The objective basis of the Pure Land gospel, the ontological mystery of the ultimate reality itself, should clearly be given priority in Shinran. This is why Shinran began his remark on the Pure Land tradition, which we have cited earlier, with Amida's Primal Vow and not with Hōnen, through whom he came to know the Vow. Shinran does not say, "If Śākyamuni's teaching is true and real, Amida's Primal Vow cannot be lies," but instead, "If Amida's Primal

Vow is true and real, Śākyamuni's teaching cannot be lies."

Why then, we have to ask anew, is this internal drama of Dharmakāya necessary? Why does the formless have to take the form of Dharmākara and Amida Buddha? Because, Shinran answers, without the manifestation of forms out of formlessness, there is no way for sentient beings attached to the world of forms to realize the world of formlessness. Without the development of a story out of the reality without story, we human beings are forever unable to reach the world beyond time and causality. Without the mediation of the compassionate expedient means on the part of the Dharmakāya-as-suchness, the deep chasm between the Buddha and the sentient beings, the pure land and the impure land, *nirvāṇa* and *saṃsāra* can never be demolished. We need the bridge to cross over this gap, which is unbridgeable by ourselves. As we have pointed out earlier, this constitutes the most crucial difference, the fundamental dividing line, between the Pure Land path and the other forms of Buddhism, the Path of Sages. The initiative has to come from the other side, from the Other Power, not from us. Even our faith, the capacity to respond to the movement within the Dharmakāya, comes from that movement itself. And this, in turn, constitutes the crucial difference between Shinran and other teachers of Pure Land faith before him. Without this prior movement, urged by compassion, on the part of the ultimate reality itself, without this movement that is grounded upon the reality itself, all our efforts to reach it, and all our designs (*hakarai*) to liberate ourselves from what we are, surely come to grief, according to Shinran.

When the gap is completely overcome, however, by the movement coming from the other side, our eyes will be opened and enlightened, and we will realize that what appeared to be an infinite distance between ourselves and the Buddha, this land and that land, blind passions and enlightenment; in short, what appeared to be an unbridgeable gap between formlessness and form will turn out to be nothing but our ignorance and illusion. All the distinctions and discriminations oppressing the sentient beings in this world of forms will be completely gone in that world of formlessness. Not until then, however, can we afford to make light of the deep chasm confronting us; not until then should we ever be oblivious of our sinfulness and our indebtedness to the light of grace that shines upon us from yonder. For until we ourselves have merged into the light, we will never cease to be under the power of darkness in this world, says Shinran.

Thus far we have examined how Shinran deals with the apparent ontological disparity between the two realms, the formless world of Dharmakāya-as-suchness and the Pure Land story of forms and names, that is, the soteriological drama enacted by Dharmākara and Amida Buddha. Rather than being a problem, this disparity constitutes for Shinran the very foundation of human salvation. It is the outcome of the internal drama unfolding within the Dharmakāya—the manifestation of the Dharmakāya-as-compassionate-means from the formless Dharmakāya-as-suchness. As the "medium" mediating the formless Buddha and the world of sentient beings attached to forms, this Pure Land soteriological drama has to partake of our world of forms; otherwise, sentient beings dwelling in this world of forms have no hope of escaping from it. On the other hand, however, this does not mean that the world of the Pure Land story is exactly on the same ontological level as our world of forms, the defiled impure land of endless discriminations and blind attachments. The two have to be of a different ontological order. In other words, the Pure Land soteriological drama, if it is going to mediate the formless and our world of forms, has to occupy a middle ontological position between the formless Buddha and the world of forms to which sentient beings belong, and this is how Shinran understands it; it is "formless form," the expedient means by which the formless reaches down to us without being defiled by our impurities and without being drowned together with us in this vast ocean of birth-and-death. To conclude, Shinran's conception of the Pure Land soteriological drama works with three—or four, if we count the historical mediators as belonging to another ontological order—ontological dimensions: the formless, form, and the formless form. This, probably, is where it decisively differs from the Christian soteriological drama.

The Christian soteriological drama essentially operates with two dimensions instead of the three given in Shinran's understanding of the Pure Land drama. The traditional Christian theological interpretation of the Gospel has been operating basically with two ontological levels, that is, time and eternity, history and God. Despite its notion of Jesus Christ as the savior, the mediator between humanity and divinity, there seems to be nothing in Christian theology that corresponds to the Pure Land formless form. Christ has been viewed as fully divine and fully human at the same time, not as a being in between the two realms, nor as being there merely in "appearance" only. No matter how the divinity of Christ has been conceptualized, his full humanity has been beyond question, even though there have been some exceptional views (condemned as heretical), and many pious Christians do not take them very seriously. Jesus was a historical being and definitely belonged to the world of "forms."

Christian theology may be able to find something analogous to the Pure Land formless form in the internal drama of the Trinitarian deity. The traditional doctrine of Trinity tried to make intelligible the unity of the three persons and the diversity within the unity, but many still find this concept difficult to understand, at least in its traditional form. Most difficult to answer, and often not even asked, is the question of why the eternal God has to have the Son and why he allows diversity within himself in the first place. If one asserts that the trinity has been there from eternity, one can easily fall into tritheism; if, on the other hand, one says that God created for some purpose the second and the third person, one denies the trinity in essence. Here, perhaps, Shinran's concept of the internal drama of the Dharmakāya might be of some help for Christian theology. Could we suggest that it is love that leads God to "deny" or limit himself in order to have the finite but eternal form of the Son, just as out of compassion the formless Dharmakāya-as-suchness manifested the formless form of Dharmakāya-as-compasionate-means?

When we thus regard the second person of the trinity, God the Son, as a "formless form" or a finite but eternal being, Christian theology has to make a clearer ontological differentiation than it has done thus far between the Son of God in heaven (or the intratrinitarian Son, the eternal Logos or Christ) and the Son of God who walked in Galilee two thousand years ago (the earthly Jesus), between the Son as a formless form and the Son in form like us. Or, to put the matter in a theological jargon, Christian theology has to make a sharper distinction between the immanent Trinity and the "economic" Trinity (the Trinity of the economy of salvation), inseparable as they are. Be that as it may, one thing we can say firmly is: God, being love, always exists in self-negation (*kenosis*), self-limitation, and in relationship with something other than Himself, just as the Dharmakāya-as-suchness negates itself to manifest the formless form of Dharmakāya-as-compassionate-means, Amida Buddha. As Moltmann says:

> God is unselfish love. Kenosis is the mystery of the trinitarian God. By virtue of God's unselfish love, God permeates all creatures and makes them alive. In this way God lives in the creation community and allows

176

the community of all God's creatures to live in God. In reciprocal per-
meation everything that is exists and lives. The unselfish empathy of God
awakens the sympathy of all creatures for each other. Perichoresis is also
the mystery of the creation.[35]

If the eternal Logos and the Jesus of history are to be more sharply
distinguished, then Christian theology has to recognize at the same time
two kinds of divine kenosis: the eternal kenosis of the immanent Trinity
and the "historical" kenosis of the economic trinity (Phil. 2:5–8).

At any rate, the "form of a servant" in which the Son appeared on
earth is clearly the Jesus of Nazareth, and it has hardly been possible for
Christians to think about God and the intratrinitarian mystery apart from
this lowly man who "suffered under Pontius Pilate." The two-dimensional
nature of the traditional Christian soteriological drama chiefly accounts
for its tragic character, with its story of God involving himself in the
conflicts of human history, being crucified on the Cross like a criminal!
From the Buddhist perspective, including the Pure Land soteriological
viewpoint, the story of the dead-serious involvement of the Son of God in
human history is likely to be perceived as a form of blind attachment to
this transient world of ever-shifting forms and conflicts. It would even
appear cruel (the nailing and blood on the Cross!) and not sublime
enough, as Suzuki reminds us from his Buddhist perspective. The
Buddhist piety would have difficulty in perceiving a saving power in the
story of the Cross.

From the Christian perspective, on the other hand, the Pure Land
soteriological drama would appear somehow not "dramatic" enough but
airy and play-like, lacking in realistic seriousness. The beautiful and
magnificent world of the Pure Land "formless forms" would somehow
seem not to take history, the "real" world of forms, seriously enough in
its raw and brutal facticity. It does not seem to be in real touch with history, the world of sentient beings with blind passions. The question can
be raised: Can the formless form really mediate and save the real world of
naked forms where we suffer in flesh and blood?

More fundamentally, it would appear from the Buddhist perspective
that the Christian idea of God is not really "formless" to begin with, and

---

[35] Jürgen Moltmann, "God is Unselfish Love," in *The Emptying God: A Buddhist-
Jewish-Christian Conversation*, ed. by John B. Cobb, Jr. and Christopher Ives (Maryknoll,
New York: Orbis Books, 1990), 121.

thus does not exactly correspond to the Buddhist notion of the formless reality. God in the Christian drama of salvation, it would seem, is too much like human beings, attached to the world of forms like us, too deeply involved in history and its vicious circle. The idea of God as "personal" being appears from the Buddhist perspective to belong to the lower level of truth adapted to those incapable of the highest vision of truth and the ultimate reality. Does this then put an end to the talk, with the two sides ultimately having nothing in common? Are they really working from the outset with entirely different, mutually irreconcilable, understandings of the nature of ultimate reality?

It would seem so, if the Pure Land understanding of the nature of reality only talked of emptiness and wisdom. But this is not the case, as we have seen. Emptiness is fullness, and wisdom is compassion at the same time. Out of Great Compassion the Dharmakāya-as-suchness unfolds the drama of human salvation in the form of Dharmakāya-as-compassionate-means, the soteriological drama of Bodhisattva Dharmākara. "Expedient means" as it is, this story of the compassionate Dharmākara and his Vow nevertheless attests unmistakably to the compassionate nature of ultimate reality itself, the source from which the whole drama unfolds. If it were not for the compassion inherent in the Dharmakāya-as-suchness itself, how would the story be able to unfold and the drama start in the first place? Whence could the Vow be uttered, if it were not from the very depth of the reality itself, which is marked by compassion?

Here, we may be allowed to borrow the dialectical logic of *sokuhi* 即非 or the logic of self-identity in self-negation ("A" is "A" because it is not "A") in order to express the ontological mystery of the internal drama of the Dharmakāya-as-suchness. The Dharmakāya-as-suchness is itself because it is not itself but unfolds as the Dharmakāya-as-compassionate-means through self-negation, that is, through love. "In the beginning there was Great Compassion (Agape)."[36] For Shinran, the Dharmakāya-as-suchness is unthinkable apart from the Dharmakāya-as-compassionate-means, and the latter is equally unthinkable apart from the former. Shinran's Dharmakāya is neither the Aristotelian "unmoved mover" nor the Stoic deity of utter impassibility, nor the Buddha who became "extinct" in the "Hīnayāna" *nirvāṇa*. The ultimate reality, to use more of

---

[36] Akizuki Ryōmin, "'Fukaeki' ni tsuite," *Bukkyō to kirisutokyō*, ed. by Yagi Seiichi, et al. (Tokyo: San'ichi Shobō, 1981), 18.

the philosophical jargon of the Kyoto School, is none other than Absolute Nothingness (*zettai mu* 絶対無).

Pure Land Buddhists and Christians seem to share a common understanding of the deepest nature of ultimate reality as Compassion, however differently it may have been experienced and conceptualized by them throughout their long history. Whether the ultimate reality is conceived of as "emptying" itself in order to come down to us in the form of a "servant," whether it is conceived of as unfolding through its self-negation the formless form of Dharmākara and Amida, Love or Great Compassion is what impels the absolute to go out of itself and enter into relationship with the relative. It is after all through Love and Compassion that human beings are saved, if at all.

The difference between history and myth should not be made absolute. The "salvation history" (*Heilsgeschichte*) of Christianity is after all not mere history; it is a part of history, but at the same time a supra-history of divine intervention. Not only is salvation history turned into a myth every time we hear the story and become "contemporary" with it, a pure historical event, however great and miraculous it may be, cannot bring about the eternal salvation of all humankind. We are saved after all by a universal truth, not by particular events in history; by the eternal love of God, not by changing occurrences. Recalling a conversation he once had with an American philosopher, D. T. Suzuki says the following from his Buddhist perspective:

> We came to this conclusion: Myth and legend and tradition—tradition may not be a good term—and poetical imagination are actually more real than what we call factual history. What we call facts are not really facts, are not really so dependable and objective. Real objectivity is in metaphysical subjectivity, you might say, metaphysical truth or poetic legend or religious myth. So we agreed that the Amida story has more objective and spiritual reality than mere historical truth or fact, and Amida has more metaphysical foundation than objective historical fact.[37]

Whether history or myth, the story of Christ and the story of Amida both reveal the deepest nature of reality for the believers. We have to agree with John Cobb when he states:

[37] D. T. Suzuki, *Shin Buddhism*, 36.

Belief in the graciousness of reality is bound up with beliefs about the actual course of events. Equally, beliefs about the actual course of events are bound up with beliefs about reality. In the Pure Land traditions, belief about reality may play the primary role, whereas in Christianity beliefs about the actual course of events may be primary. But in both cases we deal with a circle in which both aspects are needed. Both circles center in the graciousness that characterizes ultimate reality, and both have depended for their convincing power on recounting stories believed to be true.[38]

Our "dialogue" with Shinran thus far enables us further to agree with Cobb—cautiously but irresistibly—when he concludes:

The conclusion from the above is that Amida is Christ. That is, the feature of the totality of reality to which Pure Land Buddhists refer when they speak of Amida is the same as that to which Christians refer when we speak of Christ. This does not mean that Buddhists are completely accurate in their account of this reality—nor that Christians are. It does mean that Christians can gain further knowledge about Christ by studying what Buddhists have learned about Amida. It means also that Buddhists can gain further knowledge about Amida by studying what Christians have learned about Christ. Indeed, we should be able to reflect together about many questions of concern to both of us. But truly joint work is still in our future. For the present we consider in partial separation what each can learn from the other.[39]

I have already given an example of where Christian theology "can gain further knowledge about Christ" from the Pure Land soteriology, that is, with regard to the three-dimensional understanding of the soteriological drama in Pure Land Buddhism. Another area where Pure Land soteriology and Christian theology can go into a fruitful dialogue is Christology, the central question of which is how to understand the transcendent character of earthly Jesus. The Pure Land counterpart to Jesus is not Amida Buddha but Śākyamuni Buddha, the historical Buddha who is believed to be a manifestation of Amida and to have revealed the mystery of the Pure Land way of salvation. While both Śākyamuni and Jesus are regarded as the incarnation (or manifestation) of the transcendent reality,

[38] John Cobb, *Beyond Dialogue: Toward a Mutual Transformation of Christianity and Buddhism* (Philadelphia: Fortress Press, 1982), 138–39.

[39] Cobb, *Beyond Dialogue*, 128.

Śākyamuni is not the only one for Shinran, whereas for Christians Jesus is the one and only incarnation of the eternal Logos. If Amida is Christ, then the two traditions should also recognize the common transcendent origin of the two mediators of salvation. Then Jesus can be regarded as a manifestation of Amida Buddha, the Buddha of Infinite Light and Life, and Śākyamuni Buddha as an incarnation of Christ or the eternal Logos. The Christians may well regard Jesus as the one who embodied in the perfect way the figure of Bodhisattva Dharmākara become Amida Buddha.

Both Pure Land Buddhism and Christianity are religions based upon a particular story that they regard as the decisive revelation of truth; the story of a bodhisattva in one, and the story of a Galilean in the other. Both cherish their story but do not absolutize them by identifying them with truth itself or regarding them as the end itself. For they know whence their story originates, and they know how to find their way through the story to the reality beyond story, the Infinite Light and Eternal Life, Love and Compassion.

Approaching the end of our study, two items of significant divergence between Pure Land Buddhism and Christianity need to be mentioned here. They concern the state and destiny of the saved ones. First, the state of the saved. As we have pointed out earlier, those who are born (*ōjō*) in the Pure Land will completely shed their finite and impermanent forms, their individualities, and be one with the formless Dharmakāya-as-suchness. According to the traditional Christian eschatological hope, however, the faithful will still retain their individuality in some form (the glorious, imperishable, "spiritual body"), and the distinction between them and God will remain as ever, although they will then be able to see God "face to face" (I Cor. 13: 12).

We have also seen that for Shinran enlightenment and *nirvāṇa* are not the end of the soteriological drama. There is a return of the saved ones from the Pure Land to this impure land, again through the working of Amida's *ekō*, which is based upon the fulfillment of his Vow (the twenty-second Vow) called "the Vow of directing virtue for our return to this world." Once an individual merges into the formless world and sheds his individual form, he or she can freely assume any form and any individuality again and come back as a bodhisattva to the world of suffering sentient beings in order to deliver them from their sin and evil, just as he or she had once been delivered by others before. Coming from the world of infinite wisdom and compassion, they repeat in their own ways the soteriological drama of Bodhisattva Dharmākara, his eternal archetypal story, except that it takes place in this world of defiled forms, not in the pure world of "formless form" as with Dharmākara. Unlike the Christian understanding of salvation, liberation in Shinran does not mean arriving at the final point of no return. For there is no such a thing as finality, the eschaton, in the Buddhist cyclical view of time. The soteriological drama as conceived by Shinran is a never-ending story. It is the story of the mutual engagement of the formless, form, and the formless form, which will last as long as there remains even a single being lost in this world of birth-and-death.

Bibliography
and Index

Bibliography

I. PRIMARY SOURCES

A. SHINRAN'S WORKS

Dai Nihon koku zokusan ō Shōtoku taishi hōsan 大日本國粟散王聖德太子奉讃 [Hymns to Prince Shōtoku, Monarch of the Millet-Scattered Islands of Japan]. *SSZ* (*Shinshū shōgyō zensho* 真宗聖教全書, Shinshū Shōgyō Zensho Hensansho, ed.), vol. IV.

Goshōsoku shū 御消息集 [Collection of letters]. *SSZ*, vol. II.

Gutokushō 愚禿鈔 [Gutoku's notes]. *SSZ*, vol. II.

Ichinen-tanen mon'i 一念多念文意 [Notes on once-calling and many-calling]. *SSZ*, vol. II.

Jōdo monrui jushō 浄土文類聚鈔 [Selected passages on the Pure Land way]. *SSZ*, vol. II.

Jōdo sangyō ōjō monrui 浄土三經往生文類 [Passages on the modes of birth in the three Pure Land sūtras]. *SSZ*, vol. II.

Jōdo wasan 浄土和讃 [Hymns on the Pure Land]. *SSZ*, vol. II.

Kyōgyōshinshō 教行信證, or *Ken jōdo shinjitsu kyōgyōshō monrui* 顯浄土真実教行證文類 [The true teaching, practice, and realization of the Pure Land way]. *SSZ*, vol. II.

Kōsō wasan 高僧和讃 [Hymns on the masters]. *SSZ*, vol. II.

Kōtaishi Shōtoku hōsan 皇太子聖德奉讃 [Hymns in praise of Prince Shōtoku]. *SSZ*, vol. II.

Mattōshō 末燈鈔 [Lamp for the latter age]. *SSZ*, vol. II.

Mida nyorai myōgō toku 彌陀如来名號德 [On the virtues of Amida Tathāgata's name]. *SSZ*, vol. II.

Nyorai nishu ekō mon 如来二種廻向文 [Passages on the two aspects of Amida's directing of virtue]. *SSZ*, vol. II.

Nyūshutsu nimon geju 入出二門偈頌 [Hymns on the two gates of entrance and emergence]. *SSZ*, vol. II.

Saihō shinan shō 西方指南抄 [Notes showing the way to the west]. Words of Hōnen, compiled by Shinran. *SSZ*, vol. IV.

Shōzōmatsu wasan 正像末和讃 [Hymns on the right, semblance, and last Dharma-ages]. *SSZ*, vol. II.

Songō shinzō meimon 尊號眞像銘文 [Notes on the inscriptions on sacred scrolls]. *SSZ*, vol. II.

Tannishō 歎異抄 [Notes lamenting deviations]. *SSZ*, vol. II.

Yuishinshō mon'i 唯信鈔文意 [Notes on "Essentials of faith alone"]. *SSZ*, vol. II.

B. ENGLISH TRANSLATIONS OF SHINRAN'S WORKS

Essentials of Passages on the Pure Land Way: A Translation of Shinran's Jōdo monrui jushō. Shin Buddhism Translation Series. Kyoto: Hongwanji International Center, 1982.

Hymns of the Pure Land: A Translation of Shinran's Jōdo wasan. Shin Buddhism Translation Series. Kyoto: Hongwanji International Center, 1991.

Hymns of the Pure Land: A Translation of Shinran's Kōsō wasan. Shin Buddhism Translation Series. Kyoto: Hongwanji International Center, 1992.

The Jōdo Wasan: The Hymns on the Pure Land. Ryukoku Translation Series IV. Kyoto: Ryukoku University Translation Center, 1965.

The Kōsō Wasan: The Hymns on the Patriarchs. Ryukoku Translation Series VI. Kyoto: Ryukoku University Translation Center, 1974.

The Kyō Gyō Shin Shō (Ken Jōdo Shinjitsu Kyōgyōshō Monrui): The Teaching, Practice, Faith, and Enlightenment (A Collection of Passages Revealing the True Teaching, Practice, and Enlightenment of Pure Land Buddhism). Ryukoku Translation Series V. Kyoto: Ryukoku University Translation Center, 1966.

Letters of Shinran: A Translation of Mattōshō. Shin Buddhism Translation Series. Kyoto: Hongwanji International Center, 1978.

Notes on "Essentials of Faith Alone": A Translation of Shinran's Yuishinshō-mon'i. Shin Buddhism Translation Series. Kyoto: Hongwanji International Center, 1979.

Notes on Once-calling and Many-calling: A Translation of Shinran's Ichinen-tanen mon'i. Shin Buddhism Translation Series. Kyoto: Hongwanji International Center, 1980.

Notes on the Inscriptions on Sacred Scrolls: A Translation of Shinran's Songō shinzō meimon. Shin Buddhism Translation Series. Kyoto: Hongwanji International Center, 1981.

The Shōshin Ge: The Gāthā of True Faith in the Nembutsu. Ryukoku Translation Series I. Kyoto: Ryukoku University Translation Center, 1962.

Shōzōmatsu Wasan: Shinran's Hymns on the Last Age. Ryukoku Translation Series VII. Kyoto: Ryukoku University Translation Center, 1980.

Tannisho: A Shin Buddhist Classic. Trans. by Taitetsu Unno. Honolulu: Buddhist Study Center Press, 1984.

Tannishō: A Primer. Trans. by Dennis Hirota. Kyoto: Ryukoku University Translation Center, 1982.

The Tanni Shō: Notes Lamenting Differences. Ryukoku Translation Series II. Kyoto: Ryukoku University Translation Center, 1962.

The True Teaching, Practice and Realization of the Pure Land Way: A Translation of Shinran's Kyōgyōshinshō. 4 vols. Shin Buddhism Translation Series. Kyoto: Hongwanji International Center, 1983–1990.

C. OTHER CLASSICAL TEXTS

Amida kyō 阿彌陀經 [Smaller sūtra of immeasurable life]. *SSZ,* vol. I.

Anjin ketsujō shō 安心決定鈔 [Notes on the settling of faith]. *SSZ,* vol. III.

Anraku shū 安楽集 [Passages on the (land) of happiness]. By Tao-ch'o [Dōshaku]. *SSZ,* vol. I.

Daimuryōju kyō 大無量壽經 [Larger sūtra of immeasurable life]. *SSZ,* vol. I.

Eshinni shōsoku 恵信尼消息 [Letters of Eshinni]. *SSZ,* vol. V.

Gaijashō 改邪鈔 [Notes rectifying heresy]. By Kakunyo. *SSZ,* vol. III.

Godenshō 御傳鈔 [The biography]; *Honganji Shōnin Shinran denne* 本願寺聖人親鸞傳繪. By Kakunyo. *SSZ*, vol. III.

Hanjuzanmai kyō 般舟三昧經 [The sūtra of the samādhi of direct encounter with the Buddhas; *Pratyutpannasamādhi-sūtra*]. *Taishō shinshū daizōkyō* #417, #418.

Kangyōshichō sho 觀經四帖疏 [Commentary on the *Contemplation Sūtra*]. By Shan-tao [Zendō]. *SSZ*, vol. I.

Kanmuryōju kyō 觀無量壽經 [Sūtra of contemplation on the Buddha of immeasurable life]. *SSZ*, vol. I.

Ōjōraisange 往生禮讚偈 [Hymns on the birth (in the Pure Land)]. By Shan-tao 善導 (Zendō). *SSZ*, vol. I.

Ōjōronchū 往生論註 [Commentary on the treatise on the birth (in the Pure Land)]. By T'an-luan 曇鸞 (Donran). *SSZ*, vol. I.

Ōjōyō shū 往生要集 [Passages on the essentials for birth (in the Pure Land)]. By Genshin 源信. *SSZ*, vol. I.

Rokuyōshō 六要鈔 [Notes of essentials on the six (fascicles)]. By Zonkaku 存覚. *SSZ*, vol. II.

Senjaku hongan nenbutsu shū 選擇本願念佛集 [Passages on the nenbutsu selected in the Primal Vow]. By Hōnen. *SSZ*, vol. I.

Shinran denne. See *Godenshō*.

Shinran muki 親鸞夢記 [A record of Shinran's dreams]. *Teihon Shinran Shōnin zenshū* 定本親鸞聖人全集, vol. 4. Ed. by Shinran Shōnin Zenshū Kankōkai. Kyoto: Hōzōkan, 1969–1970.

Wago tōroku 和語燈録 [Japanese record of the lamp]. By Hōnen 法然. *SSZ* vol. IV.

II. SECONDARY SOURCES

A. WORKS IN WESTERN LANGUAGES

Abe, Masao. "Kenotic God and Dynamic Sunyata." In *The Emptying God: A Buddhist-Jewish-Christian Conversation*. Ed. by John B. Cobb, Jr. and Christopher Ives. Maryknoll, New York: Orbis Books, 1990.

_____. *Zen and Western Thought*. Ed. by William R. LaFleur. Honolulu: University of Hawaii Press, 1985.

Andrew, Allan A. *The Teachings Essential for Rebirth*. Tokyo: Sophia University, 1973.

Anesaki, Masaharu. *History of Japanese Religion*. Tokyo: Charles E. Tuttle Company, 1963 (reprint).

_____. *Nichiren, The Buddhist Prophet*. Cambridge, Mass.: Harvard University Press, 1916.

Barth, Karl. *The Epistle to the Romans*. Trans. by Edwyn C. Hoskyns. London: Oxford University Press, 1933.

Bellah, Robert N. "Ienaga Saburo and the Search for Meaning in Modern Japan." In *Changing Japanese Attitudes toward Modernization*. Ed. by Marius Jansen. Princeton: Princeton University Press, 1965.

_____. *Beyond Belief: Essays on Religion in a Post-Traditional World*. New York: Harper & Row, 1970.

Bloom, Alfred. *Shinran's Gospel of Pure Grace*. Tucson: University of Arizona Press, 1965.

_____. "The Life of Shinran Shōnin: The Journey to Self-Acceptance." *Numen*, 15 (1968).

Chappell, David W. "Chinese Buddhist Interpretations of the Pure Lands." In *Buddhist and Taoist Studies*. Ed. by Michael Saso and David W. Chappell. Honolulu: The University Press of Hawaii, 1977.

Coates, Harper Havelock, and Ishizuka, Ryugaku, trans. *Hōnen, the Buddhist Saint*. 2 vols. New York and London: Garland Publishing, Inc., 1981. Originally published in 1925 (Kyoto: Chionin).

Cobb, John B., Jr. *Beyond Dialogue: Toward a Mutual Transformation of Christianity and Buddhism*. Philadelphia: Fortress Press, 1982.

Cobb, John B., Jr. and Christopher Ives, eds. *The Emptying God: A Buddhist-Jewish-Christian Conversation*. Maryknoll, New York: Orbis Books, 1990.

Dobbins, James C. "From Inspiration to Institution: The Rise of Sectarian Identity in Jōdo Shinshū." *Monumenta Nipponica*, 41/3 (Autumn 1986).

_____. *Jōdo Shinshū: Shin Buddhism in Medieval Japan*. Bloomington and Indianapolis: Indiana University Press, 1987.

Eliot, Sir Charles. *Japanese Buddhism.* London: Routledge & Kegan Paul, 1959 (reprint).

Gadamer, Hans-Georg. *Wahrheit und Methode.* 4th Auflage. Tübingen: J.C.B. Mohr, 1975 (1960).

Gira, Dennis. *Le Sens de la conversion dans l'enseignement de Shinran.* Paris: Editions Maisonneuve et Larose, 1985.

Gomez, Luis O. "Shinran's Faith and the Sacred Name of Amida." *Monumenta Nipponica*, 38/1 (Spring 1983), 73–84. Rejoinder by Ueda Yoshifumi and Dennis Hirota; surrejoinder by Gomez: "Correspondence." *Monumenta Nipponica*, 38/4 (Winter 1983), 413–27.

Groner, Paul. *Saichō: The Establishment of the Japanese Tendai School.* Berkeley: Berkeley Buddhist Studies Series, 1984.

Hirota, Dennis, trans. *No Abode: The Record of Ippen.* Kyoto: Ryukoku University Translation Center, 1986.

Ishihara, John. "Luther and Shinran: *Simul justus et peccator* and *nishu jinshin.*" *Japanese Religions*, 14/4 (1987).

Kasulis, Thomas. "Letters of Shinran." *Philosophy East and West*, 31/2 (1981).

King, Winston L. "An Interpretation of the *Anjin Ketsujōshō.*" *Japanese Journal of Religious Studies*, 13/4 (1986).

Kitagawa, Joseph M. *Religion in Japanese History.* New York: Columbia University Press, 1966.

Lubac, Henri de. *Amida.* Paris: Editions du Seuil, 1955.

_____. *Aspects of Buddhism.* Trans. by George Lamb. New York: Sheed and Ward, 1954.

Matsunaga, Daigan and Alicia. *Foundation of Japanese Buddhism.* 2 vols. Los Angeles and Tokyo: Buddhist Books International, 1974–1976.

Morrell, Robert E. *Early Kamakura Buddhism: A Minority Report.* Berkeley, California: Asian Humanities Press, 1987.

_____, trans. *Sand and Pebbles (Shasekishū): The Tales of Mujū Ichien, A Voice for Pluralism in Kamakura Buddhism.* Albany: State University of New York Press, 1985.

Nakai, Gendo. *Shinran and His Religion of Pure Faith.* Kyoto: Kanao Bunendo, 1946.

Nattier, Jan. *Once Upon a Future Time: Studies in a Buddhist Prophecy of Decline*. Berkeley, California: Asian Humanities Press, 1991.

Nishida, Kitarō. *Last Writings: Nothingness and the Religious Worldview*. Trans. by David. A. Dilworth. Honolulu: University of Hawaii Press, 1987.

Nishitani, Keiji. *Religion and Nothingness*. Trans. by Jan Van Bragt. Berkeley: University of California Press, 1982.

Nobuhara, Tokiyuki. "Sunyata, Kenosis, and Jihi or Friendly Compassionate Love: Toward a Buddhist-Christian Theology of Loyalty." *Japanese Religions*, 15/4 (1989).

Odin, Steve. "Abe Masao & The Kyoto School on Christian *Kenōsis* & Buddhist *Śūnyatā*." *Japanese Religions*, 15/3 (1989).

_____. "*Kenōsis* as a Foundation for Buddhist/Christian Dialogue: The *Kenotic* Buddhology of Nishida and the Kyoto School in Relation to the *Kenotic* Christology of Thomas J. J. Altizer." *The Eastern Buddhist* (Spring 1987).

Ohtani, Lady Yoshiko. *Eshin-ni: The Wife of Shinran Shonin*. Kyoto: Honpa Hongwanji, 1970.

Rogers, Minor Lee. "Rennyo and Jōdo Shinshū Piety: The Yoshizaki Years." *Monumenta Nipponica*, 36/1 (Spring 1981).

_____. "The Shin Faith of Rennyo." *The Eastern Buddhist*, 15/1 (Spring 1982).

Rogers, Minor L. and Rogers, Ann T. *Rennyo: The Second Founder of Shin Buddhism. With a translation of his letters*. Berkeley, California: Asian Humanities Press, 1991.

Ryukoku University Translation Center, trans. *The Sutra of Contemplation on the Buddha of Immeasurable Life as Expounded by Śākyamuni Buddha*. Kyoto: Ryukoku University, 1984.

Sansom, George B. *A History of Japan to 1334*. Stanford, California: Stanford University Press, 1958.

_____. *Japan: A Short Cultural History*. New York: Appleton-Century-Crofts, Inc., 1934.

Smith, Wilfred Cantwell. *The Meaning and End of Religion*. New York: Harper & Row, 1978 [1962].

Suzuki, Daisetz T. *Collected Writings on Shin Buddhism*. Kyoto: Shinshū Ōtaniha, 1973.

_____. *Shin Buddhism*. New York: Harper & Row, 1970.

Takahatake, Takamichi. *Young Man Shinran: A Reappraisal of Shinran's Life*. Waterloo, Ontario: Wilfred Laurier University Press, 1987.

Takizawa, Katsumi. *Reflexionen über die universale Grundlage von Buddhismus und Christentum*. Frankfurt am Main: Verlag Peter D. Lang, 1980.

Tanabe, Hajime. *Philosophy as Metanoetics*. Trans. by Takeuchi Yoshinori with Valdo Viglielmo and James W. Heisig. Berkeley: University of California Press, 1986.

Tanaka Eizo, trans. "Anjin Ketsujo Sho: On the Attainment of True Faith." *The Pure Land*, 2/2–5/2 (December 1980–December 1983).

Ueda, Yoshifumi and Hirota, Dennis. *Shinran: An Introduction to His Thought*. With Selections from the Shin Buddhism Translation Series. Kyoto: Hongwanji International Center, 1989.

Unno, Taitetsu and Heisig, James W., eds. *The Religious Philosophy of Tanabe Hajime: The Metanoetic Imperative*. Berkeley, California: Asian Humanities Press, 1990.

Unno, Taitetsu, ed. *The Religious Philosophy of Nishitani Keiji: Encounter with Emptiness*. Berkeley, California: Asian Humanities Press, 1989.

Waldenfels, Hans. *Absolute Nothingness: Foundations for a Buddhist-Christian Dialogue*. Translated by James W. Heisig. New York: Paulist Press, 1980.

_____. *Faszination des Buddhismus: Zum christlich-buddhistischen Dialog*. Mainz: Matthias-Grünewald-Verlag, 1982.

Weinstein, Stanley. "Rennyo and the Shinshū Revival." In *Japan in the Muromachi Age*. Ed. by John Whitney Hall and Toyoda Takeshi. Berkeley: University of California Press, 1977.

_____. "The Concept of Reformation in Japanese Buddhism." In *Studies in Japanese Culture*. Vol II. Ed. by Saburō Ōta. Tokyo: Japan Pen Club, 1973.

Yamamoto Kosho. *An Introduction to Shin Buddhism*. Ube: Karinbunko, 1963.

_____, trans. *The Words of St. Rennyo*. Ube: Karinbunko, 1968.

B. WORKS IN JAPANESE

Akamatsu Toshihide 赤松俊秀. *Kamakura bukkyō no kenkyū* 鎌倉仏教の研究. Kyoto: Heirakuji Shoten, 1957.

————. *Shinran* 親鸞. Jinbutsu sōsho, no. 65. Tokyo: Yoshikawa Kōbunkan, 1961.

————. *Zoku Kamakura bukkyō no kenkyū* 続鎌倉仏教の研究. Kyoto: Heirakuji Shoten, 1966.

Akamatsu Toshihide and Kasahara Kazuo 笠原一男, eds. *Shinshūshi gaisetsu* 真宗史概説. Kyoto: Heirakuji Shoten, 1963.

Chiba Jōryū 千葉乗隆, Kitanishi Hiromu 北西 弘, and Takagi Yutaka 高木豊. *Bukkyōshi gaisetsu: Nihon hen* 仏教史概説: 日本篇. Kyoto: Heirakuji Shoten, 1969.

Fugen Daien 普賢大円. *Shinshū gairon* 真宗概論. Kyoto: Hyakkaen, 1950.

Futaba Kenkō 二葉憲香. *Shinran no kenkyū* 親鸞の研究. Kyoto: Hyakkaen, 1970.

Hattori Shisō 服部之總. *Shinran nōto* 親鸞ノート. Tokyo: Fukumura Shuppan, 1970 (reprint).

Hoshino Genpō 星野元豊, Ishida Mitsuyuki 石田充之, and Ienaga Saburō 家永三郎, eds. *Shinran* 親鸞. Nihon Shisō Taikei 11. Tokyo: Iwanami Shoten, 1976.

————. *Jōdo no tetsugaku. Zoku—Jōdo* 浄土の哲学. 続・浄土. Kyoto: Hōzōkan, 1975.

————. *Jōdo* 浄土. Kyoto: Hōzōkan, 1957.

————. *Shinran to jōdo* 親鸞と浄土. Tokyo: San'ichi Shobō, 1984.

Ienaga Saburō. *Chūsei bukkyō shisōshi kenkyū* 中世仏教思想史研究. Kyoto: Hōzōkan, 1955 (revised and enlarged edition).

————. *Nihon shisōshi ni okeru hitei no ronri no hattatsu* 日本思想史における否定の論理の発達. Tokyo: Kōbunkan, 1940.

————. *Tanabe Hajime no shisōshiteki kenkyū: sensō to tetsugakusha* 田辺元の思想史的研究: 戦争と哲学者. Tokyo: Hōsei Daigaku Shuppankyoku, 1973.

Ienaga Saburō, Akamatsu Toshihide, and Tamamuro Taijō 圭室諦成, eds. *Nihon bukkyōshi* 日本仏教史. 3 vols. Kyoto: Hōzōkan, 1967.

Inoue Mitsusada 井上光貞. *Nihon kodai no kokka to bukkyō* 日本古代の国家と仏教. Tokyo: Iwanami Shoten, 1971.

_____. *Shintei Nihon Jōdokyō seiritsushi no kenkyū* 新訂日本浄土教成立史の研究. Tokyo: Yamakawa Shuppansha, 1975.

Ishida Mitsuyuki. *Jōdokyō kyōrishi* 浄土教教理史. Kyoto: Heirakuji Shoten, 1977.

_____. *Shinran kyōgaku no kisoteki kenkyū* 親鸞教学の基礎的研究. Kyoto: Nagata Bunshōdō, 1970.

_____. *Shinran kyōgaku no kisoteki kenkyū 2*. Kyoto: Nagata Bunshōdō, 1977.

Kasahara Kazuo. *Rennyo* 蓮如. Jinbutsu Sōsho, no. 109. Tokyo: Yoshikawa Kōbunkan, 1975.

_____. *Shinran to Rennyo—Sono kōdō to shisō* 親鸞と蓮如—その行動と思想. Nihonjin no Kōdō to Shisō, no. 40. Tokyo: Hyōronsha, 1978.

_____. *Shinran to tōgoku nōmin* 親鸞と東国農民. Tokyo: Yamakawa Shuppansha, 1975.

_____. *Shinshū ni okeru itan no keifu* 真宗における異端の系譜. Tokyo: Tōkyō Daigaku Shuppankai, 1962.

Kiritani Junnin 桐渓順忍. *Kōza Shinshū no anjin rondai* 講座真宗の安心論題. Tokyo: Kyōiku Shinchōsha, 1983.

Matsuno Junkō 松野純孝. *Shinran—Sono shōgai to shisō no tenkai katei* 親鸞—その生涯と思想の展開過程. Tokyo: Sanseidō, 1959.

_____. *Shinran—Sono kōdō to shisō* 親鸞—その行動と思想. Nihonjin no Kōdō to Shisō, no. 2. Tokyo: Hyōronsha, 1971.

Miyazaki Enjun 宮崎圓遵. *Shinran no kenkyū* 親鸞の研究. *Miyazaki Enjun chosakushū* 宮崎圓遵著作集 I. Kyoto: Shimonkaku Shuppan, 1986.

_____. *Shinran to sono montei* 親鸞とその門弟. Kyoto: Nagata Bunshōdō, 1956.

_____. *Zoku Shinran to sono montei* 続親鸞とその門弟. Kyoto: Nagata Bunshōdō, 1961.

Mochizuki Shinkō 望月信亨. *Chūgoku Jōdo kyōrishi* 中国浄土教理史. Kyoto: Hōzōkan, 1942.

_____. *Ryakujutsu Jōdo kyōrishi* 略述浄土教理史. Tokyo: Nihon Tosho Center, 1977 (reprint).

Nakamura Hajime 中村 元. *Bukkyōgo daijiten* 仏教語大辞典. 3 vols. Tokyo: Tōkyō Shoseki, 1975 (reprinted in one volume, 1981).

Okamura Shusatsu 岡村周薩, ed. *Shinshū daijiten* 真宗大辞典. 3 vols. Kyoto: Nagata Bunshōdō, 1972 (reprint).

Ryūkoku Daigaku Shinshūgaku Kenkyūkai 龍谷大学真宗学研究会, ed. *Shinran Shōnin chosaku yōgo sakuin*. 親鸞聖人著作用語索引, 2 vols. Kyoto: Ryūkoku Daigaku Shinshūgaku Kenkyūshitsu, 1966, 1971.

Shinshū Shōgyō Zensho Hensansho 真宗聖教全書編纂所, ed. *Shinshū shōgyō zensho* 真宗聖教全書. 5 vols. Kyoto: Ōyagi Kōbundō, 1941.

Takeda Ryūsei 武田龍精. *Shinran jōdokyō to Nishida tetsugaku* 親鸞浄土教と西田哲学. Kyoto: Nagata Bunshōdō, 1991.

Takeuchi Yoshinori 武内義範. *Kyōgyōshinshō no tetsugaku* 「教行信証」の哲学. Tokyo: Ryūbunkan, 1987 (reprint).

Takizawa Katsumi 滝澤克己. *Bukkyō to kirisutokyō* 仏教とキリスト教. Kyoto: Hōzōkan, 1964.

————. *Zoku bukkyō to kirisutokyō* 続仏教とキリスト教. Kyoto: Hōzōkan, 1979.

Tamura Enchō 田村圓澄. *Hōnen Shōnin den no kenkyū* 法然上人伝の研究. Kyoto: Hōzōkan, 1972.

————. *Hōnen* 法然. Jinbutsu Sōsho, no. 36. Tokyo: Yoshikawa Kōbunkan,1959.

————. *Nihon bukkyō shisōshi kenkyū: Jōdokyō hen* 日本仏教思想史研究: 浄土教篇. Kyoto: Heirakuji Shoten, 1959.

Tanabe Hajime 田辺 元. *Zangedō to shite no tetsugaku* 懺悔道としての哲学. Tokyo: Iwanami Shoten, 1946.

Yagi Seiichi 八木誠一, Abe Masao 阿部正雄, Akizuki Ryōmin 秋月龍珉, Honda Masaaki 本田正昭, eds. *Bukkyō to kirisutokyō: Takizawa Katsumi to no taiwa o motomete* 仏教とキリスト教: 滝澤克己との対話を求めて. Tokyo: San'ichi Shobō, 1981.

Yagi Seiichi. *Bukkyō to kirisutokyō no setten* 仏教とキリスト教の接点. Kyoto: Hōzōkan, 1975.

————. *Pauro, Shinran, Iesu, Zen* パウロ, 親鸞, イエス, 禅. Kyoto: Hōzōkan, 1983.

Yūki Reimon 結城令聞, gen. ed. *Gendaigoyaku Shinran zenshū* 現代語訳親鸞全集. 10 vols. Tokyo: Kōdansha, 1974.

Index